W9-DED-894

THE BEATLES LYRICS

THE BEATLES LYRICS

The Stories Behind the Music, Including the Handwritten Drafts of More Than 100 Classic Beatles Songs

HUNTER DAVIES

LITTLE, BROWN AND COMPANY
NEW YORK BOSTON LONDON

Little, Brown and Company
Hachette Book Group
237 Park Avenue, New York, NY 10017
littlebrown.com

First Edition: September 2014
Published simultaneously in Great Britain by Weidenfeld & Nicolson, September 2014

Little, Brown and Company is a division of Hachette Book Group, Inc.
The Little, Brown name and logo are trademarks of Hachette Book Group, Inc.

The publisher is not responsible for websites (or their content) that are not owned by the
publisher.

The Hachette Speakers Bureau provides a wide range of authors for speaking events.
To find out more, go to hachettespeakersbureau.com or call (866) 376-6591.

Every effort has been made to trace the owners of copyright material. The publishers will be
pleased to rectify any errors or omissions in all future editions.

ISBN 978-0-316-24716-0
Library of Congress Control Number: 2014940357

10 9 8 7 6 5 4 3 2 1

IM

Printed in Italy

CONTENTS

When, in a generation or so, a radioactive cigar-smoking child, picnicking on Saturn, asks you what the Beatles affair was all about – 'Did you actually know them?' – don't try to explain all about the long hair and screams. Just play the child a few tracks from this album and he'll probably understand what it is all about. The kids of AD 2000 will draw from the music much the same sense of well being and warmth as we do today. For the magic of the Beatles, is I suspect, timeless and ageless. It has broken all frontiers and barriers. It has cut through differences of race, age and class. It is adored by the world.

Derek Taylor, sleeve notes for the *Beatles For Sale* album, 1964

INTRODUCTION

The Beatles, so young, so keen, in their suite at the George V Hotel in Paris in late January/early February 1964. While there, they heard the news that 'I Want To Hold Your Hand' had got to number 1 in the USA. It was also in the suite that Paul created 'Can't Buy Me Love'. Left to right: Ringo, John, Paul, George. (**Photograph@ Harry Benson** 1964)

One of the strange things about the Beatles phenomenon is that the further we get from them, the bigger they become. Their influence and our interest in them seems to grow all the time. When their old stuff is repackaged it often becomes even more successful than it was when first released. The scruffiest scrap of paper signed by them is worth a small fortune. All round the world there are universities studying their oeuvre – something I would have dismissed as ridiculous, back in the sixties.

Apple, the Beatles organization formed in 1968, never employed more than fifty people during its early years. I reckon that across the world today there are at least five thousand people making their living out of the Beatles: writers, researchers, dealers, academics, conference organizers, tourism and museum people, souvenir manufacturers, plus members of the several hundred or so tribute bands who dress up as Beatles and play their music all around the world, all year round. It is the music that turns them on – though it is of course excellent fun to go and worship at the tourist sites, attend a Beatles fair and buy rubbishy souvenir tat or have your photie taken on the crossing at Abbey Road.

If it is the music that matters, where did it all come from? How did they create their songs when they had no musical training and could not read or write music? What were their influences and inspirations? Even more mysterious, having got started, how come they suddenly metamorphosed, discarding childish, hackneyed, borrowed forms to blossom into the most admired, most studied, most gifted songwriters of our age – or perhaps of any age? All artists develop, but in the case of the Beatles the transformation was dramatic. Who would have thought that the minds responsible for 'Love Me Do' and 'Please Please Me' would go on to produce 'Eleanor Rigby' and 'Across The Universe'?

Their music – the notes and chords, tunes and rhythms – has been well studied, well analysed, well applauded, almost from the moment they received any national attention. Exceedingly clever musicologists have taken apart the quavers and crotchets, dissected the harmonies, revealed the musical tricks and instruments used, numbered and marked all parts of the musical body. We now know exactly which notes were being played and by whom and for how long in that crashing, earth-shaking crescendo at the end of 'A Day In The Life'. But what of the words?

The lyrics have, in comparison, been neglected. (Do note, by the way, it is the lyrics that mainly concern us here, not the melodies.) Can lyrics be pinned down and pulled apart? And even if they can, will it make them any better, any more interesting? Should we presume to analyse when most artists admit they themselves don't always know where those words came from; or should we hold back, just let them be? After all, these are only pop lyrics not Shakespearean sonnets, so why do we need explanations or primers?

Because the creative process is always fascinating. Explanations are not necessary to our enjoyment of the piece, but information that helps to illuminate the process only adds to that enjoyment. So I decided to examine the original versions of their songs, discover how and when those words were first written down, how lines were changed or discarded along the way to the recording studio.

This was to become my self-imposed, self-created mission: to track down as many of the original manuscripts of the Beatles' songs as possible. To look at their lyrics, both in first drafts and finished versions, and try to explain the meaning, the references, the names and places, phrases and expressions. To unveil them, as much as I could.

Can their lyrics be described as poetry? In one sense, no. They are part of songs – an art form where words and music fuse together and are complimentary. The lyrics were not intended to be considered as separate entities, so it is perhaps unfair to judge them on their own.

Unlike some songwriters, the Beatles never began a song with a complete set of verses, all written down. Mostly, they started out with scraps of words or phrases, or only the title. This was John's normal practice. In Paul's case, whole tunes did sometimes come to him, but the words came later.

Words mattered to both of them, though not so much in their early years and in their early songs, when they were following the formula of the time. It was the tune that mattered most. You don't dance to words. The hook, the arresting phrase, was often enough. John was writing real poetry from an early age, in his own fashion, but these were inscribed on different pages, a different part of his brain; he never thought he could get away with writing what he really wanted to in something aimed at the mass market – or the meat market, as he often described it.

But John and Paul did have a literary bent, read widely, appreciated good writing and knew exactly what they didn't like. They also, along with George, passed the eleven-plus exam and went to very good grammar schools and had a grounding in Eng literature, even if at the time they rubbished a lot of it, and the teachers.

The other day, in a moment of boredom, I studied the faces on the famous *Sgt. Pepper* cover – all people they admired or had been influenced by – and was surprised to find there were nine writers: Lewis Carroll, Edgar Allan Poe, Dylan Thomas, Aldous Huxley, Terry Southern, William Burroughs, H.G. Wells, George Bernard Shaw, Stephen Crane. The musical total came to only three: Bob Dylan, Stockhausen and Bobby Breen, a Canadian singer, born 1927, whom I must admit I had never heard of.

When John was gowing up, and was asked what he would like to do if he ever properly grew up, he would often answer: journalist. This was not the truth. He really wanted to be a poet, but thought it would sound unreal and pretentious to say so. In a 1975 interview with *Rolling Stone* magazine, asked what he thought he'd be doing in his sixties, John pictured himself writing children's books. He wanted to write the sort of books that had given him such pleasure and inspiration as a boy – *The Wind in the Willows*, *Alice in Wonderland*, *Treasure Island*.

The fact that someone has literary interests does not mean they have literary talent. I personally think John and Paul did. And it was the main reason I wanted to meet them and why in 1966 I first went to interview Paul. 'Eleanor Rigby' had just been released and I was amazed not just by the tune but by the words. In *The Sunday Times*, I described the lyrics as the best of any contemporary pop song. As if I was qualified to pronounce on anything to do with English Lit.

I still can't claim qualifications to examine literary text, no more than I have the knowledge and expertise to examine the music – though I can read music, having gone to violin lessons for five years as a child, which is five years longer than John or Paul ever managed. But I felt and still feel sufficiently emboldened to write about what I personally like and think about their songs, what I enjoy. This is partly because I am of their generation and background, growing up in the same sort of houses, attending the same sort of Northern grammar school, and also being around them for a short spell (as their biographer 1966–68). I therefore like to think – though it may possibly be my own fantasy – that I have some idea about what might have been in their minds, where the words might have come from.

The danger in writing about their songs, be it the words or the music, is to over-analyse and over-intellectualize. I find so many of the Beatles musicology books unreadable – not just because of the jargon, but because they are writing for specialists, often to impress and score points. The same has happened, to a much lesser extent, with the words. And it's been mainly the more fanatical fans who have got carried away, finding hidden meanings and messages, drug references where none was intended. Quite often, as they progressed, John did throw in meaningless phrases, just to baffle and confuse listeners, and to amuse himself.

One of the attractions of popular music is that you don't really have to know or understand or even like the words. They insinuate themselves into your skull and never leave. I remember as a child learning the words of a really rubbish wartime song called 'Mairzy Doats' – just as John and Paul did, for I recall discussing it with them. It was only years later I discovered the words were 'mares eat oats and does eat oats and little lambs eat ivy'. All nonsense, but no more so than many nursery rhymes that we all have lodged in our heads.

John thought most analysis of music was pretty much nonsense. In his letters, he rarely wrote about his music-making. There were no descriptions of the agonies of composition, the struggles he was going through to create – which is a common preoccupation in the correspondence of poets and the more literary of novelists. Only after the event did he occasionally give clues as to how and when a song got written, and even then only if asked.

No one really, truly knows where words come from. 'Songs are like rabbits: they like to come out of their holes when you're not looking,' according to Canadian singer-songwriter Neil Young. T.S. Eliot said that the words in a poem were there to 'divert' the mind. This is even more the case with lyrics, which often get chosen for their sound, to fit the musical mood, rather than to convey precise meanings, which tends to make analysing them rather a challenge.

However, this has not put off the academics. One of the earliest and most comprehensive studies of Beatles lyrics was published by Colin Campbell and Allan Murphy: *Things We Said Today: The Complete Lyrics and a Concordance to the Beatles' Songs 1962–1970*. Campbell, later to become Professor of Sociology at York University, was teaching at a university in Vancouver at the time. They transcribed all the lyrics on to a computer – which in the seventies must have been a massive task in itself, as computers were about the size of Wembley Stadium – and then analysed them. The results allowed them to reveal to the world the most frequently mentioned colour in the Beatles' lyrics: blue, with 35 mentions, followed by yellow, 32. This does not take into account the fact that half of the 'blues' refer to the mood rather than the colour, and most of the yellows feature in a single song. As with all statistics, the answers often lead to further questions.

Campbell and Murphy's book did, however, feature an excellent introduction in which they traced the development of the lyrics, highlighted the use of homophones (such as, should it be 'I say high, you say low' or 'I say "Hi", you say "'Lo"'?) Listening to the songs, it's hard to know which meaning they intend – and in many cases it might not occur to the listener that there could be an alternative meaning – but I am sure the Beatles did it consciously, loving double meanings.

The academic musicologists, almost from the beginning, were so intent on comparing Beatles tunes with Schubert and Schuman that they gave little thought to the words and whether they might be up there with any of our great poets. Campbell and Murphy in their study started by making a case for Robert Burns as a rough literary equivalent – a songwriter with a lyrical gift, who wrote love ballads, often in the vernacular. They then went on to declare that the most fitting comparison would be Wordsworth – which I think is pushing it, as the traditions of his times were so different.

It's true that Wordsworth wrote about his own life in *The Prelude*, and as a Romantic he advocated letting Nature be our teacher – just as Lennon, particularly in his later songs, asked us to look around and let Love be our teacher; it's also true that Wordsworth came up with some fairly banal lines, such as his description of a pond: 'I measured it from side to side/'tis three feet long and two foot wide.' While working on a Wordsworth biography I raised this with the Dove Cottage experts; their response was defensive, asserting that since Wordsworth was a genius all his compositions, even that one, must be subjected to serious study and consideration and not mocked.

I suppose the same defence can be used when studying the Beatles' lyrics. The lyrics of 'Love Me Do' might seem banal, but should not be dismissed.

It is part of their oeuvre – and more importantly, it was how they began.

But of course we must avoid too much analysing. It will only annoy John, sitting up there.

'Listen, writing about music is like talking about fucking,' as he told *Playboy* magazine in 1980. 'Who wants to talk about it?'

The reasons why a book using the original manuscripts of their lyrics has not appeared before is primarily because of the dreaded laws of copyright. When I edited *The John Lennon Letters* it was relatively simple: all I had to secure was the permission and agreement of Yoko Ono, owner of the Lennon copyright, which she gladly gave. Then find the letters.

When I first embarked on this project, I thought the copyright of any original manuscripts must still belong to Paul McCartney and the Lennon estate, and some to the Harrison estate. I contacted Paul and Yoko and each seemed interested in the project, and appeared willing to help.

Then, after legal soundings, and a lot of casting about, I was informed by Sony/ATV that the publishing copyright of almost every Beatles' song is owned by them and it covers *all versions* of their songs, even ones they do not know exist.

Before mechanical recording of songs came in, a music publisher was someone who physically published the music and words of a song in the form of sheet music. That's how people in the nineteenth and early twentieth centuries would learn the latest songs, playing them on an instrument or singing them. From around 1900 onwards, the publisher – who of course was spending money and taking all the risks – owned the copyright and took 50 per cent of all proceeds. When gramophone records came in, the system continued and until 1952 it was sales of sheet music which determined the UK's weekly hit parade. After that, the sales and influence of sheet music declined, but the power of the music publisher remained.

The Beatles' music publisher from almost the beginning of their career was Dick James, under the banner of Northern Songs. He owned 50 per cent, the traditional split, while the other half was divided between John and Paul and Brian Epstein, their manager, with minor shares belonging to George Harrison and Ringo Starr.

In 1969, Dick James sold his share to Lew Grade of ATV – and the Beatles were persuaded to do the same. At the time, they were paying income tax at around 90 per cent in the pound and this was a way of making a quick tax-free gain.

In 1985, the rights came up for sale again. Paul and Yoko had not been on the best of terms, but they were interested and tried to get the price down. While they hesitated, in stepped Michael Jackson – and bought the lot for a reported sum of £24 million. In 2005, Jackson had money problems and did a deal with Sony, receiving around £60 million for half the ownership. Since his death, Sony/ATV has been controlling all the rights.

Throughout this period, ever since Northern Songs sold out, every time Paul has performed 'Yesterday' in public he has been required to pay a copyright fee – even though he is singing his own song, one he composed. Though as a performer, like all performers, he still gets a performance fee, administered by the Performing Rights Society.

The next major hurdle was locating the manuscripts. I happen to have acquired nine of them, back in the sixties, which is how my interest in them first began. While I was in the studio at Abbey Road, late at night, there would often be scraps of paper lying around. Many of these were just left at the end of the night for the cleaners to burn. Now and again, if I had been following a particular song from the beginning and knew I was going to write about it in the book, I would ask if I could have them. And they would say yes, of course, otherwise they will only be binned.

The Beatles, at that stage, had no interest in where they had come from or what they had done so far, only in the next thing. They were very young, still in their mid-twenties, an age when you rarely think of keeping stuff. Anyway, the point of being in the recording studio was to record; once the new song was captured on tape, why keep the scribbled words? It was just scrap paper to them.

Whenever I visited their homes, I would ask if they had lyrics of any earlier songs that I wanted to write about, and they would rummage around and give me the odd scrap. All of these I kept, long after the book was published, just as I kept the memorabilia and ephemera – from football programmes to guide books of the forts on Hadrian's Wall – picked up while doing my other forty or so non-fiction books. None of the latter has turned out to be at all valuable. But the Beatles memorabilia? Towards the end of 1981, I woke up one day to discover that Sotheby's had had their first auction of Beatles bits – and that my nine lyrics were worth more than my house.

The first major auction of Beatles material was held at Sotheby's in London in December 1981.

I rang the British Museum, offering the collection to them on permanent loan, thinking they might say, Nah, we don't do pop music, but they were pleased to accept it. When the new British Library building opened in 1997 in Euston Road, my collection was transferred to their Manuscript Room, where it remains to this day, next to Magna Carta and the works of Shakespeare, Beethoven, Wordsworth and a host of other creative greats. In my will, they will go permanently to the British Library – as some of them already have done. If I were to sell them on the open market, I know they would end up in the USA or Japan. I want them kept together, as a collection, here in the UK, available to be seen and studied.

It was not until I began this project that I learned mine is the largest known collection of Beatles lyrics in a public archive. (We don't know precisely what Paul and Yoko themselves own – but both have private archives.) I have discovered, though, another equally important and almost as extensive collection in the USA, at Northwestern University in Illinois, gathered together by John Cage (1912–92), the American composer whose most famous piece was called '4'33"' – because it lasted exactly 4 minutes and 33 seconds. The piece, which had to be performed in silence, still receives regular performances around the world. It was the sort of avant-garde music and art that by 1966 Paul and John, now they had become London arty types, were interested in.

Back in 1966 Cage was collecting original musical scores and lyrics to benefit the Foundation of Contemporary Performance Arts. Yoko Ono, a friend of Cage's, managed to persuade John (whom she had recently met although they were not as yet together) to hand over six lyrics. The Beatles were by then in the middle of *Revolver*, and the manuscripts were from that album. Then Yoko turned up at Paul's one day and got from him the coloured manuscript of 'The Word' from *Rubber Soul* (see pages 123–25).

Cage's seven Beatles lyrics were acquired by Northwestern University in 1973–74. 'Today they are some of the most valuable items we hold,' says D.J. Hoek, the present head of the Music Library. 'They are the initial expression of a musical idea on paper.'

Aside from Northwestern, I have been unable to find any other proper collections of Beatles lyrics, at least not in known or public hands, but there could be some billionaire with a stash of them in his den. I doubt it, somehow; these days, they very rarely come up and prices start at around $250,000 – and on two occasions they have reached the $1,000,000 mark. But there must be individual collectors who bought a lyric relatively cheaply when they first started appearing for sale in the 1980s. And also people like me, who were given them by John, Paul and George many years earlier. Those people who went on to sell them, often did so privately, through dealers rather than in the public auction rooms, so no records are available. I do know of one person, a friend of Paul's, who was trying to sell seven lyrics back in the 1970s, offering them to various institutions (including Northwestern); in the end he sold them at a London auction house. They are now dispersed around the world, owned by various individuals.

The Quarrymen in November 1957. Paul and John are at the microphones, in white jackets, indicating that they are the joint leaders.

In trying to track down original manuscripts of the lyrics, I did the obvious things: approached all the main auctions houses, such as Sotheby's, Christie's and Bonhams, and the main memorabilia dealers, such as Tracks in the UK. I also contacted collectors who might have any, even copies, and also Beatles experts, researchers and academics who have made a life study of Beatles music. Fortunately, many of those I contacted had kept good scans, which they were kind enough to let me have. (They don't of course own the publishing copyright; that belongs to our dear friends at Sony.)

I also made contact with several private collectors who own original lyrics, but in almost every case they requested no publicity. They don't want to run the risk of being burgled, or for people to know what they own.

Some of the manuscripts are mere scraps, some hard to read, and some almost identical to the recorded lyric, but these remain of interest, to me anyway, if only to see their handwriting. The most difficult to locate have been the lyrics from the early years, perhaps because they were rarely written down in those days. 'Love Me Do', for example, has very few words, so there was little need to write them down. Those early recordings were done quickly, with the band in and out of the studio in as short a time as possible, with few people around. No one thought of preserving scruffy scraps of paper.

When it came to the later albums, circa 1965 and onwards, I managed to track down more and more, till eventually – as in the case of *Sgt. Pepper* – I had succeeded in tracing some sort of manuscript version of every number on the entire album. So in the end I did reach my target of one hundred Beatles songs.

How many songs are there in total? It depends how you define a Beatles song. My definition is a song composed and recorded by the Beatles, during the period they were the Beatles, i.e. until the band finally split in 1970. So that precludes recordings of songs composed by other people – something they often did in their early days; songs they composed but gave to others to perform and never recorded themselves; songs created after the Beatles ceased to exist and they became solo artists; songs without lyrics, i.e. instrumentals such as 'Flying' on the *Magical Mystery Tour* album; variations of the same song, such as the reprise of the *Sgt. Pepper* title song or 'Revolution'. By that reckoning, my total of Beatles songs comes to 182.

I have almost always tried to arrange them chronologically in the order in which we, the fans, heard them, which was not necessarily the order in which they were written or recorded. Roughly speaking, there was little divergence until the very end when *Let It Be*, the film and the album, came out chronologically last, for various complicated reasons, while the real last album, the final one they worked on and gave to us, was *Abbey Road*.

Where I have secured a manuscript, by which I mean an image of an original handwritten version, I have also included the final recorded and published version, so you can compare the two. With the lyrics – i.e. the final recorded version – also note that when there are endless repetitions of the chorus, or verses, or the same lines, I did not always include the repetitions, just to save space.

In considering them chronologically, I have also tried to tell the story of the band's music-making and its development. Their music comes out of their lives, just as their lives and feelings and emotions got reflected back into their music. So in some ways it has become the story of their lives as told through their music.

Paul and John – and George: a Brief Musical Biography

Paul and John met through music – and for no other reason. They didn't attend the same school or even live in the same area, in fact they had never even met prior to Saturday, 6 July 1957, when John's little schoolboy group, the Quarrymen, played at a church fête in Woolton, Liverpool, and Paul was brought along by a mutual acquaintance, Ivan Vaughan, a friend of John's who attended the same school as Paul.

Paul, just turned fifteen, brought his guitar along, and after watching the Quarrymen perform he was introduced to John, the group's leader, and proceeded to demonstrate his expertise on the guitar, playing a number called 'Twenty Flight Rock'. John was impressed, but of course tried not to show it, being tough, being the boss. He realized that Paul knew more chords and was probably a better guitarist than him, so for a week he pondered whether it would be a good idea to introduce a rival into the group. On reflection, he decided yes and invited Paul to join. A year later, George Harrison, who was at the same school as Paul, a year younger but already as good a guitarist as either of them, was introduced by Paul to John and he too became one of the Quarrymen.

GARDEN FETE
ST. PETER'S CHURCH FIELD

WOOLTON PARISH CHURCH   Rector: M. Pryce Jones.

Saturday, 6th July, 1957
at 3 p.m.

ADMISSION BY PROGRAMME:
CHILDREN 3d.

PROCEEDS IN AID OF CHURCH FUNDS.

John with the Quarrymen in 1957.

Looking back, it was remarkable that three people we now consider to have been such talented performers and composers should have grown up together at the same time, in the same place, and then joined together, and stayed together, for the next thirteen years. There was every chance they might never have met – or met very briefly and then gone their separate ways. There were thousands of youths of their age in the Liverpool area, let alone the rest of Britain, all loving the same sort of music, trying to play it, joining little groups, breaking up and moving on to other ventures. One of the original Quarrymen, the drummer Colin Hanton, went on to become an upholsterer. Another, Rod Davis, who became head boy of Quarry Bank School and later went on to Cambridge, was at the time, back in 1957, just as proficient a musician as John and the others.

So what was it in John, Paul and George that made them persevere when for a long time the world showed no interest in what they were doing – which was mainly begging for humble engagements at parties and village halls.

John always said that, but for the Beatles coming along, he would have ended up like his dad, doing nothing very much, or failing that, a tramp. Paul, who was always more calculating, more clued up, did have some paper qualifications, having sat his A levels, and could well have gone on to training college and become a teacher, which would have pleased his father. But he, along with John and George, eventually became obsessed with making music, ignoring the advice of most adults and family members who warned that they would never make a living at it.

In 1964, Paul gave an interview to an American Beatles magazine, just before their USA tour, in which he said that his ambition had always been to get into some sort of group and stay in it for a few years – hopefully till the age of twenty-five. Then he would give it up and go to art college, the one John had attended, 'And hang out there for a few years.'

I remembered his father, Jim, telling me that as a boy Paul had been just as interested in drawing and painting as he had been in music. Similarly, John, when he was growing up, had spent most of his spare time writing stories and poems, drawing cartoons and pictures. So that subsequent total passion for music, which came about in their teenage years, had not been an all-consuming factor when they were growing up.

As youngsters, both John and Paul had been offered music lessons by devoted and caring parents, but both later admitted that they simply couldn't be bothered, they were too lazy, moreover they hated people telling them how to do things. So where did the talent for music come from?

In the case of John – born 9 October 1940, and brought up by his Aunt Mimi after his parents split – there was a vague musical background in the family. His father, Freddie, who went off to sea, had a good singing voice (so he told me, and of course I believed him) and would entertain his friends at get-togethers with a song or two, but he never did it for a living. His own father, also called John Lennon, had for a time toured the USA as part of a group of Kentucky minstrels. It proved to be nothing more than an interlude in his early life; at the end of the tour he returned to Liverpool, where he spent the remainder of his working days as a clerk.

John's mother, Julia, played the banjo well enough to teach John some basic chords and encourage him to continue. She also played the accordion, according to her daughter Julia Baird (John's half-sister) and had a good singing voice, but could not read music. 'She was forever singing,' remembers Julia. John was fifteen when his mother died in a car accident, just as she was coming back into his life again.

John's Aunt Mimi was so against him playing guitar that she made him practise outside in the porch. She appears to have had no interest in music, at least popular music. 'I think the maternal side of our family,' says David Birch, John's cousin (son of his Aunt Harriet), 'can fairly be described as tone deaf – apart from his mother Julia.'

Pauline Lennon, now Pauline Stone, the widow of Freddie, John's father, says that Freddie couldn't play an instrument or read music. 'But he had excellent pitch and rhythm and loved to sing. In fact he was always singing. It was impossible ever to feel down with him around. Mainly it was popular ballads, like "Smile" or "Blue Moon" but also a bit of opera – I also remember him singing "Nessun Dorma". He had a tenor voice, but I'd describe him as a "crooner".'

John also learned to play the mouth organ as a young boy, after a fashion. His Uncle George (husband of Mimi) had given him a cheap one and he took it with him on a bus trip to Edinburgh to stay with his aunt, playing it for the entire journey. The bus driver told him to come back to the bus station next day – and presented him with a much better one.

Paul, born 18 June 1942, had a much stronger musical heritage. His father,

Jim, although never a full-time professional musician (he spent his working life as a cotton salesman), did have his own little jazz band before the war: Jim Mac's Band. Paul remembers as a boy loving all the family gatherings where his uncles and aunts would sing songs and play instruments. In this the McCartneys were fairly typical; most extended working-class families could boast at least one amateur musician able to play the piano or the fiddle – self-taught – always on call for a good old-fashioned family knees-up.

Jim played the piano and the trumpet – until his teeth went – and they had instruments in the house, but because he played by ear he felt unable to teach Paul how to play, not knowing the rules and the language. Paul did have a couple of lessons, then gave up. But his aptitude was clearly always there, encouraged by Jim, who told him that if he learned the piano he would always be invited to parties.

As for George, born 25 February 1943, neither of his parents appear to have been very musical. George's father, a bus driver, had owned a guitar at one time, during the war, but he does not appear to have played it while George was growing up. George's mother Louise enjoyed a sing-song and, unlike John's Aunt Mimi, she actively encouraged George when he joined the Quarrymen, going along to watch them play.

Both Paul and George grew up in homes where the radio was blaring out all the time, usually popular music, whereas John's Aunt Mimi preferred silence. It was one of the reasons John was rather impressed by their musical knowledge in the early days.

In 1963, the *Record Mirror* submitted seventy-eight questions to each of the Beatles. (The results were never published, presumably because only Paul and Ringo filled them in properly, while the other two mucked about and didn't answer them all.) One of the questions asked them to name their biggest musical influence; Paul's answer – in John's handwriting – is 'John'. Why? 'Because he's great'. Paul has then scored this out and written 'My Dad'.

Asked what his Dad thought of his music, Paul responded: 'My Dad likes it, but he thinks we are away a bit too much.' Did he encourage your music? 'Not half. He suffered my practising for years.' Asked what else his parents would have liked him to be, 'Clever,' replies Paul.

Paul's mother Mary died in 1956 from breast cancer. Paul was fourteen at the time and his younger brother Michael recalls it was around then that Paul's obsession with the guitar began, throwing himself into learning to play it. Was it a compensation mechanism? Would it have happened otherwise? The first song Paul remembers writing was 'I Lost My Little Girl' which he thinks he wrote when he was about fourteen. He played it to John, not long after they first met.

Mary McCartney, like George's mother, was Roman Catholic, but neither

Paul nor George were sent to Catholic schools. In fact, they attended Church of England Sunday schools, as did John. Paul was a keen choirboy, and he had a good clear singing voice, as did his younger brother Michael. Though none of the Beatles' parents was overtly religious or even regular church-goers, the boys followed working-class conventions of forties and fifties Britain whereby children were sent to church or Sunday school on a Sunday, giving their parents a break and perhaps the opportunity for a bit of a Sunday-morning cuddle.

The Beatles in 1960, then called the Silver Beetles, auditioning before Larry Parnes, which led to their first tour, two weeks as a backing group to the north of Scotland. Far left is Stu Sutcliffe, who had just joined the group. The drummer, looking pretty bored, was a stand-in. Left to right: John, Paul and George.

Did their Catholic mothers – in the case of Paul and George – and regular Church of England attendance have any influence on their musical tastes and knowledge? A case has been made out for the effect of religion on their music. But I think it is fairly minimal.

And what of their Irish ancestry? Paul and John both had Irish roots, as did George, through his mother. The Irish, so we are always told, are very musical. But then so, traditionally, are Merseysiders. In fact we all are, if we go back far enough. The folk tradition of stories and songs passed on orally from one generation to the next exists in every culture.

There is another minor element in their inherited make-up, which did come out in their music, and that is humour. Merseyside humour is built on mockery, irony, sarcasm, satire, not taking yourself too seriously, or others. According to the late Ian MacDonald, author of an excellent book on the Beatles records, mainly about their music, 'Liverpool is a designated area of outstanding natural sarcasm'. As their lyrics progressed, there is a lot of humour, as we shall see, jokes, puns, word-play, pastiche. Even when being terribly serious and preachy – which they could be at times, delivering morals and messages – they usually ended with a laugh, mocking themselves.

Even if we agree that John and Paul inherited some musical talent from one or other of their parents, and that their family life and upbringing in Liverpool did have an influence on their music, we all know that that is not quite enough to account for their genius, otherwise loads of us would have written 'Yesterday'. One of the common clichés about genius is that it is 10 per cent inspiration to 90 per cent perspiration.

The Beatles certainly worked extremely hard. When they first appeared, in London and later in New York, they were assumed to be overnight sensations who had come from nowhere. In fact they spent the six years leading up to 1963 unknown and mostly unpaid, struggling to be the Beatles, which equals the six years they spent as the world-famous Fab Four until the band broke up in 1969.

Paul might later have exaggerated how many songs they wrote in those early years, but they did write loads. And the songwriting didn't fall off when they became famous. Far from sitting back on their laurels, idly counting their money and gold discs, or lazily repeating a tried-and-trusted formula, they continued onwards and upwards – and occasionally sideways and backwards. The important thing was to evolve, move on, try something new. Their output from 1963–1965 was prodigious. While travelling hundreds of thousands of miles, performing hundreds of live concerts, recording films, TV shows and interviews, they still managed to bring out album after album of new and wonderful songs.

Their musical talent may have been something they were born with, but arguably the most important elements in the creation of the Beatles' music were hard work and dedication. Without those ingredients, their legacy would have been puny.

The spark that first brought the band to life, that drew out what was lurking inside, was skiffle. This was home-made, do-it-yourself music, the kind anyone could have a go at, even if they couldn't play an instrument, or didn't even have an instrument. Lonnie Donegan's 'Rock Island Line', which was a hit in 1956, was a huge influence, encouraging the untrained and the unmusical to have a go, even if all they did was scrape a washboard with a thimble or twang a tea-chest bass. That same year, Elvis Presley's 'Heartbreak Hotel' went to the top of the charts in fourteen countries. Then there was Bill Haley with his 'Rock

Around The Clock', the theme tune for the film *Blackboard Jungle*, which had British teenage audiences ripping up cinema seats. Suddenly, the young John, Paul and George had new musical idols whose records they rushed out to buy or borrow, to listen to and work out how it was done.

Their first instinct was to copy. How could it not be? They wanted to reproduce the noises they liked and the words being sung. As they progressed, and they got a bit better on their guitars, their tastes progressed. They became desperate for the latest American rock and roll records.

What was unusual about the coming together of Paul and John was that they moved on almost at once from copying to creating their own versions. But they still followed the format of the day when it came to what constituted a pop song. It had to be just under four minutes long and preferably about boy–girl love. The words didn't really matter as long as it had a hook, a catchy title or phrase, and an exciting beat or infectious melody. Happy, hopeful, romantic love was the preferred subject matter, though you could also write about the opposite side of the coin – unhappy, miserable love, tears and pain – but not too often or your audience would get fed up and go elsewhere. Regardless of what the song was about, it was vital that you could dance to the tune. Even the unhappy, slow ones. That was about it, really.

John and Paul began writing songs when Paul was still only fifteen, not long after they first met. He would bunk off school and go home to their empty council house at 20 Forthlin Road while his father was at work. John would join him. It became easier for John to spend time there after he started art college in 1958. Nobody, least of all Mimi, knew where he was most of the time.

They would play their guitars, head to head, watching each other, learning new chords, trying out different fingering, copying and criticizing each other. As they made up songs they wrote the titles down in a school exercise book, sometimes with an attempt at trying to list the chord sequence so they would remember it, using their own made-up notation. Each song was marked as 'another Lennon and McCartney original'. Within a year or so, Paul was boasting that they had already written between seventy and one hundred songs – the number varied, and was usually greatly exaggerated.

There is an early photograph, taken by Paul's brother Michael, that shows them in the front parlour at Forthlin Road, which was where the piano was, though that can't be seen in the photograph. They are sitting side by side in front of the fireplace, both in black, like mirror reflections – Paul, being left-handed, holds the guitar under his left arm, while John has his under his right. They seem joined together, one body with two heads. Both are leaning forward, looking down at the notes for a song written in an exercise book lying on the floor in front of them. According to Michael, the song they were playing that day was 'I Saw Her Standing There'. He says that he once blew the photo up and could see that the first words were in fact 'He' and then 'She', but these were both crossed out before they settled on 'I' saw her standing there.

At one time, John and Paul decided to write a play. 'It was a serious play,' so John recalled in a *New Musical Express* interview in 1963. 'It was about Jesus coming back to earth today and living in the slums. We called the character Pilchard. It fell through in the end.'

They also wrote short stories together, which indicates that their creative urges were not solely directed towards pop songs. John of course was writing nonsense verse, joke and cartoons from an early age – many of which later emerged in his two books of poems.

Paul and John, left- and right-handers, like mirror reflections, caught composing together by Paul's brother Michael in 1962. On the floor is an exercise book with their earliest songs.

Their joint song writing continued and it led to them making their first primitive record. One day, some time in the summer of 1958, they walked into the little DIY recording studio of an elderly gentleman called Percy Phillips in the Kensington area of Liverpool. On one side they recorded 'That'll Be The Day', Buddy Holly's 1957 classic, and on the other their own composition, 'In Spite Of All The Danger'.

It cost them seventeen shillings and sixpence, which worked out at three shillings and sixpence each for the five Quarrymen who took part that day. It was the most they could afford, and they ended up with only one copy of their record. They took turns to have it, a week or so at a time, to show it off to friends and family. The last one to have it was John Duff Lowe, a member of the Quarrymen at the time, a school pal of Paul's, who played the piano. He kept it for the next two decades, by which time it had been as good as forgotten. When I was interviewing John, Paul and George in 1966–68 for the biography, not one of them mentioned it.

John Duff Lowe, now a retired businessman living in the West Country, remembers it well:

I can clearly recall rehearsing 'In Spite of All the Danger' at Paul's house during our Sunday afternoon rehearsals, and Paul showing me how he wanted me to play bluesy accents – playing a black key with an adjacent white one – which you can clearly hear on the recording.

It ran for four minutes, which we were not supposed to do. This had Percy Phillips pulling his finger across his throat, indicating we had to stop at three minutes fifty seconds. When the original is played, the needle rises a millisecond after George's last chord, a single strum. He probably did it in the heat of the moment, knowing we had run out of time.

The first recorded song, 'In Spite Of All The Danger', by the Beatles, then the Quarrymen, in 1958. Only one copy was ever made.

When the record reappeared in the 1980s it was obvious that, as a unique part of early Beatles history, it was a worth a fortune. It was all set to go to auction but Paul stepped in and bought it privately. Today it is often described as the single most valuable record in history and would be worth a small fortune if it ever came on the market again. In 1995 it was heard for the first time on the Beatles' *Anthology* album.

The interesting thing about the record is the fact that they included a self-composed number. The home-made disc label credits the composers as 'McCartney, Harrison'. In reality, it was all Paul, trying to do an Elvis-type ballad, but George got a credit for helping with the arrangement. John is the lead vocalist on both songs with Paul and George backing up on harmonies.

The lyrics are fairly unmemorable: 'In spite of all the danger / In spite of all that may be / I'll do anything for you / Anything you want me to / If you'll be true to me.'

I have always been intrigued by the precise meaning. If it is just a boy–girl love song, as it appears, then why would there be any danger? It's almost as if an illicit affair was going on, perhaps with a married woman, but how could that be, for a teenage boy in 1958, when sex had not yet been invented?*

Paul might well have been subconsciously thinking of his first sexual experience, which he later told me about, and which I used in my 1968 biography: 'I got it first at fifteen. She was older and bigger than me. She was supposed to be babysitting while her mother was out.' So that could have been the danger.

In August 1960 they made their first of five trips to play in Hamburg, a stage in their life seen as vital for their development as performers, helping them to create their own distinctive sound. It is interesting to wonder whether that would have come about if Paul's mother had lived? As a trained nurse and midwife, she was keen on her sons' education and on their economic and social improvement. She might well have insisted that he stayed on at grammar

---

* Philip Larkin in his 1974 poem 'Annus Mirabilis' famously said that sexual intercourse began with the Beatles' first LP in 1963.

school to complete his studies. John's Aunt Mimi had less influence in his life after he became an art student, while George, who had already left school and started a fairly pointless apprenticeship, was encouraged by his mother in all his musical activities. Mary McCartney, however, might well have put her foot down. And Paul, being a dutiful son, might well have given in. Then what would have happened? Would John and George have gone to Hamburg without Paul, splitting the Lennon–McCartney partnership before it had even begun?

In Hamburg they got their second experience of a recording studio, but only as the backing group for a singer called Tony Sheridan. I have a copy of the contract they signed with Bert Kaempfert Produktion dated 1 July 1961. Clause 7 states that John is 'authorized as the Group's representative to receive the payments'. John was the leader, as he had started the group. Whereas Paul's full name, James Paul McCartney, is given, John Winston Lennon is listed as John W. Lennon. Pete Best was their drummer at the time, before the change to Ringo.

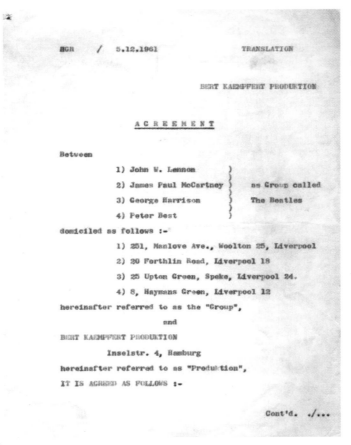

German contract for the Beatles, 1961, as a backing group, giving their home addresses.

BORN 9th OCT 1940 (age 20.)
EDUCATED QUARRY BANK GRAMMER SCH
THEN LIVERPOOL COLLEGE OF ART
(THROWN OUT). WENT TO SCOTLAND
TOURING WITH A BRITISH SINGER
WENT TO HAMBURG (AUG 1960) FOR 4
MONTHS WITH THE GROUP. RETURNED
AGAIN 1961 TO TOP TEN CLUB.
STARTED THE GROUP ABOUT 4 YEARS
AGO (SKIFFLE) PAUL JOINED THEN
GEORGE. HAD ONE OR TWO DRUMMERS
PETE JOINED 2DAYS BEFORE OUR
1ST VISIT TO HAMBURG WITH HALF
A DRUM KIT — WE ONLY HAD LITTLE
AMPLIFIERS BUT BOUGHT BETTER
ONES IN HAMBURG.
INSTRUMENTS PLAYED GUITAR
(PIANO) GUITAR BASS
WRITTEN A COUPLE OF SONGS WITH
PAUL
AMBITION. TO BE RICH.
JOHN . W. LENNON (LEADER)

PAUL McCARTNEY
BORN 18 . 6 . '42 . LIVERPOOL.
Educated. Liverpool INSTITUTE Grammar
school. Left 1960 to tour
Scotland, then came to Hamburg,
then back to Liverpool, and
then to "Top Ten" Club Hamburg,
returning to Liverpool at the
end of time.
Been in the group (formerly
a skiffle group — "The
Quarry men" —) for around
4 years; but, with "the Beatles"
for almost 2 years.
Instruments: Guitar,
piano, guitar bass.
Hobby — pastime.
Music, etc....
Songs written: With John
(LENNON) — around 70 songs

Biog notes, written by John, Paul and George, for their German recording company in 1961. John signs himself 'Leader'.

Polydor, the recording company, asked each of the group to write out a little biography. In his, John lists his ambition as 'to be rich' and signs himself 'John W. Lennon (Leader)'; he mentions in passing that he has 'written a couple of songs with Paul'. The biography Paul prepared is more detailed and effusive. Under a separate headline, 'Songs Written', he states 'with John (Lennon) – around 70 songs'.

NAME GEORGE HARRISON
BORN IN LIVERPOOL — ENGLAND — 25/2/43
EDUCATED AT LIVERPOOL INSTITUTE
HIGH SCHOOL — THEN WORKED AS ELECTRICIAN
FOR 3 MONTHS — BUT FINISHED WORK
TO TOUR SCOTLAND PLAYING ROCK +
ROLL. AUGUST 1960 CAME TO HAMBURG
TO PLAY AT KAISERKELLER. RETURNED
TO LIVERPOOL DECEMBER AS I WAS
ONLY 17 YEARS OLD AND THE POLICE
SAID I WAS NOT ALLOWED TO WORK.
APRIL 1961 RETURNED TO HAMBURG TO
PLAY AT TOP TEN CLUB REEPERBAHN.

This record was to find its way to Liverpool and NEMS record shop, run by Brian Epstein, which led to Brian meeting them and going on to become their manager. In a five-year contract between Brian and the Beatles, signed on 1 October 1962, John and Ringo sign in their own names but Paul and George, still being under twenty-one, also had to obtain the signatures of their fathers.

The band agree that Brian, as their manager, will receive 25 per cent of 'all moneys in consideration of their services as Artists'. The list of these services, covering how and where they might be performing or working, is interesting. It includes 'vaudeville and review' and also 'balls, dances and private parties'. There is no mention of the possibility of any income as composers. Did Brian not expect them to make much money writing their own stuff, seeing them only as performers? Or was there no point in mentioning income from songs when they had yet to become recording artists?

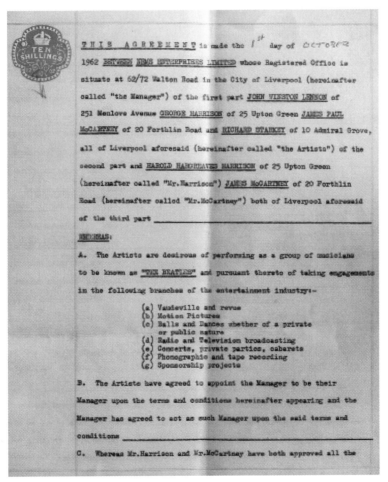

Contract with Brian Epstein's company, NEMS, 1962, in which they are desirous of performing at vaudeville, balls, dances, phonographic recordings.

One of their earliest engagements, before Brian took over, was at a strip club in Liverpool. When the stripper came on, she handed down her sheet music for them to play her backing tune. Unable to read it, they played something they did know, which was 'Ramrod'. So, if they had been able to read music, would they have gone a different route, becoming session musicians, perhaps not bothering to write their own songs? Of course not. Their view was that being properly trained would only hold them back. Not knowing the rules allowed them to break the rules.

Paul never seems to have composed with George, or even thought about it, yet while they were both at the Liverpool Institute, he would often go back to George's house, where his mother Louise was always welcoming, and they would practise chords, learn new tunes and techniques. But neither remembered writing together.

George was young for his age, which was very young anyway, as everyone remarked upon at the time, observing him walking like a lapdog ten yards behind John. He looked up to Paul as the clever one, and John as the leader, and tended to fade into the background rather than push himself forward. At sixteen, he had left school and started work as an apprentice electrician in a local department store. He probably felt intellectually inferior to Paul, the sixth former, and John, the art college student. When it came to composing songs, he left that to John and Paul, concentrating on playing the guitar properly.

Right from the beginning, Paul and John hit it off as joint composers. There was clearly some chemistry there. They were competing while co-operating, supporting while criticizing, rivals yet fans, loving each other while bitching. It was in the act of making music that they were at their closest.

Paul, George and John, recording in Abbey Road Studios, July 1963.

Partnerships were the norm when it came to composing popular songs, usually with one person responsible for the lyrics while the other did the music – for example Gilbert penned the words and Sullivan the music; Elton John's songs had words written by Bernie Taupin; Mick Jagger did most of the words while Keith Richards composed the music. There have of course been notable exceptions, such as Noël Coward and Cole Porter, who did it all. (Cole Porter used to irritate Rodgers and Hammerstein by saying 'How can it take two men to write one song?')

Aside from the fact that they both wrote words and music, the other unusual aspect of Lennon and McCartney's partnership was that they were performers as well as composers. Most composers, joint or otherwise, take a back seat, handing over their babies for others to bring into public life. Elvis never wrote his own songs, nor did Frank Sinatra. Dylan is an exception, writing words and music as well as performing, and his example inspired Paul and John.

There was one interesting and rather mysterious break in their joint song writing, which had been so productive from almost the first time they met, turning out, supposedly, 100 original new songs. During their early spells in Hamburg – covering roughly a year, 1960–61, they don't appear to have written much, if anything. They were together all the time, not having to rely on finding an empty house in order to sit and work on a new song, as they had done in their early years at home in Liverpool, so in theory they should have produced more.

They were of course busy performing, almost nonstop, taking pills to keep awake, so didn't have much spare time. But the more likely explanation is that when they first went to Hamburg, John was more involved with his art college friend Stu Sutcliffe, whom he had talked into joining the Beatles. Paul felt a bit a jealous, rather excluded, and for a while his relationship with John was not quite as intense. In July 1961, Stu, now engaged to Astrid Kirchherr, stayed on in Hamburg and left the group. He died tragically after a brain hemorrhage in April 1962.

By then, John and Paul had started writing songs together again, especially when there seemed to be a possibility, thanks to Brian Epstein's hard work, that Decca or someone else might really offer them a recording contract.

There has always been a prejudice in the recording industry against performers getting above themselves, imagining they are creative artistes. Audiences can be unreceptive too; when an artist they know and love announces he or she is going to sing a song they have just written, the reaction from the fans is liable to be a moan of 'Spare us'.

The other bias in Britain was that home-grown songs were, well, home-grown, and therefore inferior to the American variety, hence our native composers had to copy American music, producing pastiche country and western or phoney blues songs, and the singers had to adopt a mid-Atlantic accent. British pop music, such as it was in the fifties and early sixties, was also London-centred, with a prejudice against provincial towns and cities, especially Northern ones like Liverpool – the assumption being that nothing noteworthy had ever come from there.

The Beatles had to break all these barriers down – and it took time.

So it's all the more surprising that, when at long last they did get a break – the chance of a recording contract, in London – they dared presume or at least hope to be allowed to perform one of their home-grown original numbers …

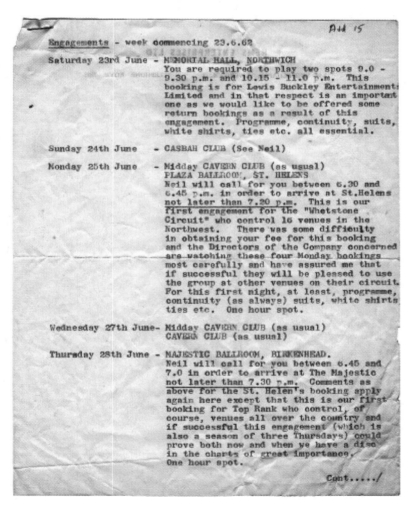

Brian Epstein's instructions for some of their exciting engagements, June 1962, – for which suits and ties were essential.

The Beatles, January 1963, make a personal appearance at NEMS musical store in Liverpool, signing copies of their new single 'Please Please Me'.

I

LOVE ME DO

Early singles and the first LP, *Please Please Me*

October 1962–August 1963

I have been unable to find a handwritten version of the words to 'Love Me Do'
– not a good start to this venture. Paul originally jotted down the words in a
school notebook. They had been singing it together for at least four years, from
Liverpool to Hamburg and back, and the words are simple and repetitious. It's
hard to forget them, even after a few drinks or some funny pills, so no need to
write out any copies.

Considering the simplicity of the song, the recording history of 'Love Me
Do' is complicated. It was one of thirty-three numbers that Brian Epstein
typed out and offered to George Martin for their EMI audition on 6 June 1962.

I have always called it an audition, which is how the Beatles approached it,
but Mark Lewisohn in volume one of his masterly history of the Beatles (*The
Beatles Tune In*, 2013) says that EMI had already signed the Beatles. Behind the
scenes, their publishing company (Ardmore and Beechwood) had heard the
tapes of the Beatles' failed Decca audition and liked the sound of their original
compositions, such as 'Like Dreamers Do', and wanted to acquire publishing
rights, so George Martin was being leaned on to sign them up.

Despite all this, listening to them in the studio, George would presumably
still have decided he personally did not want to work with them, if he had
considered they were rubbish.

For the test recording, which is what we shall call it, Brian Epstein
suggested a play list including seven original numbers, five of which feature
Paul as the main singer, so we must presume he wrote them: 'PS I Love You',
'Love Me Do', 'Like Dreamers Do', 'Love of the Loved' and 'Pinwheel Twist'.
There were also two to be sung by John: 'Ask Me Why' and 'Hello Little Girl'.
The rest were all well-known standard pop numbers of the day – or in some
cases, yesterday. At the top of the page, Brian suggested a medley of three as
their opening offering – none of which were written by them.

During the session, they recorded four songs in all: the first number on

Brian's list, 'Besame Mucho', and three of their original compositions: 'Love Me Do', 'P.S. I Love You' and 'Ask Me Why'.

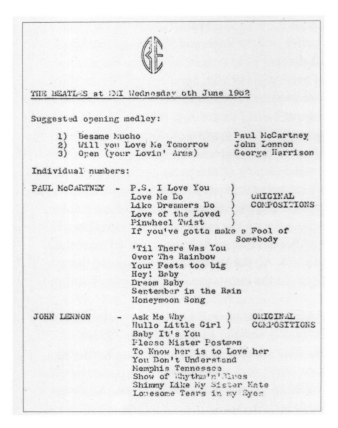

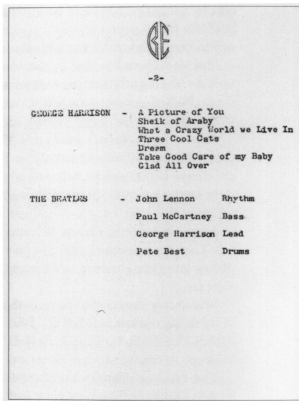

THE BEATLES at EMI Wednesday 6th June 1962

Suggested opening medley:

1) Besame Mucho — Paul McCartney
2) Will you Love Me Tomorrow — John Lennon
3) Open (your Lovin' Arms) — George Harrison

Individual numbers:

PAUL McCARTNEY — P.S. I Love You)
Love Me Do) ORIGINAL
Like Dreamers Do) COMPOSITIONS
Love of the Loved)
Pinwheel Twist)
If you've gotta make a Fool of Somebody
'Til There Was You
Over The Rainbow
Your Feets too big
Hey! Baby
Dream Baby
September in the Rain
Honeymoon Song

JOHN LENNON — Ask Me Why) ORIGINAL
Hullo Little Girl) COMPOSITIONS
Baby It's You
Please Mister Postman
To Know her is to Love her
You Don't Understand
Memphis Tennessee
Show of Rhythm'n'Blues
Shimmy Like My Sister Kate
Lonesome Tears in my Eyes

-2-

GEORGE HARRISON — A Picture of You
Sheik of Araby
What a Crazy World we Live In
Three Cool Cats
Dream
Take Good Care of my Baby
Glad All Over

THE BEATLES — John Lennon Rhythm
Paul McCartney Bass
George Harrison Lead
Pete Best Drums

Brian Epstein's (BE) suggested list of what the Beatles might play to impress George Martin, 6 June 1962.

George Martin was interested, but not wildly impressed, being particularly worried about Pete Best's drumming. When he asked, after they had finished the session, whether there was anything *they* didn't like, George Harrison replied in his dead-pan, guttural tones, 'Your tie.' Fortunately, George Martin laughed, as did the other engineers.

After a wait which, to the Beatles, afraid they would not be given a second chance, had seemed to drag on for an eternity, they were called back to the EMI recording studios three months later, on 4 September. George had a black eye that day, having been punched in the Cavern by some girl's jealous boyfriend. Ringo had by this time joined them on drums. They did 'Love Me Do' again and also recorded a song George Martin was very keen on, 'How Do You Do It?' written by Mitch Murray. Martin was convinced it was going to be a number one hit (which it was the following year, recorded by Gerry and the Pacemakers.)

They performed 'How Do You Do It?' as requested, but recorded it without too much enthusiasm, still preferring their own, home-made songs for their debut. Paul has said that he was embarrassed by 'How Do You Do It?' and feared he would be mocked in Liverpool if that became their first record.

George Martin had them back again a week later and this time agreed to have another go at 'Love Me Do' – but he had hired a session musician, Andy White, to play on drums – a fairly normal procedure in recording studios, but a massive disappointment for Ringo.

They were all nervous, and fiddled with their headphones, which they had never used before. Paul was particularly worried when George Martin decided that he, Paul, should sing the solo vocal line 'Love, love me do' on his own, rather than John, which was how they had always done it on stage. John for years had managed to play his harmonica after he had sung the line, but Martin felt he was garbling the last word, so it was coming out as 'Love love me waahhhh ...' He therefore suggested that Paul should sing that line instead, on his own, which worried Paul as he knew that his voice was not as deep as John's. Listening carefully to it now, you can detect Paul's nerves, forcing his voice lower.

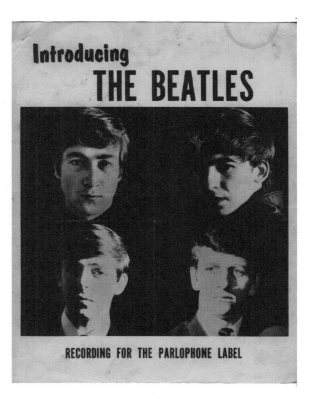

Parlophone's first press handout for the Beatles, October 1962, for 'Love Me Do'.

'Love Me Do' was released on 5 October 1962, with another of their own songs, 'PS I Love You' on the other side. 'Love Me Do' crept quietly into the charts. It was rumoured that Brian Epstein gave it a push by buying ten thousand copies for his own record store, though probably it was no more than 2,000 – but it only ever got as far as number 17. However, this was good for a debut. In the USA, Capitol Records initially did not release it – nor did they fancy 'Please Please Me', the Beatles' second single, released in January 1963.

Please Please Me, their first album, was recorded in a single day, 11 February

1963, at the Abbey Road Studios.* The big achievement with this first tranche of songs was to have done it – to have got the tracks recorded and released. The other, more interesting element is that they had got away with recording so many of their own compositions, despite being a brand-new band, unknown outside Merseyside.

On that first album, all they did was repeat their stage performances, recording most of them in a single take. There was no double tracking in those days. And if you made a mistake, you had to do the whole thing again.

Technical tricks and facilities were few, but George Martin, being an experienced producer with the benefit of an education in classical music, worked hard to get the sound he required, dictating what he did and did not like, instructing them on what he wanted – such as using a different drummer, or having Paul take over a solo – and suggesting arrangements.

What he did not do – and never did, even later on – was mess around with their words. There is no evidence, and none of them has any recollection, of George Martin ever being unhappy with their lyrics – certainly not to the extent of making them change words or work on lines. Perhaps he didn't really care; lyrics to pop songs were considered trivial and inconsequential. Perhaps Martin was satisfied that John and Paul seemed to know what they were doing when it came to their lyrics –

EMI exhort the trade to take orders for their first LP, Please Please Me, *in May 1963.*

and to have fairly strong opinions – so he was content to let them get on with it.

The most interesting aspect of these early lyrics, rereading them now, is not their subject matter – romantic boy–girl love, or miserable romantic boy–girl love – but the lack of sexual content.

When the Beatles made their breakthrough, they were generally thought to be attractive – why else would girls be screaming at them? Parents, however, feared that they might be a corrupting influence with their long hair and

---

* That same day, just a few streets away, Sylvia Plath, aged thirty, committed suicide in her flat in Primrose Hill. The juxtaposing of these two events was recalled some years later in a poem by the Liverpool poet Paul Farley, Professor of Poetry at Lancaster University, entitled '11 February 1963', published in *The Ice Age* in 2002.

loud music. Many parents went so far as to consider them dangerous, which now seems laughable. If you study the actual lyrics now, they are almost entirely wholesome, healthy, benign. Compared to Elvis, Chuck Berry, Little Richard (or Mick Jagger, when he arrived on the scene a year later), all of whom deliberately emphasized the sexual element in their songs and stage performances, aiming to be raunchy, the Beatles seem positively chaste.

Professor Colin Campbell, in his exhaustive 1980 concordance of the lyrics, established that the word 'sex' or 'sexy' appears only once in the entire Beatles canon ('Sexy Sadie', and even then it is not about sex at all, as we shall see). Only once, in all those lyrics. I was surprised. It is true there is a smutty double entendre in 'Penny Lane', but you have to be from Liverpool to spot it.

In addition to being clean, in the sexual sense, Beatles lyrics are awfully well-mannered. The word 'please' features in seven of their early songs: 'Love Me Do', 'Please Please Me', 'Don't Bother Me', 'I Want to Hold Your Hand', 'You Can't Do That', 'If I Fell', 'When I Get Home'. How polite is that?

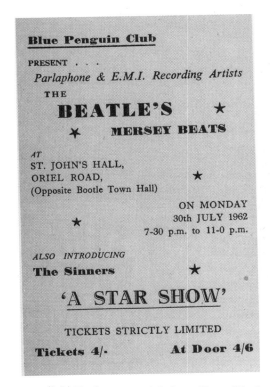

(left) Early poster, with the spelling of Parlophone and Beatles still a bit of a puzzle.
(right) National tour in 1963 with Billy J. Kramer.

Love Me Do

With 'Love Me Do', the Beatles were at last out, in the shops, on the streets, in the air, on the jukeboxes, though not many people at the time could possibly have imagined that so much would develop from such a simple, basic song. Even though I have traced no manuscript, it is still worth printing all the words, hang the expense, including all the repetitions, just to see how basic they were.

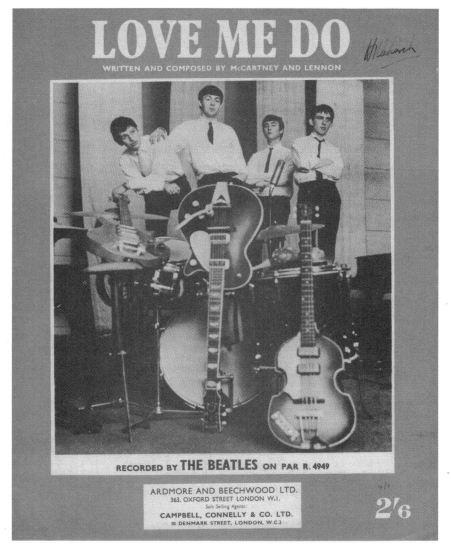

Sheet music for their first record, 'Love Me Do', October 1962. Ardmore and Beechwood were EMI's publishing company, who first wanted to sign them. Note carefully George's black eye.

Love, love me do.
You know I love you,
I'll always be true,
So please, love me do.
Whoa-ho love me do.

Love, love me do.
You know I love you,
I'll always be true,
So please, love me do.
Whoa-ho, love me do.

Someone to love, somebody new.
Someone to love, someone like you.

Love, love me do.
You know I love you,
I'll always be true,
So please, love me do.
Whoa-ho, love me do.

Love, love me do.
You know I love you,
I'll always be true,
So please, love me do.
Whoa-ho, love me do.
Yes, love me do.
Whoa-oh, love me do.
Yes, love me do

The late Professor Wilfrid Mellors, an eminent musicologist who wrote one of the earliest academic studies of Beatles music (*Twilight of the Gods*, 1973), described the words of 'Love Me Do' as 'vacuous – but life affirming'.

I once dared to criticize the lyrics to John – around the time of 'Strawberry Fields Forever', when everyone with an Olevel was busily analysing every Beatles lyric – and he defended them. He maintained that the words of 'Love Me Do' were just as good, just as true and meaningful as 'I Am the Walrus': 'They're all just words.' As for the record itself, he thought at the time it was 'wet, compared with Little Richard'.

'Love Me do' was one of the earliest songs that Paul ever wrote back in 1958, aged fifteen or sixteen, at home in Forthlin Road. He played it to John, who is said to have contributed a middle verse, but this is so flimsy and meagre – consisting of 'Someone to love, somebody new, someone to love, someone like you' – that it scarcely registers as a development. The basic four lines are in fact repeated *four* times, which does seem self-indulgent. They were very young – and pop lyrics of the time were simple and repetitive.

The best thing about the lyrics is the title 'Love Me Do' – which was originally 'Love, Love Me Do' after the first line, but was simplified when they came to issue the record. The construction 'Love me do' is rather archaic and stilted English, as if it has been somehow reversed and really it should be 'Do you love me', which would be more natural and colloquial.

What probably attracted them was not the unusual grammar but that hidden in the first line is a double meaning. The first 'love' can be seen as a proper noun, the way you might address someone as 'Darling' or 'Dear' instead of using their name, while the second is the verb. So that's quite clever. However, George

Martin was apparently not very impressed by any of the lyrics.

The unique selling point – well, fairly unusual selling point, both then and now – was not the words but John's harmonica, which is what distinguishes the song and gives it its own flavour. His harmonica playing is raw, basic, unflashy, with none of the warbling or tremulous vibratos used by harmonica maestros of the time such as Max Geldray – who featured in *The Goon Show* – and Larry Adler.

The feeling conjured by the song is one of honesty, simplicity, naturalness as opposed to the slickness, smoothness and syrupiness of Cliff Richard and the Shadows, then enormously popular in the UK, with their exaggerated echoes.

In the line 'somebody new' John pronounces it as 'noo' in the American fashion, trying to be bluesy. I am quite surprised George Martin allowed that, as it is the only word where he is clearly aping the Yanks. But then most British singers of the fifties, such as Dickie Valentine and Frankie Vaughan, and Cliff in the sixties, affected a mid-Atlantic accent, convinced that was the way to acceptance.

PS I Love You

The B side of 'Love Me Do' was written by Paul in Hamburg in 1961–62 and supposedly addressed to Dot Rhone, his girlfriend at the time, a sweet young girl from Liverpool, who along with Cynthia, John's girlfriend, came out to visit Paul in Hamburg. But Paul has since denied that he had any particular girl in mind. It was just that a letter was a popular theme for a pop song. The words are basic, no development, a sweet song with no story, no angst, but Paul sings it nicely, enunciating carefully, very English and clear. (Printed here without the repeats, to save space.)

I have found a manuscript version, of a sort, but it is a bit of a mystery. It looks as if it was written down by someone at the time and subsequently corrected by Paul. So only one line is in Paul's hand: 'these few words 'til we're together'. Was it transcribed by someone who was present in the studio during the recording? I contacted Andy White, the drummer who was brought in to replace Ringo, who is now retired and living in the USA. I thought perhaps the words might have been written out by him, as he was new to the group and their songs, but when I sent him a scan he said the handwriting was not his: 'I was only in the studio for three hours, ten a.m. to one p.m. During this time we recorded three songs: "Love Me Do", "PS I Love You" and "Please Please Me". All our time was taken up learning the songs. There was no written music or lyrics.'

'PS I Love You' – in the hand of a Swedish fan, with corrections by Paul.

The handwriting looks a bit girlish, and the spelling of Beatles at the top appears to be Beetles, a mistake people were still making at the time. It might have been someone from their fan club (which had been formed in Liverpool as early as 1961) or perhaps a foreign fan who had copied out the lyrics, mishearing one of the lines, and then got Paul to correct it. In that case it probably dates from 1963, when the Beatles made their first foreign tour – to Sweden – and a Swedish fan, having copied out the words by listening to the record, then showed them to Paul.

As I write this letter,
Send my love to you,
Remember that I'll always,
Be in love with you.

Treasure these few words 'til we're
    together,
Keep all my love forever,
PS, I love you.
You, you, you.

I'll be coming home again to you, love,
And 'til the day I do, love,
PS, I love you.
You, you, you.
I love you.

Please Please Me

Their second single got to number 1 in most charts, and so did better than 'Love Me Do'. It was written by John at Aunt Mimi's house. 'I remember the day I wrote it and the pink eiderdown over the bed.' He was playing around with the word 'please', as used in a thirties song by Bing Crosby, which had the line 'please, lend your ears to my pleas'. Music-wise, as he admitted later, he was trying to come up with a song like Roy Orbison's 'Only the Lonely'. Except it didn't turn out like either of these songs – which is often the case. The original inspiration, for a novel, a poem or a song, can totally evaporate and become hidden from sight, if not from the mind of the creator.

The singer is complaining that his girl is not pleasing him the way he is pleasing her. If there was a deliberate sexual connotation, then that would rather ruin my assertion that Beatles lyrics are fairly sexless, but if it is there, it was quite well hidden. We are much quicker these days to detect sexual meanings. All he seems to be saying is that he is being nice to her but she is not being nice to him.

After the lovey-doveyness of 'Love Me Do' and 'PS I Love You', there is an element of unhappiness and moaning – all of it rather self-centred, blaming the girl, which might not be acceptable in this feminist age. He says she is making him blue, rhyming 'blue' with 'you', which is pretty weak – as John must have realized, but he didn't care, not at the time; it's just a pop song. The only interesting phrase in the lyrics is 'there's always rain in my heart'. But this was borrowed from the Buddy Holly song 'Raining in My Heart'.

The crescendo when they get to 'Come on, come on, come on, come on' makes it an exciting song. OK, that *is* clearly sexual – an early exception that proves the general rule. I think in their minds they were trying to differentiate themselves from the totally limp and soppy lyrics of Cliff Richard and the Shadows, who were their deadly rivals in the charts back in 1962–63, with 'The Young Ones', 'Bachelor Boy' and 'Summer Holiday'.

Ask Me Why

A return to romantic love – he begins by telling her 'I love you' – but it's a hurried, rather jumbled song which John knocked off quickly. It was used to fill the B side of the 'Please Please Me' single. It has some slack rhymes, and he falls back on feeling blue again, but there is a trace of real angst, which is unusual in such an apparently perky pop song. 'My happiness still makes me cry, And in time you'll understand the reason why … I can't believe it's happened to me. I can't conceive of any more misery.'

He doesn't tell us what happened. Or whether he means that he would be miserable if he wasn't with her – or that he's miserable because he is with her? And was he thinking of Cynthia, whom he had fallen madly in love with – judging by his early letters to her – when he first met her at art college in 1958?

I Saw Her Standing There

The first track on their first LP, *Please Please Me*, 'I Saw Her Standing There' was written by Paul at the end of 1961 or early 1962, supposedly inspired by a girlfriend, Iris Caldwell, sister of Rory Storm, whose group Ringo had drummed for. Iris was a trained dancer and obviously impressed Paul with her movements – but Paul has denied he had any particular girl in mind. And if Michael McCartney is correct, and early versions began with 'She/He saw her standing there', then it would suggest there was no one girl – just girls in general. Most of their fans in and around Liverpool were girls of that age. Paul may have wanted to write a song they could all identify with – and dance to.

When he first played it to John, composing together at Forthlin Road, the working title was 'Seventeen' and the first two lines were 'She was just seventeen, never been a beauty queen'. John made a face and Paul agreed it was a bit corny. He'd been thinking of beauty contests at places like Butlins holiday camps. But it did imply that she wasn't very attractive. John suggested the line 'know what I mean'; it's a fairly meaningless, throat-clearing phrase, popular with Liverpudlian and British youth in general, but it does have a nudge-nudge quality, suggesting sexual experience. OK, so that's another possible example.

The rhyming of 'standing there' with 'way beyond compare' sounds a bit forced – something they might have avoided a few years later, when they began to put away childish things like rhyming couplets.

It proved a very popular song and became a standard part of their repertoire; it was one of the five the songs they played on *The Ed Sullivan Show* in February 1964.

Misery

Written mainly by John in late January 1963, backstage at the Kings Hall, Stoke-on-Trent, hoping Helen Shapiro would sing it – but she never did. She was the star on their first nationwide tour, which started 2 February 1963 – though by the end of it, their single 'Please Please Me' having gone to number 1, the Beatles had taken over as the prime attraction.

Sixteen-year-old Miss Shapiro was a rather old-fashioned, staid, young woman who had become a sensation with a series of hits sung in a surprisingly deep, jazz-type voice. I interviewed her when she had her first number 1, and she seemed rather stunned by it all. I accompanied her out into Oxford Street to buy some shoes, where she was spotted by a gaggle of teenage girls, one of whom asked her, 'Are you Alma Cogan?'

While Paul's 'I Saw Her Standing There' had been optimistic and happy, John's 'Misery' was … well, miserable, and mournful at the way the world was treating him. If offers us a clue to their different personalities, though we were not quite in tune with their tunes at the time, unaware of who had written which lyric, how and why.

Programme for the Beatles' first national tour, supporting Helen Shapiro, which started in February 1963 – by the end, they were the main attraction.

Do You Want To Know A Secret

Written by John, who was by this time living with Cynthia in a flat owned by Brian Epstein. The secret could have been that he had found out he did still love her; or that she was pregnant; or that they had secretly married on 23 August 1962 (Brian wanted it kept secret from the fans). The title and idea came from a song which John's mother Julia used to sing from Walt Disney's *Snow White* which included the line 'wanna know a secret'. It's very short, just two minutes, with limited lyrics. (And the secret? I'm in love with you.)

John wrote it and then gave it to George to sing, maintaining that it suited George's voice. 'It only had three notes,' said John, 'and he wasn't the best singer in the world.' It was a sop to the youngster having a vocal solo, and a reward for all his hard work on the guitar. He also took the lead vocal on 'Chains' – not written by them – on the *Please Please Me* LP.

There's A Place

Another new song written for the *Please Please Me* album, which had not appeared already on a single. It has a hurried feeling, as if bashed out quickly. Aside from the usual 'I love you' sentiments, John is feeling blue for the third time (after 'Please Please Me' and 'Ask Me Why'). We know they were working under pressure by now, doing national tours, knocking their new songs out quickly, but this dependence on 'blue' for an easy rhyme was becoming a bit slack.

Poster for that tour supporting Helen Shapiro, February 1963.

John does however manage a slight progression in his lyrics. The 'place' in the title – apparently suggested by Leonard Bernstein's 'Somewhere (There's a Place for Us)' from *West Side Story* – turns out not to be a physical location. The place where he goes when he feels low, when he feels blue, tra-la, is … his mind. Which was quite neat. According to Wilfrid Mellers, this was the first lyric that made him aware that 'John might be an oral poet'. He liked the tune as well. 'Long tied semibreves flowing into minims and into crotchet triplets – here is seed for later development in Beatles music.'

From Me To You

Their third single, which came out just after the *Please Please Me* album. It was written on 28 February 1963 while they were travelling by coach between York and Shrewsbury on what was still billed as the Helen Shapiro tour. John and Paul were keen to have some new songs ready to confound Tin Pan Alley – heart of London's pop music world – where they were being dismissed as an overnight success, who had come from nowhere and would soon disappear back there.

As they sat side by side, playing their guitars, looking for a catchy line or title to get them started, inspiration came in the form of the *New Musical Express* letters column 'From You to Us', which the band were reading on the coach. The main story in that week's issue concerned Cliff and Elvis and whether Cliff was doing better.

Considering the speed at which it was written, 'From Me To You' was neatly thought through and has a development of sorts – something few of their early songs had. Having come up with the notion of something going from me to you, they then list the possibilities: a heart that's true, arms to hold you, lips to kiss you, everything you want in fact, which he will send along, from me to you. George Martin, when they came to record it, had John get out his harmonica again and Paul threw in a few falsettos, just to get the girls going.

Looking back, Paul remembers being quite pleased with the song, feeling it showed progress, with a beginning, a middle and an end – a sign that they were getting better. But the critics at the time were not impressed: *New Musical Express* deemed it 'below par'. John remember feeling furious, but at the same determined to try harder. 'That's when I first realized you've got to keep it up.'

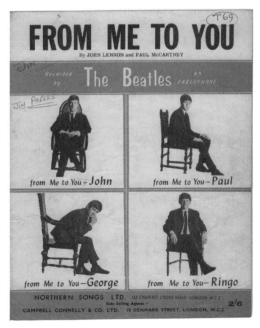

Sheet music for 'From Me To You', released April 1963. Northern Songs was now the publisher.

Press handout from Parlophone for their new chart-topping, infectious tune, April 1963.

Thank You Girl

The B side of 'From Me To You' was not as well realized. There is no story,
no catchline, poor rhymes – and the dreaded 'feeling blue' makes its fourth
appearance. It was supposedly meant to be a genuine 'thank you' to their girl
fans. They sound a bit bored and embarrassed by such a mechanical piece of
pop. No wonder it got relegated to the B side.

I'll Get You

Another B side, which I had long forgotten. It was a joint composition – written at Menlove Avenue, which was most unusual; as a rule, Mimi did not let Paul in to make music. Paul looks back on the song with affection and it was popular in their live shows. He even likes the words, suggesting they were reminiscent of Lewis Carroll, which is hard to see, his only example being the use of the word 'imagine'. In the second line, John sings 'Imagine, I'm in love with you'. Which is reminiscent of a Lennon song to come. The 'I'll Get You' bit refers to the fact that he is sure he is going to get the girl in the end. When he thinks of her, he is never ever – wait for it – blue. It was the A side of this single, written a few days later, which caused all the real excitement …

She Loves You

This came out as a single after the release of the *Please Please Me* album in August 1963, and turned out to be a belter.

It was another of those songs written on tour; they had just played a concert at the Majestic Ballroom in Newcastle and had one of their rare days off before the next gig, in Leeds. Paul remembers them in a room at the Turk's Head Hotel, sitting on separate beds, each with their guitar. John agrees it was Newcastle – but in his recollection they composed it in the back of the van.

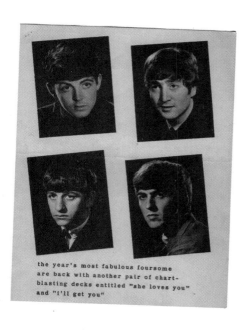

the year's most fabulous foursome are back with another pair of chart-blasting decks entitled "she loves you" and "i'll get you"

Their first three singles – 'Love Me Do', 'Please Please Me' and 'From Me to You' – aside from all having 'Me' in the title, were all simple love songs, a declaration of love between the singer and someone else. This time they decided to remove themselves, get rid of the first person, and write about third-person love, with the singer as the go-between trying to reconcile two lovers, one of whom (the boy) has been cruel and hurtful. He is told to apologize – he should know he is on to a good thing, because she loves him.

Is there a hint of a threat – that if the boy does not apologize, the singer, i.e. John, might step in? Only perhaps by a slight suggestion in his voice, not the words, but it did give an undercurrent of menace, for those looking for it.

When they were practising the falsetto oooh-oohs on the tour bus, one of the other singers, Kenny Lynch, warned that they might sound feminine. Real men did not sing in high-pitched voices, but the Beatles had found it went down well in 'From Me To You'. They were oooh oohing for fun, amusing themselves – and the girls.

The other distinctive feature of 'She Loves You' were the yeah yeah yeahs, which John later said were originally just to fill gaps in the lyrics. When Paul first sang the song to his dad, back in Forthlin Road, Jim said he would like it much better if they sang 'yes yes yes'. This was a common reaction among an older generation brought up during the war; at school in the fifties I remember teachers telling me off for saying OK and yeah, expressions which they considered American and not proper English.

The Beatles were not the first pop artists to use 'yeah yeah' as a gap-filler. Elvis had done it a few times, though more of an aside; the Beatles' yeah yeahs were a prominent feature of the chorus, which was kept up all the way through.

The lyrics followed the same old theme of boy–girl love, albeit in the third person; the same emphasis on rhyme; the phrasing was straightforward and the mood was resolutely upbeat, with only a hint of anguish. But then, who cared

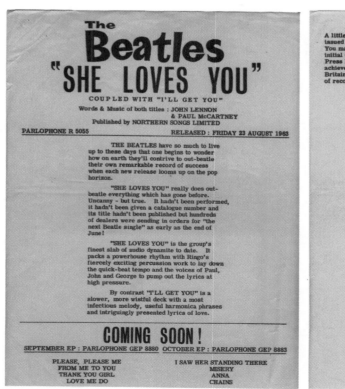

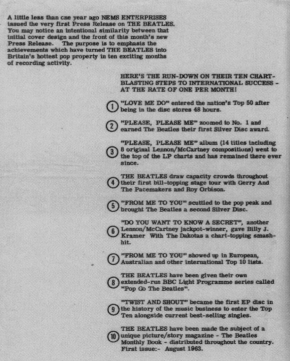

Pretty pink paper for Parlophone's press info for 'She Loves You', August 1963.

about the words? Interviews with the Beatles from that period seldom focus on the lyrics, how they were written, what they meant. It's all about their hair, their next record, their clothes, will Paul now get married?

The yeah yeah yeah angle was a gift to the headline writers in all the national papers, referring to them as the Yeah Yeah group. The general public, who had either been unaware of the Beatles till then or had dismissed them as just one more noisy, shouty pop group, now found it impossible to avoid them. They were everywhere. And whether you liked them or not, if you listened carefully it was obvious that there was something a bit different about them, their sound was distinctive.

Pop music followers, and writers in the music press, had found 'Love Me Do' somewhat crude and unpolished. The tune was a pleasant enough and they liked the harmonica, but the group's vocals and playing sounded hesitant, lacking in confidence. The same could not be said of 'She Loves You'. The performance was bursting with energy, confidence and strength, with great harmonies and some full-blooded oooh-oooh falsettos, plus the yeah yeahs. The Beatles had finally found their own musical voice.

The song seemed to sum up the essence of this new group from Liverpool: their energy and beat, their melodies and harmonizing, their wit and confidence. And yes, their sex appeal, shaking their mop tops as they reached the climax of the song, creating hysteria among girls in the audience.

'She Loves You' went straight to number 1 – their second number 1, after 'From Me to You'. Sales outstripped anything they had done so far, or anything any of their rivals were doing. By the end of 1963 over 1.3 million copies had sold in the UK. John's old running joke about getting to the toppermost of the poppermost had come true. It was the song that announced and then defined the birth of Beatlemania.

Proud boasts in the music press for a very good first year.

2

WITH THE BEATLES

Second album and fifth single

November–December 1963

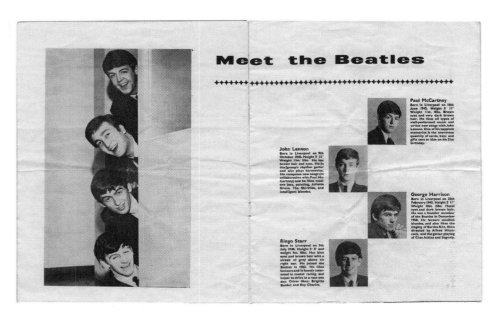

The Beatles had hardly been to London until 1963, and then only on a handful of visits, but in the summer of 1963 Brian found them a rented flat in Mayfair where they had a bedroom each, for when they were staying in the capital – though John and Cynthia, having a baby, had a flat on their own in Kensington, directly above Robert Freeman, the photographer.

In April 1963 Paul met a seventeen-year-old actress called Jane Asher through a BBC programme and then in a photo-shoot for the *Radio Times*. They became friends and he started hanging around her house – eventually moving into an attic room in her family home in November 1963.

It was a huge cultural and social and artistic shock for Paul. Shock is perhaps the wrong word; 'sensation' would be better, as Paul was impressed, fascinated and stimulated by the middle-class, bohemian, artistic Asher household and absolutely loved being a part of it. Having been brought up on a Liverpool council estate, he had no experience of such a life and such a home. This is not to suggest that his father was rough or uncultured; Jim was well dressed, charming, socially at ease in most company – like Paul himself – but their house was small, money was short, books and amenities few.

The Ashers lived in a large, rambling Georgian terrace at 57 Wimpole Street, traditionally London's medical area, but also with literary associations (Elizabeth Barrett Browning had lived a few doors along at number 50). Jane's mother was a professor of music and her father an eminent doctor. They were cultured, intellectual, and encouraged their children to be creative and express themselves. Their house was filled with paintings, books and scientific journals.

Paul lived there as a lodger, very simply, for around two years, which is surprising, when he was suddenly making so much money. He could have afforded a posh house of his own, out in the suburbs, which is what John, Ringo and George all opted for. But he loved Jane and the Ashers, their lifestyle, their friends. Being in central London meant he was handy for avant-garde galleries and exhibitions – and the night clubs – with no need for a long trail back home afterwards.

The influence of this new social and cultural world in which Paul was moving soon began to have an effect on his writing. But he wasn't the only one open to new experiences; once they moved to London, John and George began broadening their horizons too. They were not intellectually intimidated by the new circles in which they found themselves – after all, the Beatles weren't the stereotypical overnight pop sensations who had left school at fifteen to become lorry drivers or labourers before hitting the big time. John, Paul and George had gone to excellent grammar schools, which meant they had to be clever enough to pass the entrance exams, and though they may have disliked school at the time, it had exposed them to Chaucer and Shakespeare as well as modern art and literature.

When they weren't in London they were rushing round the UK on tours, or doing TV and radio appearances, but in the summer of 1963 they managed to find time to start work on their second album, *With the Beatles*, which eventually came out in November of that year, just eight months after their first album.

The recording sessions were spread over three months, as opposed to one day for *Please Please Me*, but this was due to their busy schedule. Double-tracking was now standard, so the sound is better and stronger, but once again only half the fourteen tracks were composed by them.

The cover of the first album had featured a snap of them standing on a staircase at EMI's London offices in Manchester Square, wearing inane smiles, as if in a school photograph – you can almost hear the photographer* shouting, 'Cheese!' For their second album, they wanted a much artier photograph. They had always admired the portrait of Stu Sutcliffe that Astrid Kirchherr had taken in Hamburg, with its dramatic half-light and half-shadow, but she had not photographed all the Beatles. So Robert Freeman was commissioned to do similar shot featuring all four of them. The result, shot in a hotel in Bournemouth, makes them look serious and sombre, and it was so successful that for a while Freeman became their official photographer.

On both albums, press officer Tony Barrow wrote the sleeve notes in the breathless style that typified early sixties pop prose. 'Pop picking is a fast n' furious business these days', runs his first sentence on *Please Please Me*. He describes Paul and John as the band's 'built in tunesmith team' and quotes one radio presenter as declaring that they are 'musically the most exciting and accomplished group to emerge since The Shadows'. By the second album, they are being hailed not only as 'remarkably talented tunesmiths' but also 'cellar stompers of Liverpool … sure-fire stage show favourites … rip roarin' … fabulous foursome …'

The second album was made up of yet more love songs, happy or otherwise, still following the traditional pop format, but the interesting development was that at long last, after recording twelve of their own songs (plus twelve by other composers), young George was finally allowed to have one of his own compositions included on the album.

---

* Angus McBean (1904–90), a well-known theatre and society photographer of the day.

It Won't Be Long

Written by John, and recorded as a single to follow 'She Loves You'. They decided it wasn't up to it, so used it to kick off the new LP instead. And it isn't up to much, really, though the title leads into a nice play on words: 'It won't be long, yeah yeah – till I belong.' Not belonging fits the mood of the song, but neither the tune nor the words develop or have an obvious hook to make the song lodge in your brain. Another one-dimensional song – about a one-dimensional problem: someone at home, waiting for their lover, dejected and rejected, though we don't know why.

You could of course read into it that John's rejection was not caused by some unknown girlfriend but by his own parents, who abandoned him at the age of five to be brought up by his aunt. When his mother did eventually reappear in his life, she was cruelly taken away from him – killed in a traffic accident. Perhaps this is why he feels that the world is against him. Seen in this light, the lyrics can be read as a genuine cry of anguish.

The characters of John and Paul are forever being contrasted, with Paul typified as the happy, cheerful, optimistic one, and John the tortured soul, thanks to his troubled background. But Paul had his own traumas, most notably the loss of his mother at a young age, so why did that not make him a misery guts? Or did the loss make him determined to overcome such a blow by putting on a cheerful front?

Despite losing his mother, Paul was brought up in a happy family, with a loving caring constant father. John, regardless of things he said later, also had a happy childhood, at least until he was about twelve, and was lovingly and well cared for. It was as a teenager that he rebelled against school and teachers and the strict, unbending Aunt Mimi, maintaining he wasn't really loved and his genius not recognized.

Paul and John are indeed very different characters, and this difference, as the years went on, was reflected in their songs, but I find it hard to agree that it was circumstances that made them the way they were and formed their general outlook on life. I prefer to think that that was how each was born, though it took a while for their innate differences to emerge.

All I've Got To Do

John wrote this in 1961, at a time when he was trying to sound like Smokey Robinson and the Miracles, so he is attempting his sweetest, smoothest voice and nicest harmonies. It ends on a few bars of humming, which doesn't sound much like him. One can imagine him laughing at himself as he did it. The words are equally unoriginal: 'Whisper in your ear, the words you want to hear.' There is a reference to 'calling on the phone', which enforces the American influence – as few people in Britain had telephones.

All My Loving

Paul with Jane Asher, to whom he got engaged on Christmas Day, 1967.

Another love song, this time by Paul, and probably the best love song they had produced to date. The words are fairly conventional, sending all his love to someone who is away, promising he will always be true, rhyming 'kissing' with 'missing', 'you' and 'true', but it rings sincere and genuine. It's the tune that really makes it, the first four bars being especially haunting. So it's strange that, according to Paul himself, it all began with the words and not the tune. 'It was the first song I ever wrote where I had the words before the music.' They came to him while shaving, and he wrote the words down as a poem.

The girl he was missing was Jane Asher, his new London girlfriend.

Don't Bother Me

This is the first George song – though not all Beatles fans registered how unusual it was to have George singing his own song. I certainly didn't, assuming at the time it was another Lennon–McCartney composition. This was partly because it didn't lead to a spate of George songs – that came very much later – so it was easy to forget it had ever happened.

George wrote it in August 1963 while on tour, at the Palace Court Hotel in Bournemouth where Robert Freeman shot the cover photo. George had fallen ill, and was recovering by staying in bed, so decided to try and write a song, just to see if he could do it. It was the first song with lyrics he had ever written on his own. In 1967, when I was doing the biography, George was dismissive about it: 'It was a fairly crappy song. I forgot about it completely once it was on the album.' He said he gave up all thought of writing songs for another two years – he was too involved with other things.

In his memoirs *I Me Mine*, published in 1980, he repeated the assertion that it wasn't much of a song, 'It might not even be a song at all, but it showed me that all I needed to do was keep writing and then eventually I would write something good.'

Perhaps the lyrics suggested themselves because at the time he wrote the song he did not want to be bothered, by anyone, as he was feeling poorly, but he turns it into a love song. He is missing his love, who has left him all alone, so please keep away. The sex of the person bothering him is not stated – one assumes it began with one of the other Beatles knocking on his bedroom door – but in the lyrics it sounds as if it could have been a girl who was after him.

Bill Harry, editor of *Mersey Beat*, has another theory. Whenever they met in Liverpool, Bill would ask George if he was going to compose another instrumental like 'Cry for a Shadow', the tune he had co-written back in 1961. George's response would always be, 'Don't bother me.' According to Bill, George later told him that this phrase had lodged in his mind – and that he had turned it into a song. The phrase certainly sounds typical of George. He could be very serious, concentrating hard on whatever he was doing, and didn't like being interrupted or asked idiot questions.

It's a good song, as good as anything the Beatles had written up to that time, which was why I had assumed it was a Lennon–McCartney composition. George's voice gets a bit low at times, till you fear he will hit the floor. It has a vaguely Latin American rhythm, with Ringo on bongo and drums, which trundles it along.

The manuscript is in George's hand, without any changes or corrections, so it was presumably written out neatly at some stage. George's hand looks young and hesitant, rather childlike compared with the bolder handwriting of Paul and John, as if perhaps he was not used to writing stuff down. Which was roughly the case. John had been writing reams of poems and stories as well as songs since about the age of ten; likewise Paul had written hundreds of songs. George, despite having gone to the same grammar school as Paul, had not knuckled down to his essays and schoolwork, abandoning sixth form and A levels by leaving at sixteen to take on a fairly menial job. 'Don't Bother Me' was written at a time when he felt he couldn't write lyrics, unlike the fab two.

'Don't Bother Me', George's first composition, in George's handwriting – released on the LP With The Beatles, *December 1963.*

Since she's been gone I want no one to talk to me.

It's not the same but I'm to blame, it's plain to see.

So – go away, leave me alone, don't bother me.

I can't believe that she would leave me on my own.

It's just not right when every night I'm all alone.

I've got no time for you right now, don't bother me.

I know I'll never be the same if I don't get her back again.

Because I know she'll always be the only girl for me.

But 'till she's here, please don't come near, just stay away.

I'll let you know when she's come home. Until that day,

Don't come around, leave me alone, don't bother me.

Don't bother me.

Little Child

A sad and lonely boy wants someone to dance with him – it sounds very much like John, but the song was a joint effort. Why though would he be asking a little child to dance with him? Did it really mean a child, as in some sort of game, or did it mean a young girl, a babe, with whom he was going to have some teenage fun? You wouldn't get away with such a title today.

The song follows a pattern set by other Beatles songs – particularly in the repetition of 'come, come on, come on' and 'feel so fine', and of course the harmonica, with John playing quite an extensive solo. It was supposedly written with Ringo in mind, for him to sing, as it was a simple song, then John decided to sing it himself.

The manuscript would appear to be an early version, written in Paul's hand. It varies slightly from the finished version; the line which became 'If you want someone to make you feel so fine' was originally 'If you want someone to have a ravin time' (though in writing it out he has missed out the word want). The word 'ravin' does rather jar, and doesn't fit in with the notion of a little child, which probably explains why it was dropped.

The terminology Paul has used is quite interesting. He describes the first bit as the chorus (rather than writing it out, he simply puts 'chorus'); then we have two verses, although rather than use the word 'verse' he numbers the two sets of five lines as 1 and 2 – with the chorus in the middle and then the chorus again at the end.

Wilfrid Mellers, in his analysis of Beatles songs, described their typical song pattern as 'Edenic' – by which he meant they began with the Verse, consisting of four or five lines, then the melody was reprised with another set of words, which Mellors termed the Repeat. This was followed by the Middle, before ending with the Da Capo, which I take to be another repeat of the Verse. It does seem to complicate a simple song, and Paul's divisions between Chorus and Verse are perfectly adequate. As their songwriting progressed from a simple repetition of chorus, verse, chorus, they began to elaborate on the basic formula.

When the Beatles referred to the 'middle' or the 'middle eight', they meant the middle section, the development of the tune, and some new words, before they repeated the beginning. This was often the hardest part to write. Getting the beginning – the initial theme, in words and music – often came to them quite quickly, but they tended to struggle with the next bit. Particularly John, who would often leave songs unfinished, undeveloped, because he was stymied by the middle bit.

John and Paul had come to songwriting with no knowledge of how others had done it. Their approach was simply to study songs they liked, breaking them down into components, and then copy the format. Since they couldn't read music they were incapable of transcribing the notation, but they got round that obstacle by jotting down the chords, for example G D E, to remind themselves how they had played it.

In this example, the progression of a chorus (which is actually repeated twice on the record) followed by a verse, chorus, verse, chorus, follows one of the traditional patterns of composition.

'Little Child' in Paul's hand, from the LP With The Beatles, *December 1963, includes some lines that never made it.*

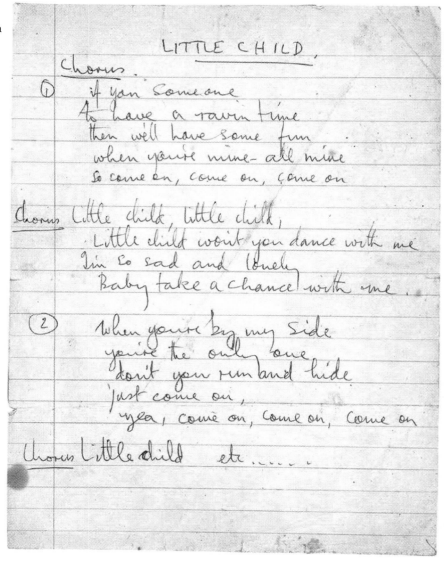

Little child, little child,
Little child, won't you dance with me?
I'm so sad and lonely,
Baby take a chance with me.

If you want someone
To make you feel so fine,
Then we'll have some fun
When you're mine, all mine,
So come, come on, come on.

When you're by my side,
You're the only one,
Don't you run and hide,
Just come on, come on,
So come on, come on, come on.

Little child, little child,
Little child, won't you dance with me?
I'm so sad and lonely,
Baby take a chance with me.

Hold Me Tight

This number was influenced by the Shirelles, an all-girl group from New Jersey who had several hits in the early sixties. On their early albums the Beatles did cover versions of a few Shirelles songs, including 'Baby It's You'. Once the Beatles had stormed the USA the following year, launching an 'invasion' of British groups, the Shirelles were one of the many American groups who fell from favour and went into decline.

The song is written and sung by Paul, who does his best with a few oooh-oooh falsettos but then seems to lose interest and the song – words and music – runs out of steam. It was written in the Forthlin Road days and when asked years later, Paul couldn't remember much about it, dismissing it as a 'work' song.

The manuscript is in Paul's hand and is an early version – written in a notebook by the look of it – with a couple of drawings, one of which is a face (could it be John?). There are several crossings outs and changes. The final version was longer, possibly because after he had played it to John they had gone on to do more work on it together. But not to much effect.

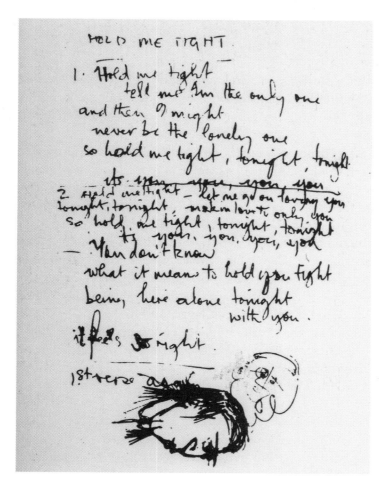

'Hold Me Tight', from the LP With The Beatles, *an early version in Paul's hand. With a drawing by him of John – possibly.*

Hold me tight,
Tell me I'm the only one,
And then I might,
Never be the lonely one.
So hold me tight, to-night, to-night,
It's you, you you you – oo-oo – oo-oo.

Hold me tight,
Let me go on loving you,
To-night to-night,
Making love to only you,
So hold me tight, to-night, to-night,
It's you, you you you – oo-oo – oo-oo.

You don't know what it means to hold
    you tight,
Being here alone tonight with you,
It feels so right now, feels so right now.

Hold me tight,
Let me go on loving you,
To-night, to-night,
Making love to only you,
So hold me tight, to-night, to-night,
It's you, you you you – oo-oo – oo-oo
You oo-oo

I Wanna Be Your Man

Paul wrote this with Ringo in mind. In most of their stage shows, there had been a Ringo number, a song chosen for him which was within his limited vocal range. But the song was never finished, barely progressing beyond the title and chorus.

Then came a chance encounter in a London street with Andrew Oldham, manager of the Rolling Stones. Oldham, who had once done some publicity work for the Beatles, told them that the Stones were looking for a new song. At that stage they had released only one record, a cover version of a Chuck Berry number. The Beatles had been to see them play live in a couple of London clubs and had become friendly with Mick Jagger and Keith Richards.

John and Paul went to where the Stones were rehearsing and played what they had written so far, telling the Stones that if they liked it, they would finish it off for them, no bother. Which they did, there and then, showing off their expertise – much to the admiration of Jagger and Richards. The Stones were roughly a year behind the Beatles in their development, but this song got them into the Top Twenty, helping to make them a major act – and of course a major rival to the Beatles from then on. It also encouraged Jagger and Richards to write and record their own songs, having seen how easy John and Paul had made it look.

When the Beatles returned to working on their own new LP, they got Ringo to sing it. The Stones might have been impressed – or desperate – enough to record the song, but it was never really finished and never gets anywhere. The title line is repeated thirteen times – which suggests an element of desperation. Later, John admitted that it wasn't one of their best: 'We weren't going to give them [the Stones] anything great, right?'

Not A Second Time

This one is wholly a John song – and typical of him in that it has him crying and hurt because some girl has let him down, and he won't be giving her a second time. But something surprising happened: the tune was picked up by William Mann, music critic of *The Times*, and subjected to the first intellectual analysis of any Beatles song. On 23 December 1963, just a month after *With the Beatles* was released, Mann extolled 'the Aeolian cadence at the end of "Not a Second Time"' raving about the Beatles' ability to 'think simultaneously of harmony and melody, so firmly are the major tonic sevenths and ninths built into their tunes'.

It must have come as a shock to those parents who were still dismissing the Beatles as long-haired talentless Scousers. John too affected surprise. He was quoted in 1965 as saying that Mann 'just used a whole lot of musical terminology and he's a twit'. But by the seventies John was admitting rather proudly that Mann's review had marked the start of intellectual analysis of their music – while the phrase 'Aeolian cadence' was picked up by newspaper columnists, none of whom had any idea what it meant, employing it as a form of shorthand to convey pretentiousness.

Listening to the tune again now, after all these decades, I still can't see anything exceptional about it musically. John sings it well, with heart, but the tune is totally unmemorable. And so are the lyrics. Beatles fans are very fond of listing their top 100 faves, but this rarely makes it.

This Boy

One week after *With the Beatles* came out they produced another single – the B side of which was 'This Boy'. It received little attention, compared with the A side. Featuring a lead vocal by John, the song was knocked out in a hotel room on tour. John dismissed it as having no content, 'just a sound and a harmony'. They were trying to do a three-part harmony, aping the Everly Brothers. The lyrics are short, staccato, with no narrative; reading them now, it can be said that they reveal John's struggle with a split personality. On the one hand there is This Boy, who is happy and loves you, on the other there is That Boy, who isn't good for you.

Despite their success in the Mersey Beat *poll in January 1962, there is still a problem spelling Paul's surname.*

I Want To Hold Your Hand

One of the attractions for Paul of staying at Jane's was that there were musical instruments all over the house. And they came in handy one day in October 1963 when Paul and John were composing 'I Want To Hold Your Hand', allowing them to try bits out on the piano and organ kept in the basement where they were working. For the most part though they were happiest carrying on the way they always had: side by side, playing their guitars.

'I remember when we got to the chord that made the song,' said John later. '"Oh you-ooo… got that something", Paul hit this chord and I turned to him and said, "That's it – do it again!" In those days we used to write like that – playing into each other's noses.'

They polished it up, quite quickly, and a day or so later, 17 October, went into Abbey Road Studios to record it. They exploded into it, loving the noise and their own excitement. They were helped by the fact that this was the first time they were able to use Abbey Road's four-track recording system – which allowed mistakes to be erased and the best bits superimposed.

In that room at the Ashers' they had already worked out the chords they were going to use, trying out some unusual changes and bridges – something not normally attempted in smooth-flowing pop songs. They also worked on a proper ending instead of the slow fade most pop records went out on.

The song has several internal crescendos, and descendos – if that is a proper word for going down the scales – as well as lots of their now familiar falsetto oohs. John, as the main singer, is at his most strident and aggressive, almost as shouty as in 'Twist and Shout'.

The music, to teenage female ears, might have sounded sexually exciting, but the words are probably the least suggestive and most soppy and simplistic of all their songs to date. They don't progress from the title, apart from telling us he will be happy if he holds her hand. He even says 'please'.

Certainly Brian Epstein must have been pleased, as the lyrics promoted a clean, healthy-living image. Parents could hardly accuse them of being a corrupting influence if all they wanted was to hold a girl's hand. Har har.

In real life, of course, in the dressing rooms and hotel rooms, they were already going a great deal further than that. Years later, John admitted he had been furious at the way Brian tidied and prettied up their image in the early days, maintaining that their dressing room on tour had resembled an orgy scene from Fellini's *Satyricon*. Their image was bullshit, they were beasts and bastards – or so he alleged, but by that time he was over-compensating, determined to shock. He was rather jealous when the Rolling Stones hit their stride and started getting away with suggestive lyrics and outrageous antics, revelling in being seen as dangerous – the antithesis of those 'nice' Beatles.

You can of course argue that the lyrics were ironic, that he is not longing to hold a hand; the excitement and intensity of the vocals makes it clear he is longing for and expecting a great deal more – which of course many fans, however innocent, would have suspected.

And they were innocent, in the fifties and sixties, with no active, penetrative sex life for the vast majority of teenagers, whether in the UK or USA. It was pre-Pill, and no one wanted to get pregnant. Before going all the way you had to get married, or at least engaged. In those long-ago, naïve times, holding hands and kissing was as far as it went for most youngsters.

The song was an instant, astounding hit – and at long last, they had a number 1 in America. Until this point Capitol, their US record company, had not issued their records, so the scale of the success took everyone by surprise. When the news came through in January 1964 the band were in Paris, staying at the George V Hotel after their first appearance before a French audience (who had reacted fairly coolly). By the time they moved on to America the following month, to play *The Ed Sullivan Show* and their first US concert, they had become an overnight sensation.

The manuscript below (now in the British Library) was neatly written out for me by Paul in 1967 – hence he has added 3/10, as if he is a teacher, marking it. In another version (see next page), also in Paul's handwriting, the words are the same but the penmanship is shaky, especially on 'think 'and 'to'. It also looks as if he is spelling 'yeah' as 'yea' – as if he was thinking of using the biblical spelling.

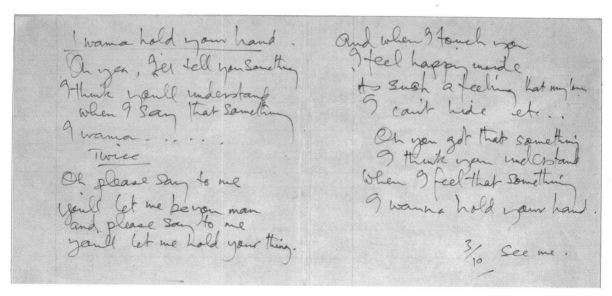

'I Want To Hold Your Hand', which came out as a single in November 1963 – in Paul's hand, written out neatly for me, hence he added '3/10 See me'.

Oh yeh, I'll tell you something
I think you'll understand
When I say that something
I wanna hold your hand
I wanna hold your hand
I wanna hold your hand

Oh please, say to me
You'll let me be your man
And please, say to me
You'll let me hold your hand
Now let me hold your hand
I wanna hold your hand

And when I touch you I feel happy
Inside
It's such a feeling that my love
I can't hide
I can't hide
I can't hide

Yeh, you've got that something
I think you'll understand
When I say that something
I wanna hold your hand
I wanna hold your hand
I wanna hold your hand

Another, earlier version of 'I Want To Hold Your Hand' – in Paul's hand.

3

A HARD DAY'S NIGHT
Album and singles 1964

It was the custom in the early sixties when a pop star or group had any half-decent success to stick them in a film so as to cash in on their name and their following. Elvis of course was the brand leader, while Cliff Richard turned out a couple of box office hits, such as *The Young Ones* (1961) and *Summer Holiday* (1962). Even minor songsters of the time, such as Adam Faith, Billy Fury and Terry Dene, now barely remembered, made it on to the silver screen. Films must have been cheaper to make in those days – or perhaps they were just quick, low-budget, mass market films, watched by millions who had less competition for their attention than today.

The Beatles were lucky in that they secured a good, intelligent, vaguely avant-garde director named Dick Lester, who managed to capture their character despite working at a frenetic pace, and a screenwriter, Alun Owen, who was able to reflect a lot of their humour, although there wasn't much of a plot. It was during the film that George first met Pattie Boyd, a young model who appeared in one scene as a schoolgirl.

The Beatles wrote seven new songs especially for the film, and came up with a further six for the album. *A Hard Day's Night* was their first album to be wholly self-composed. Ten out of the thirteen tracks were John songs – i.e. mainly written by him, and sung by him – an indication that he was still very much the leader, as he had been since the beginning. The songs are all still primarily about love – and why not? In the summer of 1964, John was still only twenty-three, Paul had just turned twenty-two and George was only twenty-one. But with this album the emotions were getting stronger, more revealing, and more care had been taken with the words.

The title song, and the title of the film, was only agreed upon at the last moment. Until then there had been a number of working titles, including 'Beatlemania', 'Let's Go' and 'On the Move'. The agreed explanation for the unusual title, handed down over the decades, is that it was a Ringo malapropism. 'It just came out,' he said in 1964 when the film was released.

'We went to do a job and we worked all day and night and I came out, thinking it was day, and I said "It's been a hard day …" I saw that it was dark, and so I added "day's night".'

However, John had used the same phrase in his book *In His Own Write* in a story called 'Sad Michael': 'There was no reason for Michael to be sad that morning, (the little wretch); everyone liked him (the scab). He'd had a hard day's night that day.' The book was published in March 1964, so presumably the story must have been written some time earlier, whereas the date usually given for Ringo coming out with the phrase was April 1964. So did John use it first? Had he forgotten? Or was it just a phrase that he and Ringo had each used at some time. Or did he pinch it from Ringo?

Anyway, once it was suggested as a title, John went off and wrote the song, knowing it was going to be the title song, kicking off the film and the album, so he wanted to be the lead singer. And boy, did he get both off to a great start.

One of the many joys for Beatles fans, back in the sixties, was that by listening to their albums so many times you got to know a single introductory chord, which became a friend, a familiar figure of sound that you could recognize in a second and know what was coming. Listening to them on the album, in the order in which the Beatles had intended them to proceed rather than a later, mixed-up compilation, you also knew the moment one song faded, even though all you could hear was nothing but a pregnant pause, what the next song was going to be, and the note on which it would start.

A Hard Day's Night probably has the most recognizable opening chord in the entire Beatles canon, possibly in any piece of popular music: a strident, crashing, magnificent, explosive opening chord. It seems a shame, and somehow dehumanizing, to use the technical definition: G eleventh suspended fourth. We will leave all other such descriptions to the music academics. We are here assembled purely for the lyrics.

A Hard Day's Night

The words are quite well thought out. After the opening chorus, John wrote two verses, with the chorus repeated in between, then back to the chorus at the end. Another of the standard formats for a pop song.

Reading the words now, and probably trying too hard to work out exactly what he is trying to say, it would seem the message is simple: work hard, bring the money home, and you will get marital bliss. There is a slight hint of a chauvinism when he moans that he is working all day for money so she can buy things.

The lines I am not quite clear about are: 'And it's worth it just to hear you say / You're gonna give me everything.' Is this her saying 'Give me all your money?' Or does he mean that, now he's handed it over, he knows she's going give him everything, i.e. hot meal and leg-over?

Maureen Cleave of the London *Evening Standard* was one of the first journalists to write intelligently and revealingly about the Beatles. She happened to be interviewing John on the day they were to record the song and went with him to Abbey Road in a taxi. During the journey, John showed her the words of the song, written down on an old birthday card given to Julian – he had recently had his first birthday – with an illustration of a little boy on a toy train.

'I said to him that I thought one line of the song was rather feeble. It originally said, "But when I get home to you, I find my tiredness is through, then I feel all right." ' Seizing my pen, John immediately changed the second line of it and came up with the slightly suggestive "I find the things that you do, will make me feel all right".'

Maureen remembers the recording session consisting of a lot of humming, 'They would put their heads together, hum for three hours, and then the song seemed to materialize, as if by magic.

'At the end of the recording session, when almost everyone had left, I saw the card sitting there on a music stand. I asked John if I could have it and he said what did I want it for. I said I wanted it because I'd suggested the alternate line for the song. End of riveting story.'

Maureen inadvertently went on to cause John and the Beatles quite a bit of bother. Two years later, in March 1966, she published an interview with John in which he remarked that the Beatles were now more popular than Jesus. The quote attracted little comment when it first appeared in the *Evening Standard*, but four months later it was picked up by an American magazine and the ensuing furore led to radio stations banning the Beatles, and their records being burned all over the Bible Belt. The Beatles finished the tour of America they were then on, but never toured again.

The lyrics of 'A Hard Day's Night' received a deft backhanded compliment when Peter Sellers produced a record in which he recited all the words in the manner of Laurence Olivier declaiming Shakespeare. It was very convincing.

The manuscript is on show today in the Manuscript Room at the British Library, along with several others on permanent loan from a kind person. The colours of the birthday card train are still remarkably vivid. You can also see where John changed the words at Maureen's suggestion – though the original words are not totally clear. There is also an amendment towards the end: 'everything's right from the start' was dropped, along with a line that appears to read 'I hope you realize with my heart'.

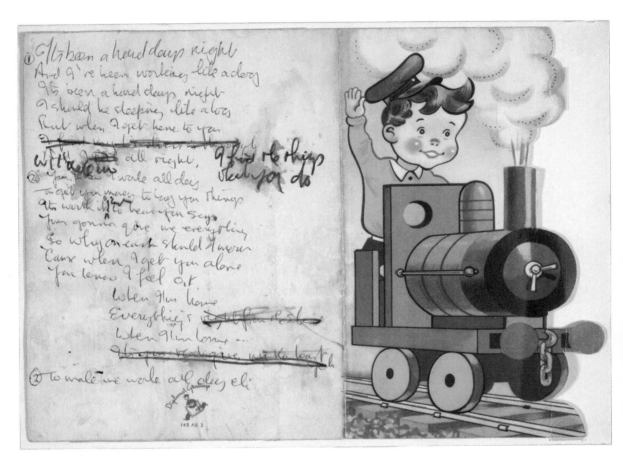

'A Hard Day's Night', released on the LP, July 1964, in John's hand. He changed the sixth line, after Maureen Cleave told him it was pretty feeble.

It's been a hard day's night
And I've been working like a dog.
It's been a hard day's night,
I should be sleeping like a log.
But when I get home to you,
I find the things that you do
Will make me feel all right.
You know I work all day
To get you money to buy you things.
And it's worth it just to hear you say,
You're gonna give me everything.
So why on earth should I moan,
'Cos when I get you alone
You know I feel okay.
When I'm home everything seems to be right.
When I'm home feeling you holding me tight, tight, yeah.

It's been a hard day's night
And I've been working like a dog.
It's been a hard day's night,
I should be sleeping like a log.
But when I get home to you,
I find the things that you do
Will make me feel all right.
You know I feel all right,
You know I feel all right.

I Should Have Known Better

This is John doing a straightforward love song, with no moans, no misery. He drives it along by himself, starting with a bit of Dylanesque harmonica to get us in the mood. The music is simple with few chord changes, though John does try a bit of falsetto when he plays with the word 'mine', turning into it my-i-ine … as if he has decided to copy Paul.

The only mystery or unusual feature is the title. It's as if he was going to write a moany, miserable song about regrets, then thought better of it. There is no regret, once we get into the lyrics – other than that he should have known he would love everything she does, tra la. The song gets few outings today, but I find it charming.

If I Fell

One reason why 'I Should Have Known Better' did not attract much attention might be that the following track, 'If I Fell', is so much richer, deeper and more complicated. This is John's first ever ballad. 'It shows that I wrote sentimental love ballads – silly love songs – way back then,' as he said in 1980. He also admitted it was semi-autobiographical, though few were aware of it at the time. Considered by many – OK, by me at least – as their most beautiful song up to that time.

It is now clear that he was thinking of leaving his wife for another woman, though Cynthia is not named and no clue is given to the identity of the other woman. He wants to be sure that she will love him more than his present woman – which is a tad presumptuous. How can anyone be sure? There's an element of gloating in the last two lines, picturing her crying when she learns he is leaving her for someone else.

The lyrics don't make clear what stage the new love is at – has he left his present one already, or is he just thinking about it? We know that John was having fairly serious but short-lived affairs by this time, though Cynthia was never aware of it. 'I was a coward,' he later admitted. And so his married life trundled on, keeping its secrets.

The lyrics, however, clearly express John's personal agonies giving no details, but at the same time giving everything away. They are deceptively simple, making you think about possibly deeper meanings, while the music is equally rich, with some sophisticated chord progressions that reflect the confusion and upheaval in John's mind.

The manuscript, in John's hand, is a clear, clean, version, so probably not the first he scribbled down. Possibly it was written out so that the others could read – and play. He has marked the verses 1 and 2 and has written 'Into' at the beginning, suggesting there would no opening chords, just straight into it.

The words are written on a Valentine card. So typical of John to pick up and scribble on any old scrap that came to hand. Could it have been a Valentine's card to Cynthia? Now that would have been cruel.

The manuscript was one of their first lyrics to come up at public auction; it was sold at Sotheby's in May 1988 for £8,580. Today it would easily fetch a quarter of a million.

If I fell in love with you
Would you promise to be true
And help me
Understand
'Cause I've been in love before
And I found that love was more
Than just
Holding hands

If I give my heart
To you
I must be sure
From the very start
That you're
gonna love me more than her

If I trust in you
Oh please
Don't run and hide
If I love you too
Oh please
Don't hurt my pride like her

'Cause I couldn't stand
   the pain
And I
Would be sad
If our new love was in vain

So I hope you see
That I
Would love to love you
And that she
Will cry
When she learns we are two

If I fell.

'If I Fell', from the LP A
Hard Day's Night, *July 1964, in
John's hand.*

I'm Happy Just To Dance With You

Written mainly by John but given to George so he would have 'a piece of action in the film'. This might explain why some of the lines sound as if they could have done with being polished up a bit more. No doubt if John had sung it himself, lines such as 'If somebody tries to take my place, let's pretend we can't see his face' would have been changed.

John always maintained that he had encouraged George to write his own songs, and denied that he and Paul kept him in the shadows. But John's explanations as to why George was given a certain song often sound condescending. It would 'suit his voice', for example, suggesting the vocal was designed for a voice with a limited range. John himself was often disappointed by his own voice. He didn't really like how he sounded and would ask George Martin to perform wonders by adding whatever he could to boost it – 'even tomato ketchup'.

George clearly didn't enjoy these put-downs and when he came to write his own book *I Me Mine* in 1980, he didn't mention John at all. Which pissed off John. John was genuinely upset – as his letters show – that George did not refer to him after all the encouragement he thought he had given George. 'I'm Happy Just To Dance With You' was the last song John and Paul wrote for George – from 1965 on he wrote his own.

The manuscript, in John's hand, features part of an early draft of 'If I Fell' on the same page. Some lines, such as the second line, 'would you know just what to do', were not used. He has numbered the 'If I Fell' lines '4', as if to suggest it was originally going to be verse four of 'I'm Happy Just To Dance With You' rather than a separate song.

There are quite a few interesting differences between the manuscript of 'I'm Happy Just To Dance With You' and the finished lyrics. Two lines – 4 and 5 in the manuscript – were not used, and were a bit limp anyway. 'I don't want to hear you say goodbye / I just want to dance until I fly.' And line 15: ''Cause I'd die to think this dance was ever thru.' One line he scored out, line 11, was eventually used. In line 13, 'If anybody tries to take my place' became 'If somebody tried to take my place.'

Before this dance is through
I think I'll love you too
I'm so happy when you dance with me
I don't want to kiss or hold your hand
If it's funny try and understand

There is really nothing else I'd rather do
'cause I'm happy just to dance with you

I don't need to hug or hold you tight
I just want to dance with you all night
In this world there's nothing I would
    rather do
'cause I'm happy just to dance with you

Just to dance with you

Is everything I need
Before this dance is through
I think I'll love you too
I'm so happy when you dance with me

If somebody tries to take my place
Let's pretend we just can't see his face
In this world there's nothing I would
    rather do
'cause I'm happy just to dance with you

'I'm Happy Just To Dance With You', from A Hard Day's Night, July 1964, early version in John's hand, with some lines not used.

And I Love Her

John raved about this ballad, written by Paul, saying later that it was Paul's first 'Yesterday'. He maintained that he'd helped with some of the lines in the middle – which Paul denied; a rare example of them disagreeing on their respective contributions. Usually they agreed on what proportion, and what bits, they had done. The song is essentially a Paul solo, a departure from their usual joint collaboration.

Paul was pretty pleased with the result. 'The first song I ever impressed myself with.' He particularly liked the title when it first popped into his head – a half-sentence, which was a clever and unusual way to begin a pop song.

It's a very sincere but simple love song. So was it written for Jane? He came up with the words while living at her house. Paul later said he had no one in mind when he wrote it, which I find hard to believe. I think by the time he was asked the question, the romance was over and he didn't want to talk about it.

The words are not particularly poetic, nor are they trying to be – just one notch above the level of 'Love Me Do' – with the exception of the line 'Bright are the stars that shine, dark is the sky'. And even that sounds a bit forced, as if he needed a rhyme for 'never die' at the end of the song.

For such a simple song, in words and music and arrangement, it required endless takes to get it right, trimming it back to essentials, avoiding the temptation to tart it up and add too many harmonies. The only gimmick is Ringo on bongo and claves, clicking away in the background, giving a slightly Latin American air.

Its simplicity and beauty is probably one of the reasons that it became and still is one of the most recorded Beatles songs by other artists.

Tell Me Why

A quickie, knocked off by John as a filler, but with a lot of emotion and some interesting rhymes – 'apologize' and 'eyes', 'knees' and 'pleas'. Superficially it's a moan about a lovers' row, which has led to her lying to him, then crying, with him holding back the tears. But perhaps it's not a complaint about being left alone by his girlfriend, perhaps it's about his parents and their treatment of him? That's the sort of explanation a psychoanalyst might well come up with – as indeed they have, especially later on when John told us that he was still screaming inside for the mother who had left him. (In his Plastic Ono days, he began to share with us the traumas of his mother's death.)

Can't Buy Me Love

Written by Paul, pretty much on his own, while they were staying at the George V in Paris, using a piano especially installed in his suite. They were in a hurry to record a new single for release in March 1964. It's similar to 'I Want To Hold Your Hand' – rocking, fast moving – and duly got to number 1 in hit parades around the world, establishing the Beatles in many eyes as the successor to Elvis. On 4 April 1964 the top five records in the USA's Billboard Hot 100 chart were all by the Beatles: 'Can't Buy Me Love', 'Twist and Shout', 'She Loves You', 'I Want to Hold Your Hand', 'Please Please Me' – with a further seven Beatles numbers scattered about the remainder of the top 100 list.

The lyrics of 'Can't Buy Me Love' are a bit confusing, apparently offering to buy love with diamonds and things, then saying money can't buy his love. In 1966 Paul was asked by a US journalist if it referred to a prostitute. Paul said all their songs could be interpreted in several ways – but thinking it referred to a prostitute, that was way too much, man.

The song was supposedly addressed to 'my love' in the original, which was then changed to 'my friend' to make it asexual – which is smart, but it does reinforce the theory that it was a prostitute, or someone whose name he didn't know.

'Say you don't want no diamond ring' is of course a double negative. I bet his old English teacher at the Liverpool Institute shook his head when he heard it ...

Any Time At All

Another pot-boiler, written by John. The chorus is repeated five times, with just two verses; there are no undercurrents in the lyrics, it's all very straightforward: 'if you want me, just call me'. Almost the same lyrics as 'All I've Got to Do' – 'all I gotta do is call'. John later admitted the tune was a recycling of an earlier song, 'It Won't Be Long'. Well, if you can't pinch from yourself, who can you pinch from?

When you consider how they wrote so many songs in such a short space of time, for themselves and for others, it is surprising that they did not repeat themselves more often. They did of course, and there are several songs where you can hear chords and sequences, ideas and phrases already used in earlier songs. And yet you rarely hear people, fans or otherwise, say 'Oh no, that's just the same tune again!' – a criticism frequently hurled at other successful pop groups.

The manuscript of the song, in John's hand, shows some drastic pruning. In the original version there were four verses, not two, but the final two verses were dumped, probably in the studio, as this looks like a version written for the recording session. The chorus is written out only once, in brackets, as they must all have known the words by then.

Did Paul criticize those final two verses, or did John have second thoughts? Or did George lob in a suggestion? They don't add to the story, such as it is, just repeating the same idea in slightly different words. The last line of the original verse 3 went: 'This boy's waiting here in the hope that you'll stay'. The use of the word 'boy' in this verse sounds a bit mawkish, though John had used it before in 'This Boy' (the B side of 'I Want To Hold Your Hand'). Perhaps they just wanted to keep the song short.

If you need somebody to love
Just look into my eyes
I'll be there to make you feel right

If you're feeling sorry and sad, I'd really sympathize.
Don't you be sad, just call me tonight.

Any time at all, any time at all, any time at all, all
you've gotta do is call and I'll be there.

If the sun has faded away
I'll try to make it shine,
There is nothing I won't do
If you need a shoulder to cry on
I hope it will be mine.
Call me tonight, and I'll come to you –

Any time at all, any time at all, any time at all, all
You've gotta do is call and I'll be there.

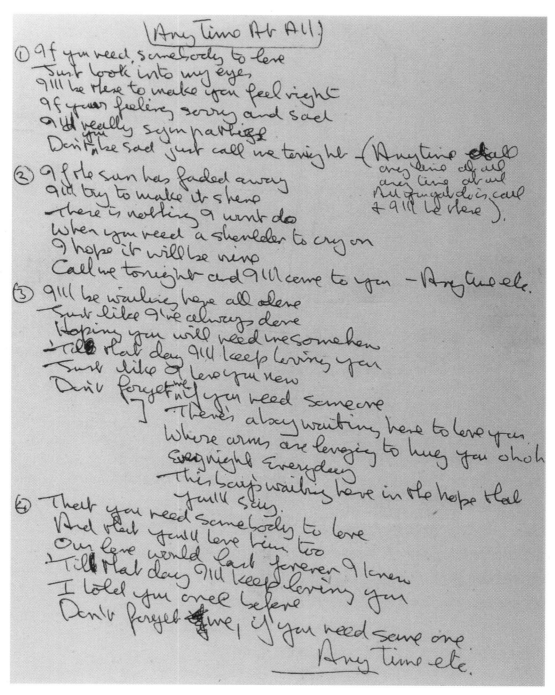

(Any Time At All)

① If you need, somebody to love
    Just look into my eyes,
    I'll be there to make you feel right
    If your feeling sorry and sad
    I'll really sympathise
    Don't be sad just call me tonight — (Anytime at all
                                          any time at all
                                          any time at all
                                          All you gal do is call
                                          + I'll be there).

② If the sun has faded away
    I'll try to make it shine
    There is nothing I wont do
    When you need a shoulder to cry on
    I hope it will be mine
    Call me tonight and I'll come to you — Anytime etc.

③ I'll be waiting here all alone
    Just like I've always done
    Hoping you will need me somehow
    Till that day I'll keep loving you
    Just like I love you now
    Don't forget me if you need someone
        There's always waiting here to love you
        Whose arms are longing to hug you ohoh
        Everynight Everyday
        This boy's waiting here in the hope that
        you'll stay.

④ That you need somebody to love
    And that you'll love him too
    Our love would last forever I know
    Till that day I'll keep loving you
    I told you once before
    Don't forget me, if you need some one.
                        Any time etc.

'Any Time At All', from A Hard Day's Night, *in John's hand, with two verses not used.*

I'll Cry Instead

This is probably the clearest indication so far of John's state of mind. We have had him crying, but now he is suggesting he can be mad, cruel – by breaking hearts. Also a suggestion that he could get himself locked up. It is a bit convoluted, as he holds back from making things too clear. We now know, from what his wife Cynthia later revealed, that he was physically cruel to her. The lyrics suggest a disturbed, tortured soul. But to conceal the angst, so we all sing along, tapping our feet, dancing away, not worrying too much about what the words might mean, he has given the song a jaunty rockabilly air.

Things We Said Today

A perfect little song written by Paul, again with an outgoing, cheerful, positive air, thanks to an aggressive acoustic guitar played by John – but on closer study there is something sad and mournful going on beneath the surface of the lyric. Wilfrid Mellers considered it 'the Beatles' most beautiful and most deep song up to this point'.

Once again it's a song for Jane, or at least about Jane, written when they had taken a break together in the Caribbean in May 1964, along with Ringo and his wife, hiring a yacht called *Happy Days*. Jane was an actress, just as busy as Paul, and their professional lives often took them apart, which clearly put a strain on the relationship: 'You say you will love me, if I have to go.' So even while he is with her, on the boat, he knows a parting will soon follow.

At the same time there is a more mature, wiser reflection in the lines: 'Some day when we're dreaming, deep in love, not a lot to say, then we will remember, things we said today.' Paul at the time was still only twenty-one, so it's quite a sophisticated thought for one so young, projecting himself into the future …

When I Get Home

On the surface, John is declaring that he is a homebody, loving coming home to 'a girl who is waiting home for me tonight', but it could also be read that he's visiting someone else in their home – why else would he be saying, 'I've got no business being here with you, this way' or 'till I walk out the door – again'. Both meanings applied: John loved being at home, doing nothing – and also playing away.

Saying he will love her 'till the cows come home' is a bit corny, but rhyming 'trivialities' with 'please' still makes me smile.

The manuscript version numbers three verses, with only a couple of minor changes from the recorded version: 'when I get home tonight' becomes 'when I get you home tonight'. He hasn't bothered to write out the three repeats of the chorus, simply putting 'oh. I. oh I. etc' – or at least, that's how it reads. On the record, it sounds more like 'Whoa-oh-aah, whoa-oh-aah', but then how do you write down such sounds, when they are more like grunts than real words?

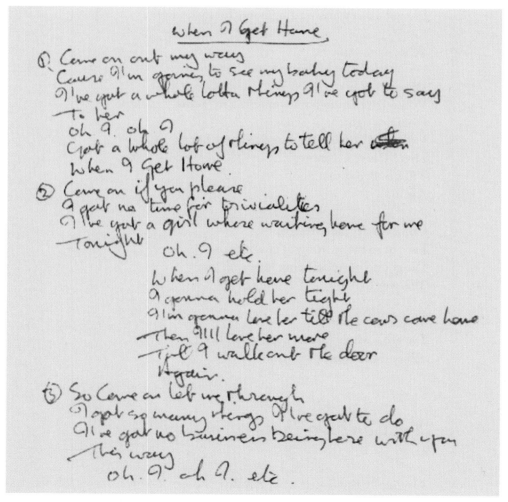

'When I Get Home', from A Hard Day's Night, in John's hand.

Whoa-ho, whoa-ho,
I got a whole lot of things to tell her,
When I get home.
Come on, out of my way,
'cause I'm gonna see my baby today,
I've got a whole lot of things I've gotta say
To her.

Whoa-ho, whoa-ho,
I got a whole lot of things to tell her,
When I get home.
Come on if you please,
I've got no time for trivialities,
I've got a girl who's waiting home for me tonight.

Whoa-ho, whoa-ho,
I got a whole lot of things to tell her,
When I get home.
When I'm getting home tonight, I'm gonna
Hold her tight.
I'm gonna love her till the cows come home,
I bet I'll love her more,
Till I walk out that door
Again.

Come on, let me through,
I've got so many things, I've got to do,
I've got no business being here with you
This way.

Whoa-ho, whoa-ho,
I've got a whole lot of things to tell her
When I get home – yeah.

You Can't Do That

Originally the B side of 'Can't Buy Me Love', this features John as lead singer
and lead guitar, demonstrating once again that he is in charge.

The lyrics also show him trying to dominate, threatening what he will do if the girl leaves him for another boy. 'Gonna let you down and leave you flat', sounds a bit like letting down a bicycle tyre, which is amusing on one level, but it could also be a physical threat, to flatten her. On the other hand, he too has suffered: 'I'll go out of my mind'. Though it could just be paranoia. In some senses, it can be seen as the Beatles' first anti-love lyrics.

Sheet music for 'You Can't Do That', from A Hard Day's Night.

I'll Be Back

John on the same theme – someone is breaking his heart and he might have to leave – but he is not threatening this time. Again, the message is a bit confused, possibly because he is trying to disguise from Cynthia, and the world, his extra-marital love life. There is no real chorus, only two lines that get repeated.

The mixed-up emotion is caught by the changing chords and descending rhythms, making it one of the more complex Beatles songs so far, although there is a flamenco-style beat that draws it all together. John said he was inspired, musically, by Del Shannon's 1961 hit record 'Runaway'.

I Call Your Name

Just before the album came out, in June 1964, they issued an EP* in the UK on which there were four songs, but this was the only one not to appear on either an LP in the UK or conventional single. John said it was about the first song he ever remembers writing, pre-Hamburg, possibly during his Quarrymen days, when he was just learning the guitar, though Paul recalls him working on it later at Menlove Avenue. The interesting thing, so far as the lyrics are

---

* What's an EP, Granddad? An Extended Play record played at 45 revs per minute, like a single, but whereas traditional 45s only had room for three or four minutes of music an EP could hold twice that, thought it wasn't as big as an LP, which held a lot more songs and played at 33 revs.

concerned – assuming it was written in those early days – is that it is not a happy love song, the sort of thing they felt they had to write back then to feed the market. John is calling her name because he can't sleep, he can't take it, he's not going to make it. The soul-searching, which came out so strongly later on, was always there.

A Hard Day's Night, released in July 1964, showed a definite progression. Despite the fact that it was conceived as part of a package with a film that was merely superficial, fast-paced entertainment for the fans, not meant to have any hidden depths, the album with its original compositions showed a greater level of depth and feeling than previous releases. John remains the leader, writing and singing most of the songs, and the subject matter is still primarily love, but the album is also notable for the emergence of the poet in Paul and the first cracks in John's cocky, cheeky façade, revealing the tortured soul beneath.

Could they keep it up, though – especially having foolishly agreed to bring out another single before the year was out, followed immediately by yet another album, all while they were rushing round the world touring. From June to November 1964, they played in fifty cities, on four continents (Europe, USA, Asia, Australia), covered 22,000 miles, giving around 100 performances on stage and TV.

4

BEATLES FOR SALE

December 1964

The Beatles met Bob Dylan for the first time on 28 August 1964 at a hotel in New York, during their second tour of the USA. He offered them some marijuana and was surprised to find they had never tried it before. He thought he'd heard them sing 'I get high', but John had to correct him and explain that, in the lyric of 'I Want To Hold Your Hand', it was actually 'I can't hide'.

Beatles lyrics, like many song lyrics, have often been misheard. Once you know them, you hear the real words immediately, but until then you can often be puzzled. On first hearing 'She's Leaving Home', I did wonder if it was about mice: 'Cheese Leaving Home'. Ok, that's a joke, but people have seriously believed that in 'Lucy In The Sky' 'the girl with colitis walks by', and in 'Strawberry Fields' 'living is easy with eyes closed' can easily sound like 'living is easy with nice clothes'. Both of those songs do have stream-of-conscious phrases and ideas, so some confusion was probably meant. Dylan thinking he had heard them singing 'I get high' is understandable as it did make sense, and was what he presumed.

In their Hamburg days, the Beatles relied on pep pills to keep going, but they had mostly been taking medicinal pills, not your actual nasty, illegal drugs. When Dylan suggested that they try a joint, they locked the doors, pulled down the blinds, put towels under the cracks, and lit up, passing it around. They all found it pretty enjoyable – especially Paul, who experienced a great release of ideas and energy.

Dylan's other influence on the band can be seen in their lyrics. They had long admired Dylan for his songs, the fact that he made the words just as important as the tunes, expressing his own emotions and thoughts. They were already beginning to follow suit, as we have seen, but encouraged by Dylan's example, Paul and John began to put more of themselves into their lyrics, to try harder, aiming for poetry not platitudes.

John had previously given a hint of his agonies in his poetry and stories, which were written in a stream-of-consciousness style. His first book, *In His Own*

Write, had been published by the distinguished literary firm of Jonathan Cape to wide acclaim and commercial success. But there remained a division in his mind between pop lyrics and his creative writing, the stuff that expressed his inner self.

A well-known TV and print journalist of the time, Kenneth Allsop, interviewing Lennon about his book on 23 March 1964, suggested to him that there should not be such a gap between his literary outpourings and his pop lyrics. Not on air, but in the BBC TV green room, he urged John to show his feelings more.

Perhaps that conversation did eventually help, along with the meeting with Dylan, or perhaps these 'interventions' were incidental and the Beatles were progressing anyway. The lyrics had progressed with each album, and they would have continued to evolve. You could also argue that the drugs didn't bring about changes either, they simply released what was there.

The big obstacle standing in the way of their development was the manic pace of life after Beatlemania took hold. Throughout 1964, they were rushing round the world, working nonstop. Occasionally they were able to take their time, reflect on things and polish material, but mostly it was a case of snatching moments where and when they could.

They knew they had to produce another album before the year was out as the fans and the industry, both in the UK and the USA, demanded it. The new album was called *Beatles For Sale* – there was no song with that title, it was one of Ringo's lines, moaning about all the demands and pressures now being made

upon them. They all felt the same way – that they were just goods, being trundled round the world and offered for sale.

Because it was such a rush job, they were unable to cobble enough original compositions together in time to fill the album; they managed only eight, then threw in six written by other people to complete the track list. So in one sense, they were going backwards rather than forwards, as the last album had been all theirs.

On the cover of the album, the photograph by Robert Freeman shows them looking a bit fuzzy and out of focus, their expressions rather worried, possibly knackered. Whereas their previous three albums had featured sleeve notes by Tony Barrow in the traditional Tin Pan Alley manner, the *Beatles For Sale* sleeve notes, written by Derek Taylor,* manage to be upbeat yet at the same time offbeat.

---

* Derek Taylor (1934–97) was probably the cleverest, most talented, most creative of all those who joined the inner Beatles gang, first as PA to Brian Epstein and then as the Beatles' PR.

I Feel Fine

The A side of their single, released on 27 November 1964, just before the album. The lyrics are fairly conventional, the sort of happy 'I love you' stuff they had been singing for years, without a trace of tears or misery or rejection or anger. 'I Feel Fine' is 100 per cent cheerful and optimistic because, well, John feels fine. The only subtext is that perhaps it's because he buys her diamond rings that she feels fine, but this is not dwelt upon.

The big attraction is the music, starting with another of the most recognizable Beatles openings ever – that long, low, sustained guitar note which resonates and vibrates because of the feedback John had deliberately worked into the recording. When using electric guitars on stage, it often happened that the amplifiers picked up the noise and sent it back. They would sometimes try to eliminate it, but other times they used it, making it part of their live act. According to John, this single marked 'the first time feedback was used on record'. Apparently he had leaned his guitar against an amp, heard what he thought was an interesting noise, and persuaded George Martin to use it. A sign that, after two years in the studio, they now considered themselves masters of their art, willing and eager to experiment, instead of waiting to be told what they could and could not do by their technical masters.

She's A Woman

The B side of 'I Feel Fine', written by Paul since John had the A side. It has a clear drugs reference – 'Turn me on when I get lonely' – just five weeks after their meeting with Dylan. Rather subtle and easy to miss, because it could be taken several ways, the reference was not publicly noticed at the time, otherwise radio stations would have banned it. It was at John's insistence that Paul shoved that line into his song – letting Dylan see a deliberate reference this time, not a mistaken one.

Paul remembers the song coming in his mind as he walked from his house – and then recording it the same day at Abbey Road. It's a good rock and roll song, though Paul's voice does get a bit high in places towards the end, when he seems to be forcing it. The lyrics included one of Pauls' worst ever rhyming couplets: 'My Love don't give me presents / I know that she's no peasant.'

No Reply

This track opened the album in a fairly mournful, downbeat way. John calls on his girl, but gets no reply. He tries to phone, but they say she is not at home – then he sees her coming out with another boy, hand in hand: 'I nearly died.'

It is the first Beatles song with a narrative, a sort of story, with a beginning and end. John admitted he had stolen the idea from 'Silhouettes', a 1957 record by a New York group called The Rays. In that song the boy watching outside knows he is being cheated on when he sees the silhouette of the lovers behind a curtain – a more subtle denouement than John's, which has him ringing up his girl and getting no reply. In real life, he never rang girls – or so he told *Playboy* in a 1980 interview. In the fifties, Paul's family were one of the minority that did have a telephone, because his mother was a midwife.

The heavy beat carries it along, like the music for an old-fashioned cowboy film, riding riding riding across the prairie – though apparently it was meant to be a bossa nova beat, which was in vogue at the time.

I'm A Loser

Written by John on a plane during their first North American tour. He is a loser because he has lost the girl, but he feels he is a loser in life anyway. Although he laughs and acts like a clown, it's all a mask, and he is frowning. The best lines are: 'I'm not what I appear to be', which he enunciates carefully, and 'Is it for her or myself that I cry?'

The song, which has some harmonica playing by John, was influenced by the Beatles' admiration for Dylan and his folk-style songs. The lyrics appear to reveal more of John's true self; he probably meant it when he sang that he was a loser, but at the same time he had always been convinced he was a genius even if no one else seemed to realize it. 'That's me in my Dylan period,' he told *Playboy* in 1980. 'Part of me suspects I'm a loser and part of me thinks I'm God Almighty.'

His singing is a bit strange, deliberately going low on the last word of each chorus, almost out of tune, sounding a bit embarrassed, as if trying to do something different and unusual, then realizing it doesn't work as he hasn't got the vocal range, and covering up by trying to make it funny.

Baby's In Black

John at his most depressive – his girl is in black, mourning for someone who will never come back, so he is blue, because she never thinks of him.

Could he have been thinking, at the back of his mind, of Astrid – the beautiful, arty, clever, talented girl they met in Hamburg and whom they all loved? She got engaged to Stu, who then suddenly died in April 1962, aged twenty-one. Astrid, when I met her in 1967, was still dressing in black, in a flat with black walls, black furniture, black candles …

The tune and the first line, 'Oh dear, what can I do?' is a steal from the old folk song 'Oh dear, what can the matter be, Johnny's so long at the fair.' Perhaps it began as a parody, before moving on to the image of a girl in black. As for the rhymes – the song contains one of their weaker lines: 'And although it's only a whim / she thinks of him.'

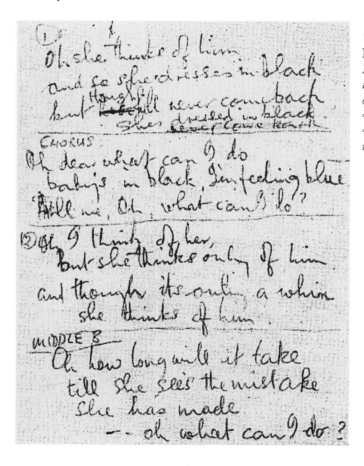

'Baby's In Black', from the Beatles For Sale *LP, December 1964 – possibly in the hand of Mal Evans, one of their two roadies, who was often given the job of writing out the lyrics in the recording studio.*

The manuscript version – possibly in the hand of Mal Evans, one of their two roadies – is an early draft. It was later expanded, but those two feeble lines were retained. Alas.

Oh dear, what can I do?
Baby's in black and I'm feeling blue,
Tell me, oh what can I do?
She thinks of him and so she dresses in black,
And though he'll never come back, she's dressed in black.
I think of her, but she thinks only of him,
And though it's only a whim, she thinks of him.
Oh how long will it take,
Till she sees the mistake she has made?
Dear what can I do?
Baby's in black and I'm feeling blue
Tell me, oh what can I do?
Oh how long will it take,
Till she sees the mistake she has made?

Oh dear, what can I do?
Baby's in black and I'm feeling blue,
Tell me, oh what can I do?

I'll Follow The Sun

One of Paul's sweetest songs, influenced by Buddy Holly, whom he was deliberately trying to copy at the time. He originally wrote it in the front parlour at Forthlin Road. It had been forgotten during their hard rocking days, but now, in October 1964, they were desperate for new material for the album, so Paul went back to this old number. And didn't do much new work on it, by the look of the lyrics. They are about the shortest of any Beatles song, just twelve lines – six of which are repeated.

It's typical of Paul's upbeat, positive but also perhaps selfish outlook: one day I will be off, my love, as I have to follow the sun. John, by contrast, in such a situation, tended to cast himself as the victim.

Eight Days A Week

Sounds like an early 1963 happy-clappy rocker dance song built round one catchy phrase. 'John and I were always looking for a title,' said Paul in the Beatles *Anthology* book. 'Once you've got a good title, if someone says "what's your new title" you're half way there. Of course the song had to be good. If we had called it "I am on the Way to a Party with You Babe" they might say, "Ok" but if you've called it "Eight Days a Week", they say "Oh that's good."'

The title sounds like a Ringoism, and it is often said to have originated with Ringo, complaining about having to work so hard. However, Paul remembers that it came from a chauffeur who was driving him to the house in Weybridge which John had moved into in July 1964. Paul asked the driver if he was busy and he replied, 'Working eight days a week.' It was the first time Paul had heard the expression.

Having got the title, and put a rhythm to it, they did little else. The lyrics do not develop beyond I am in love with my babe, and I need her eight days a week. Once they got a good hook, they felt that was enough – which had pretty much been their attitude to songwriting up until 1964.

John was later dismissive about the song, saying he was only writing for the meat market, with his professional songwriter hat on, not as a creative writer trying to express himself.

Every Little Thing

This track came as a surprise to me – playing it now, I realized I didn't know it and had no memory of having heard it back in the sixties. Little wonder, I suppose, as it is highly forgettable, a bit of dirge, with a lacklustre beat and poor words – every little thing the girl does, she does for him. Paul told Barry Miles in his 1997 biography that he had written it in his bedroom in Wimpole Street with Jane in mind, as a love song – but it can't have thrilled her much, and certainly would not today, given the implication that it is a girl's duty to serve her man.

I Don't Want To Spoil The Party

Written mainly by John on the USA tour, in hotel rooms and aeroplanes, flying between concerts – and feeling pretty pissed off, by the sound of it. A girl has been bad to him, but he'll still go to the party, in case his disappointment shows. The tune does have its fans, but the narrative is flat and static.

What You're Doing

Written mainly by Paul. Again it sounds like several other Beatles songs, before and after. There are some nice harmonies but the lyrics are repetitive – the girl is lying to him, making him cry. And yes, making him blue. Unusual for Paul to confess to crying, but it appears that his romance with Jane was running into problems. He has admitted the song was a bit of failure: 'You sometimes start a song and hope the best bit will arrive by the time you get to the chorus … but sometimes that's all you get.'

The manuscript is in Paul's hand and written on headed notepaper from the La Fayette Motor Inn in Atlantic City. It shows that there were some changes in the middle eight for the final version. It was originally 'waiting just for you', not 'here for you', and then he had two attempts at the next line which appear to read 'wondering what you gonna do / if you [something] that's true'. The last line, which was originally 'Should you want a love it's me / that's true', became 'Should you need a love that's true, it's me.'

Not exactly poetry, or even half-decent pop lyrics.

Look what you're doing, I'm feeling blue and lonely,
Would it be too much to ask of you,
What you're doing to me?

You got me running and there's no fun in it,
Why should it be so much to ask of you,
What you're doing to me?

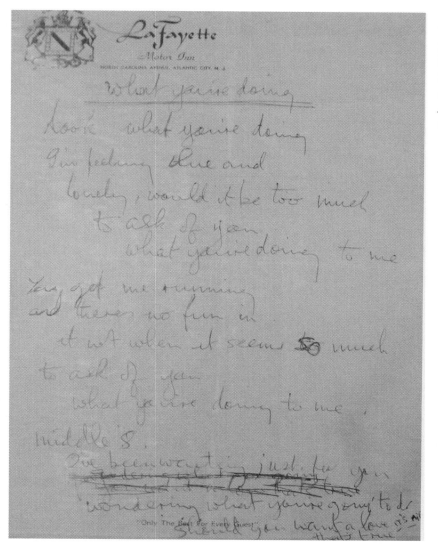

'What You're Doing', from Beatles For Sale, *December 1964, in Paul's hand on an Atlantic City motel notepaper.*

I've been waiting here for you,
Wond'ring what you're gonna do,
Should you need a love that's true,
It's me.

Please stop your lying, you've got me crying, girl,
Why should it be so much to ask of you,
What you're doing to me?

Beatles For Sale is, on the whole, a bit of a disappointment. With hindsight, we can see influences for change in their lives in 1964, but none of that is reflected in the album. Instead it betrays evidence of overwork, lack of time and limited creative energy (Paul's 'I'll Follow The Sun', arguably the prettiest song, is at least four years old), hence the need to fill it up with six songs by other composers. Though John and Paul contributed four songs each, John is still very much the leader.

They were always pretty clear-headed about which songs had worked and which hadn't – though John was later inclined to get a bit carried away, rubbishing everything: 'When I was a Beatle, I thought we were the best fucking group in the world,' he told *Playboy* in 1980. 'As far as we were concerned we were the best – but we thought that we were the best before anybody else had even heard of us, back in Hamburg and Liverpool. But I am disappointed with every record they ever fucking made. So I cannot give you an assessment of what the Beatles are.'

5

HELP!

August 1965

Ticket for Shea Stadium concert, New York, 15 August 1965, which had a world record audience for a pop concert of 55,600 and took $304,000 at the box office.

The idea of John or any of the Beatles needing help seemed potty. How could they, when they were so young, rich, famous, adored? Had they not got everything in this world they had always wanted, everything that anyone could ever want? Snap out of it, John! That was what I and probably most people at the time thought to ourselves, if we thought seriously about the meaning of the lyrics. But of course we didn't. It was just a pop song with a catchy hook, not meant to be taken seriously. Surely?

We now know, because John later told us, that this was the first really personal song he wrote – and that it truly was a cry for help.

'The only true songs I ever wrote were "Help!" and "Strawberry Fields Forever". They were the ones I wrote from experience.' So he told *Rolling Stone* in an interview in 1970.

In the 1980 *Playboy* interview he expanded on this: 'I didn't realize it at the time. I just wrote the song because I was commissioned to write it for the movie. Most people think it's just a fast rock 'n' roll song. But later I realized I really was crying out for help. So it was my fat Elvis period.'

I first met John in March 1964 on the set of *A Hard Day's Night* when the Beatles were filming at the Scala Theatre in London. I didn't get much out of him, he was just larking around, making jokes about an illuminated sign that read *Sounds On* – meaning the sound was on, so they were recording, but he was giving a thumbs up and saying 'Sounds on' – a fashionable phrase at the time to indicate that something was good, OK, right on. My interview with him never appeared, perhaps because I failed to explain the joke – or maybe it wasn't very funny in the first place.

In 1967 when I got to know him better, spending hours with him at Kenwood, his home, I could see he was often down, fed up, miserable, sitting around, doing nothing, remote, distracted. I put this down to unhappiness with his marriage; disappointment that being rich and famous turned out not to be enough, but not knowing what next to do in his life; and to taking too many nasty drugs, which were leaving him befuddled, switched off from the world.

In 1965, all these elements were already there, along with the added problem of physical and mental tiredness – they were absolutely knackered through overwork. They had done two albums in 1964, and in 1965 they did another two, three singles, plus a film. John also produced his second book. Then there was all the touring – first around Europe and then their second major tour of the USA in August, during which they met Elvis. Audiences were still screaming hysterically whenever they appeared, but now the screaming was so loud the Beatles could not hear themselves play. According to George, their nerves were being shattered by it all.

John at home at Kenwood, his house in Weybridge, Surrey, which he bought in July 1964 for £20,000.

It's interesting that in the song 'Help!' – which came out first as a single, two weeks before the album – John looks back to his childhood as a time when he didn't need help, when he was self-assured. It's a rather romantic memory.

During our long conversations he described how happy-go-lucky, cheerful, friendly and outgoing he had been up to the age of ten, which was also the memory of his Aunt Mimi. Then as a teenager he started fighting the world, teachers, authority; he felt he didn't fit in, that he was special but nobody else realized it. A not uncommon teenage condition.

Then he had the years of struggle with the band, which to them seemed to go on for ever, no one else believing that they would ever get to the top, as they always said they would. For many stars, reaching the summit can be enough, they can lie back and enjoy it, but not the Beatles. I think that was the single most surprising thing about them when I first met them – their disappointment and dissatisfaction that the thing they had longed for hadn't quite turned out the way they imagined it would be. They were still longing, looking, searching. Many intelligent creative artists do feel that way, wondering, Was it worth it? The discovery that success is all rather hollow, that you are still alone with yourself, can of course lead to self-destruction through excess, be it drink or drugs.

As with their first film, none of the songs that featured in *Help!* was written specifically for scenes in the film – they were written independently, in the way they normally wrote their songs, then slotted into the screenplay. On the album, only two of the fourteen songs ('Act Naturally' and 'Dizzy Miss Lizzy') were not written by them, so that was an improvement on the previous album. It was also a step up for George, who was allowed two songs. In addition to a good proportion of bouncy, sing-along, dance-along tunes, written against the clock, there were a couple of songs on the *Help!* album that broke new ground, giving away clues to the future. Starting with the title tune …

Help!

The song was written to order, seven weeks into shooting, when at last they decided on a title. Until then, there had been various possibilities – 'Beatles 2', 'Eight Arms To Hold You' and 'High-Heeled Kickers'. John wrote the song, mainly on his own, with help from Paul, at home in Kenwood.

The words to 'Help!' are some of the clearest, least evasive he had written up to that point, and also the strongest, with no slack or corny 'blue' 'true' rhymes or tired pop-song I love yous, dropped in for the teen market.

He also uses some rather long words, not normally found in pop songs – such as self-assurance, appreciate, independence, insecure – one result, apparently, of Maureen Cleave teasing him that all Beatles' songs seemed to be filled with one-syllable words.

There are also some excellent one-liners, such as 'my independence seems to vanish in the haze'. This is the line which sums up the drawbacks to their fame and success: being rushed around the world, not knowing where they were or who they were. Their life had changed in so many ways, hence they needed to get their feet back on the ground.

In the lyrics of 'Help!' John avoids psychobabble or second-hand Freudian analysis. In fact at one level you could take the lyrics to be another love song – wanting someone to come along and love him, take care of him, the sort of thing most people wish for in life. He does thank someone, appreciates them being 'round', which you could read as meaning he was OK really, he did have a loving wife so you didn't have to worry too much about him.

On the other hand, as John told us later, it was a personal cry of anguish. It might have been influenced by their first LSD experience, which had taken place a few weeks earlier. The phrase 'I find I've changed my mind' can be taken two ways: a simple change of opinion or a mind change due to trying life-altering drugs.

Pete Shotton, his boyhood friend, who in 1965 spent many weekends with John at his home, and later became his PA and worked for Apple, says that the line about 'appreciate you being around' referred to him – which could be true, as he rekindled memories of the laughs and pranks and daft times they'd had together as boys.

It's interesting that John later told his 'long week-end' girlfriend May Peng (assistant to John and Yoko, with whom he went off to California in 1973 for over a year) that he wished he'd performed *Help!* as a much slower, soulful song – thus making it more 'truthful'.

The manuscript of *Help!*, which John gave me, is in bold, large handwriting, with quite a few changes. 'Would' appreciate became 'do' appreciate, as it did in the final version. The first line of the verse has been crossed out. It's hard to read, but it appears to be a first attempt at the next line, 'When I was younger'. He has also written the first three lines of the recorded song at the end, as the last three lines of this version.

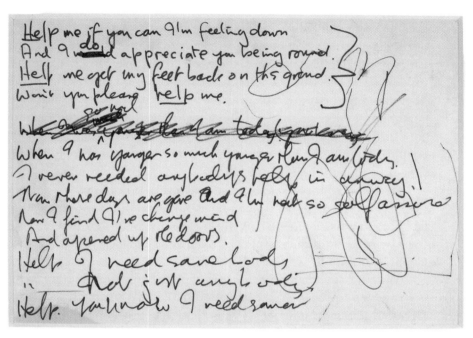

'Help!', title song for the film and LP, August 1965, in John's hand, plus some scribbles.

Help! I need somebody,
Help! Not just anybody,
Help! You know I need someone, help.

When I was younger, so much younger than today,
I never needed anybody's help in any way.
But now these days are gone, I'm not so self assured,
Now I find I've changed my mind and opened up the doors.

Help me if you can, I'm feeling down
And I do appreciate you being round.
Help me get my feet back on the ground,
Won't you please, please help me?

And now my life has changed in oh so many ways,
My independence seems to vanish in the haze.
But every now and then I feel so insecure,
I know that I just need you like I've never done before.

Help me if you can, I'm feeling down
And I do appreciate you being round.
Help me get my feet back on the ground,
Won't you please, please help me, help me, help me?

I'm Down

This was the B side of the 'Help!' single (though it doesn't feature on the album). It was one of Paul's party pieces to do a Little Richard number, usually 'Long Tall Sally', and here he performs a screaming, shouting parody of the singer – an affectionate piss-take. The Beatles appeared on stage with Little Richard in October 1962, the week after 'Love Me Do' came out, as a support act at the Tower Ballroom in New Brighton and the Empire Theatre. They asked for his autograph afterwards. Nice to know the Beatles were once autograph hunters themselves. Some years later, John gave me an autographed copy of the programme, signed for him by Little Richard, who has added his telephone number in California, in case they were over there – which at the time they thought highly unlikely.

The song is a bit of a joke, on several levels. It rather mocks John's cry for Help on the other side, moaning about being down while screaming and laughing. It also includes a comedy line – something they had not used in their lyrics before: 'You still moan "Keep your hands to yourself",' sings Paul, laughing at himself …

Although the manuscript version contains only four lines in Paul's hand, it is written on the back of a typed letter to Wendy Hanson, Brian's PA, from a US radio station in June 1965, saying that George's number 'You Like Me Too Much' is the best on their recent album.

Paul presumably picked up the letter during a visit to Brian's office in order to scribble down some of the words of his new song. On the same sheet are some neatly written lyrics I don't recognize. I think the writing is Mal Evans'; he was often given the job, in the studio and elsewhere, of making fair copies of their latest lyrics.

Four lines of the lyrics of 'I'm Down', the B side of the 'Help!' single, released in July 1965, in Paul's hand.

You tell lies thinking I can't see
You can't cry 'cos you're laughing at me
I'm down (I'm really down)
I'm down (down on the ground)
I'm down (I'm really down)
How can you laugh when you know
I'm down

(How can you laugh) When you know I'm down.

Man buys ring woman throws it away
Same old thing happens everyday
I'm down (I'm really down)
We're all alone and there nobody else
You still moan: 'Keep your hands to yourself!'
I'm down (I'm really down)
Oh, baby, I'm down (down on the ground)

Wow! Hurry up John!

Oh baby, you know I'm down (I'm really down)
I guess I'm down (I'm really down)
I'm down on the ground (I'm really down)
Whoa! Down! (I'm really down)
Oh, baby, I'm upside down
Oh yeh, yeh, yeh, yeh, yeh, I'm down (I'm really down)

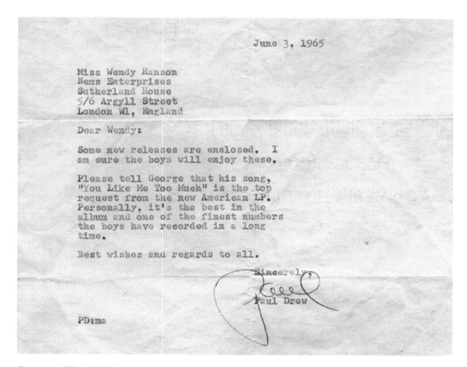

Letter to Wendy Hanson, Brian Epstein's secretary, on the reverse side of which Paul has written some of the lines for 'I'm Down'.

The Night Before

One of Paul's overlooked songs, presumably written while he was at Wimpole Street, which has not been very well rated by some critics over the years. I had to think hard to remember it, as the title seemed unfamiliar and gives little clue as to what it is about, but when I played the track, it all came back to me and I remembered that I had liked it, especially the line: 'Last night is the night I will remember you by.'

It's a jaunty but sad love song, remembering their last night together; was she telling him lies or not, before they had to part? Sounds like a farewell to Jane, going off somewhere, yet again …

You've Got To Hide Your Love Away

This is John showing that he can be as soft and sad as Paul, with more than a touch of Dylan in the use of acoustic guitar and folksy beat – the irony being that around this time Dylan himself was trying out electric guitar, having been impressed by the Beatles.

It is the first Beatles record on which they called in a musician to play an instrument that none of them could play – namely tenor and alto flutes, which come in plaintively at the end.

The words feature yet more love anguish, about a girl he has lost, leaving him now feeling 'two feet small'. Pete Shotton, who was at Kenwood when John wrote it, remembers that in the first version John had written 'two feet tall', but he made a mistake when he sang it to Paul. Paul then said he preferred it as 'two feet small'.

'I also said to them,' Pete remembers, 'that it sounded like a fucking funeral dirge – why not shout the HEY! Make it higher and give it life.'

Some people have suggested that the lyrics are not in fact about a girl John has lost, forcing him to hide his love away, but a message to Brian Epstein, who was gay. The law prohibited homosexual acts between men, so John was warning him to keep it quiet. Brian did harbour a passion for John and they once went on holiday together to Spain. John told me that they'd had a one-night stand – whatever that meant – but I didn't quite believe him, assuming he was trying to shock. Now, however … I'm not so sure. John was not gay, but he was wild enough to try anything once.

The manuscript version has the second line of what John describes as the third verse scribbled out. It appears to read 'In the state I'm in', which became the last line of that verse.

It was written by John while travelling in his Rolls with his chauffeur Anthony. He asked Anthony for something to write on and this address book was all that Anthony had to hand, so he opened it at the W section. The address book also contained scribbles by John, along with the phone numbers of the Beatles and others.

Here I stand head in hand
Turn my face to the wall
If she's gone I can't go on
Feeling two foot small

Everywhere people stare
Each and every day
I can see them laugh at me
And I hear them say

Hey! you've got to hide your love away
Hey! you've got to hide your love away

How can I even try
I can never win
Hearing them, seeing them
In the state I'm in

How could she say to me
Love will find a way
Gather round all you clowns
Let me hear you say

Hey, you've got to hide your love away
Hey, you've got to hide your love away

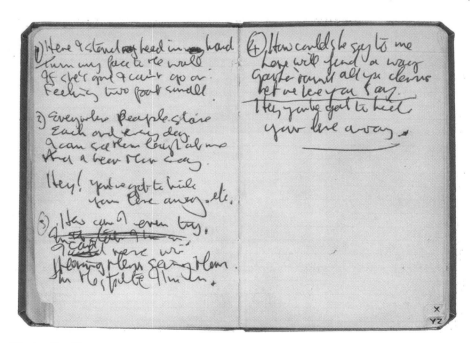

'You've Got To Hide Your Love Away', from Help!, *August 1965, in John's hand, written on the W and XYZ pages of his chauffeur's address book.*

I Need You

One of George's two songs on the *Help!* album – and now largely forgotten. It is very simple, with no tricks. It doesn't get anywhere, but it is rather haunting. The title says it all – she is off somewhere, or he is off somewhere, and he needs her, please remember how much I need you. It was written for Pattie Boyd, his girlfriend, the one he met on the film *A Hard Day's Night*, whom he would marry in January 1966. For some reason, George does not write about this song in his book *I Me Mine*, in which he mentions almost all his other songs. The only other one he omits is his second song on the *Help!* album, 'You Like Me Too Much'. Was he ashamed? Had he forgotten them? Or could he not find the original manuscripts to remind him of what he had done?

Another Girl

The title says it: the singer has got another girl. Or could it have a double meaning? The girl he is with has changed, turned into another girl? Paul wrote it while on holiday in Tunisia. A vaguely rockabilly number, nicely enunciated, with Paul picking out the syllables very carefully, fitting them exactly into the rhythm. Was it addressed to Jane? Must have been. And presumably Paul, or the singer of the song, had been playing away, for whatever reason. He's rather boastful about it in fact: 'All the girls I've met and I've met quite a few'. Which does sound like Paul – at that time, in that place. He also sounds a bit selfish: 'I don't take what I don't want.' True love, eh? Doesn't always run smooth. Especially if one of them wants to have other lovers.

You're Going To Lose That Girl

Now this is John showing off, in the lyrics anyway: if his friend does not look after his girl, he will take her out, 'And I will treat her kind.' John's track record with girls, according to the recollections of many of his girlfriends, and his first wife, do not quite tally with this rosy view of his personal history. The lyrics are an advance, story-wise, on 'She Loves You', where someone is mistreating his girl, but there is only a hint of the other boy stepping in. Catchy song, nicely sung by John with a very good falsetto, well up to Paul standards.

Ticket To Ride

One of the first Beatles lyrics to be subjected to over-analysis – and it still is today. Ian MacDonald, the music academic, practically wrote a treatise on it in his 1994 book *Revolution in the Head*. He suggested it was their 'first creative response to LSD', which they had taken for the first time early in 1965, when a dentist they were having dinner with spiked their coffee. John loved it and was soon taking it like sweets. MacDonald saw 'Ticket To Ride' as the first sign of the psychedelic records to come and detected a 'narcotic passivity' in the lyrics; he pronounced it 'psychologically deeper than anything the Beatles had done.'

At a slightly lower intellectual level, there were pundits in the pop papers who immediately declared that 'Ticket To Ride' was actually Ticket to Ryde – the name of a place on the Isle of Wight. Paul later confirmed that his cousin at one time had a pub there and he and John had visited it. There's another nice theory, put forward by the tabloid journalist Don Short, who travelled extensively with the Beatles in the early sixties. He said John told him the phrase originated in Hamburg – where the street girls had to have a medical certificate saying they were clean before they could work. I am sure that is true – that prostitutes had to be checked, and John would have made a joke about it – but I can't see how it fits into the song. Although John might well have made a joke about it afterwards, pretending it was connected.

I don't personally go along with any of the theories. It seems a very simple song to me – his girl is leaving him, going off, got her ticket, she doesn't care about him any more, living with him was bringing her down. In contrast to similar situations in earlier songs, this time he is fairly resigned, not threatening her, apart from saying 'she ought to think twice, she ought to do right by me'.

John later boasted that it was pop music's first heavy metal record. Not heavy compared with what came later, perhaps, but it has a good heavy beat and I do like the high falsetto chorus at the end on 'my baby don't care'.

The lyrics are well thought out, no dud lines or fill-ins. In fact it was one of John's best songs so far – though Paul did his bit, contributing about 40 per cent. What is agreed by all is that 'Ticket To Ride' was the longest Beatles song they had so far recorded – lasting three minutes and twelve seconds. Up to now they had mostly been 2 minutes–2 minutes 30 seconds.

In the manuscript, he has numbered just two verses – but there is a third, the second line of which he has crossed out and redone. John has written it out in capitals, as his handwriting was not always clear, so the others could sing the words without mistakes. The ninth line 'was bringing her down' became 'is bringing her down' which makes it more immediate.

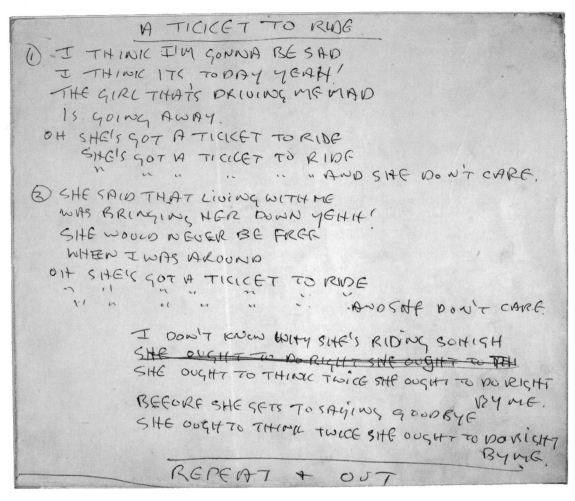

'Ticket To Ride' single, April 1965, written by John in his clearest capitals.

I think I'm gonna be sad,
I think it's today, yeah.
The girl that's driving me mad
Is going away.

She's got a ticket to ri-hide,
She's got a ticket to ri-hi-hide,
She's got a ticket to ride,
But she don't care.

She said that living with me
Is bringing her down, yeah.

She would never be free
When I was around.

I don't know why she ridin' so high,
She ought to think twice,
She ought to do right by me.
Before she gets to saying goodbye,
She ought to think twice,
She ought to do right by me.

My baby don't care, my baby don't care.
My baby don't care,

Yes It Is

This was the B side of 'Ticket To Ride' when it first came out as a single – but unlike 'Ticket To Ride', it did not appear on the album.

John is telling a girl not to wear red because 'red is the colour my baby wore', which would make you think he is referring to a previous girlfriend, though it sounds a bit dictatorial, telling any girl what to wear.

Ian MacDonald's theory was that it was a transmutation – and that really it is about John's dead mother Julia, who was red-haired. I asked Julia Baird, her daughter, if her mother wore red. 'Never never, always black black black, sometimes dark blue, but never red.' I think that answers that.

John never offered this explanation in any interview I can find, so who knows what originally inspired the song. It is deeply emotional and tender but at the same time rather lugubrious – and the lyrics are some of John's poorest. 'Red is the colour that will make me blue / in spite of you it's true / yes it is it's true.' John himself later admitted that he was embarrassed by these lines.

It's Only Love

John was also a bit embarrassed by this song, especially the rhymes, such as 'dries' and 'butterflies', and the rather lazy line: 'the sight of you makes nighttime bright, very bright.' When singing that last 'bright', you can hear him putting on a silly Scottish accent for the r, as if to let us know he realized it was a bit of a dud.

'I always thought it was a lousy song,' John told *Playboy*. 'The lyrics were abysmal.'

It's interesting that, when looking back, John was always more critical of his lyrics than the tunes, knowing he should have tried harder.

At one time, he was thinking of giving the song to another singer – Billy J. Kramer. In the end, they were desperate for material for the new album and decided to hang on to it. John's working title for the song was 'That's a Nice Hat', which suggests that he had never rated it. George Martin and his orchestra later recorded an instrumental version of it under John's original title.

The song, though short and simple with not much to it, is romantic and, by John's standards, optimistic, with only a passing reference to the fact that they have fights. 'It's Only Love' is a put-down, distancing himself, but at the same time you believe he means it, and that he is in love.

The manuscript, an early scribbled version, indicates that he did try quite hard to polish it, as there are several lines and phrases in this version that he didn't use in the end. In the third line, he has written: 'Why am I so glad when I'm beside you.' In the final version, glad becomes shy, which has a different meaning.

In the second verse, which was not used at all, he is experimenting with rhymes for 'blame' and 'complain', even if they don't quite make sense. They are hard to decipher but appear to read: 'Can't explain or name, I think it's pain, heh again / I'm ashamed the flame of love is maimed, now and then / You're to blame the same as I / I'll complain in vain, and I still love you.'

In the third verse, he has a second line, trying more corny rhymes: 'Though my plight the sight of you is bright rather tight / Write the slight away, we'll make it up girl …'

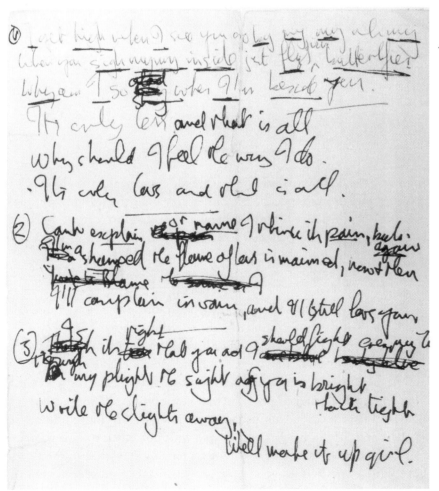

'It's Only Love, from the Help! *LP, August 1965, an early scribbled version in John's hand.*

I get high when I see you go by
My oh my.
When you sigh, my, my insides just fly,
Butterfly.
Why am I so shy when I'm beside you?

It's only love and that is all,
Why should I feel the way I do?
It's only love, and that is all,
But it's so hard loving you

Is it right that you and I should fight
Every night?
Just the sight of you makes nighttime bright,
Very bright.
Haven't I the right to make it up girl?

It's only love and that is all,
Why should I feel the way I do?
It's only love, and that is all
But it's so hard loving you
Yes it's so hard loving you – loving you.

You Like Me Too Much

George's other contribution on the album. It's an upbeat and fairly cheerful
love song to his wife Pattie, with no moans as in his previous songs. The song
sounds very Lennon–McCartneyish and is well up to their standards with
a jaunty bar-room piano accompaniment. There is one line, one thought, in
which he says, 'if you ever leave me, I will follow you', which alas foretold what
was to come. Pattie did eventually leave George, for his friend Eric Clapton
(who wrote 'Layla' and also 'Wonderful Tonight' with Pattie in mind) and they
got married in 1979.

Tell Me What You See

A simple childlike song, phrased as if asking a child a question: look into these eyes, what do you see? And the answer is me. Which is quite neat – but that's as far as it gets. There is no story, no situation unfolds. Presumably it began as another love song from Paul to Jane, telling her to trust him, even if there are some black clouds around. John helped out with the final version.

Paul, when talking to Barry Miles in *Many Years From You*, appears not to remember much about it: 'Not awfully memorable. Not one of the better songs, but they did a job, they were very handy for albums or B sides.'

'Put your trust in me' sounds vaguely biblical, the sort of verses and sayings that John and Paul would have recited at Sunday school.

John later recalled a childhood memory of a religious motto hanging on a wall: 'Big and black the clouds will be / Time will pass away / If you put your trust in me / I'll make bright your day.' They used these exact words in the lyrics.

He took the piss out of this in his second book, *A Spaniard in the Works*, at the end of the story entitled 'Silly Norman': 'However blackpool tower maybe / in time they'll bassaway / Have faith and trumpand BBC / Griffs' light make bright your day.'

In the lyrics for 'Tell Me What You See' those original religious lines are used, without any suggestion of mockery.

I've Just Seen A Face

Another of the many songs Paul composed in the music room at Jane Asher's house – along with 'And I Love Her', 'Every Little Thing', 'Eleanor Rigby', 'You Won't See Me' and 'I'm Looking Through You'. It has a vaguely skiffle beat, with some tumbling, descending chords thrown in, which Paul was quite pleased with. It was a song he played to his Aunty Gin, who liked it very much, and it was known as Aunty Gin's theme, until he knocked the words into shape.

Yesterday

Paul woke up one morning in his attic bedroom in Wimpole Street with a melody in his head that he couldn't erase. He went to the piano, beside his bed, and played it through. The tune had arrived almost intact, with the glory and the freshness of a dream (which is Wordsworth, 'Intimations of Immortality', but Paul over the years used similar phrases to recount how it had first came to him). Worried that it was someone else's tune that had crept into his subconscious, for several weeks he played it to friends, such as the singer Alma Cogan, asking if they recognized it.

He put some silly words to it, calling it 'Scrambled Eggs, supposedly followed by 'oh baby how I love your legs' just to give him some words to sing when he played it to the other Beatles. They all laughed at the words, but liked the tune.

It was during a long car drive while on holiday in Portugal with Jane in May 1965, after they had started recording the album, that he finally put some proper words to it. After fitting 'Yesterday' to the first three notes he needed a rhyme, and came up with 'all my troubles seemed so far away'. That left him needing another three-syllable word, and out popped 'suddenly'.

In many ways, the words seemed to come almost as easily as the tune, albeit spread over a longer period of time. The lyrics are short, just eleven lines, with little development.

John always thought the melody was beautiful, but the words, though good, didn't get very far and were not resolved. That in a way is a strength, leaving it vague. Why had she gone, why was a shadow hanging over her, what was the wrong thing he had said? This is never explained, leaving some analysts to suggest he wasn't in fact talking about a row with a current love, i.e. Jane, which is how it appears, but remembering the death of his

Paul and Jane Asher: it was at her house that he woke up with the tune for 'Yesterday'.

mother all those years earlier. That was a huge shadow that must have hung over him, though at the time of her death he admits he didn't grieve openly as much as he should. So was he thinking of his mother? Paul has admitted that might well have been at the back of his mind, but says he wasn't aware of it when writing the lyrics.

In the studio, when he eventually had the words and had played it to them, and they were getting down to the musical arrangement, Ringo and the others admitted they couldn't really add anything to it – it was perfect as it was. It would be best if Paul sang it on his own, accompanied on his own acoustic guitar.

George Martin suggested a string quartet, but to begin with Paul was not keen on the idea, worried that it might appear pretentious. They still saw themselves as a rock'n'roll band and didn't feel comfortable with anything that sounded too upmarket and classical. They feared that tarting it up with lush strings might make it sound schmaltzy, like Mantovani. George Martin remembers Paul saying that if they did use a string quartet, he did not want any vibrato – the throbbing, vibrating sound violinists make when pressing very hard on a string, and then vibrating their fingers, to give it richness and depth. George explained that all professional violinists play that way, but he would try to restrict it.

George Martin duly hired a string quartet – two violinists, a viola and cello – and wrote out the parts for them. It was George's first major contribution to any of their compositions, but Paul was still involved, going to George's house to discuss the arrangement and then supervising the studio recording.

'Yesterday' was the first Beatles number to be a pure solo with none of the other group members involved. It was to be their final composition on the *Help!* album, but it was not released as a single in the UK, as Paul did not want to go against the normal Beatles format, which was to have all four Beatles playing on their singles. It was, however, released as a single in the USA the following year, where it went to number 1.

This manuscript version was written out for me by Paul, very neatly, in 1967, so it has no changes or corrections – although he has added the word 'middle' just to make it clear. It went on show with other Beatles lyrics at the British Museum in 1986 then moved to the British Library. The Queen stopped to read it when she opened the new British Library building in 1998, spending much longer studying it than Magna Carta – which of course she can't read, no more than I can.

Full lyrics to the original 'Scrambled Eggs' version have appeared on the internet, with all the verses, some of them quite good, but I always suspected it might be some Beatles fan, amusing themselves by declaring they had discovered Paul's original manuscript. So I sent it to Paul himself.

'The extra words about "Scrambled Eggs" as you expected, are a spoof. I certainly didn't write them and the nearest I get to it is doing a joke on the Jimmy Fallon Show in America when we took the original verse and added a verse about waffle fries "Oh my baby how I love your thighs"!'

'Yesterday', first heard on the LP Help! *in August 1965, written out ever so neatly by Paul.*

Yesterday, all my troubles seemed so far away
Now it looks as though they're here to stay
Oh I believe in yesterday.

Suddenly, I'm not half to man I used to be,
There's a shadow hanging over me.
Oh yesterday came suddenly.

Why she had to go I don't know she wouldn't say.
I said something wrong, now I long for yesterday.

Yesterday, love was such an easy game to play,
Now I need a place to hide away.
Oh, I believe in yesterday.

'Yesterday' is now the most recorded song ever, hundreds of artists having performed it over the decades – an estimated 2,200 cover versions had been done by 2013. I still like the line 'Love was such an easy game to play', which has nicely cynical overtones.

Songs do have a life of their own. Good ones will outlive us all, travel down through the generations, and can mean different things at different times to different people.

As a song, 'Yesterday' has certainly lasted, but has it lasted intact? Has it been loved to death? Battered and bruised by all the usage and attention? Possibly. I don't think it would be in my top ten Beatles numbers to take to a desert island. Too obvious, too corny. Which I suppose is a silly thing to say. It has lasted, and been loved, because it is a perfect song.

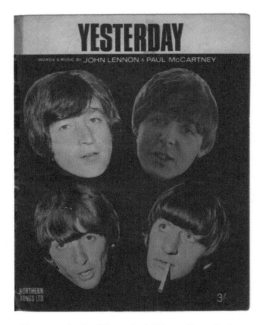

Sheet music for 'Yesterday'. They all smoked at one time, not just Ringo.

6

RUBBER SOUL

Plus singles, 1965

Was *Rubber Soul* the breakthrough? Was that when we knew the Beatles were not just another run-of-the-mill incredibly successful, highly popular, ever so enjoyable, fabulously fashionable, greatly loved band but, oh you know, there will be another excellent lot along any moment who will sell just as many and be just as popular?

They had of course broken through, in normal pop music and sales terms, back in 1963. Beatlemania was still going strong. Three years is a lifetime in popular music, as it is in politics, so they had had more than a good run already. Why would they want or try or need to change?

Looking back over those three years after they made their debut as recording artists in October 1962, there had been some great tunes to hum along and dance to – 'Ask Me Why', 'I Saw Her Standing There', 'I Want To Hold Your Hand', 'I Wanna Be Your Man' – and some half-decent lyrics, such as 'And I Love Her', 'I Feel Fine' and of course 'Yesterday'. But most of them had been love songs, fairly conventional in word and thought.

Now, in the October of 1965, as they began working on a new album and a new single, there was a definite sea change, a push forwards, sideways, upwards, outwards. It was like a coming of age; they became maturer and more confident, no longer confined by what had gone before or the conventions dictating the format of popular songs; they felt able to experiment, find their own style, express themselves, try new things in words, music and instruments.

With the lyrics, though they were still loving love songs, the big change was trying to tell stories, create narratives and scenes which had a beginning and an end – something they had not done before. They also became fond of jokes, teases, pastiches, parodies.

Most of their earlier songs had started in their heads with a phrase, a hook, an observation, two or three or four or five words which they played with, put a tune to, a musical phrase to go with the lyrical phrase. Once they liked the sound and idea, tried it on each other, they la-la'd the rest of the words, ad-libbing, using whatever came into their heads. Then they had to look for a middle eight, before getting back to the chorus, the main idea. Finally they fitted words to the tune and then wrote them down. This pattern was now undergoing a change, with John in particular, and the lyrics were starting to come first. It was part of a deliberate attempt to be himself, writing about himself, creating music the way he had created his poems, writing words down, thinking about them, then coming up with the tune later.

According to John, with *Rubber Soul*, 'We finally took over the studio. In the early days we had to take what we were given, we had to make it in two hours, one or two takes was enough, and we didn't know how you could get more bass. Then we got contemporary.' Back in 1962 they had been deferential, doffed their caps to the professionals, bowed to the men in suits. Now they were the ones calling the tune. They were like a group of workers who had got control of the factory.

The album's title is a rather weak pun – a play on soul music and rubber sole. Paul explained that he had heard some old American criticizing the Rolling Stones, saying they were good, but really 'plastic soul'. Playing with the expression, they changed it to rubber soul.

The cover photograph (taken by Robert Freeman) was an accidentally stretched photo, which elongated their faces, making them look rubbery rather than cute mop tops. It was a joke, a play on the title, but perhaps also intended to hint at deep, mystical qualities lurking inside their souls. To some, the sight of their distorted faces and glazed eyes on the front of the album supported the theory that drugs were beginning to play a part. But *Rubber Soul* is not an album about drugs, nor is it psychedelic – that came later. They did not record while under the influence; working in the studio was a hard slog given the time constraints they were under and they knew they would never get anything done if they were to indulge in pot or LSD. The drugs were taken at home. Sometimes the images that came to them in a drug-induced state did inspire songs, but Ringo always said that most of those songs turned out to be rubbish and never saw the light of day.

'The drugs are to prevent the rest of the world crowding in on you,' said John. 'They don't make you write any better. I never wrote any better stuff because I was on acid or not on acid.'

Rubber Soul can be seen as a transitional stage in the dynamics of the group. John has been the leader ever since the beginning, and on their recent albums he had written most of the songs and taken the lead in most decisions. But with *Rubber Soul* Paul began providing more songs, and they were a rather different sort of song, shifting the direction of the group. Could it have been all those nasty drugs that John later admitted he was eating like sweets, slowing him down, making him less bothered? Or was it down to problems with Cynthia and his marriage?

George has two numbers on the new album, as on the previous one, which indicates how much he was growing: 'Songwriting until then had been a bit frightening for me. John and Paul had been writing songs since they were three years old ... They'd had a lot of practice. They'd written most of their bad songs before we'd even come into the recording studios ... I had to come from nowhere and start writing.' George considered *Rubber Soul* to be their best album: 'It's my favourite, even at the time. We certainly knew we were making a good album. We were suddenly hearing sounds that we weren't able to hear before, everything was blossoming at the time, including us, because we were still growing.'

Just before the release of *Rubber Soul*, Francis Wyndham interviewed Paul for a long-forgotten publication called *London Life*. It was one of the first serious interviews, devoted to the work rather than the hairstyles. Paul talks about Robert Graves and Francis Bacon, and mentions that John is reading a book about the Christian view of pain and pleasure – revealing their wide-ranging interest in the arts generally. He says the new album – which nobody had yet heard – will contain funny stuff, and mentions 'Norwegian Wood'. He also says that he and John would like to write a whole song on one note: 'Melodic songs are quite easy to write – to write a good song on just one note is really very hard.' He also admits that they borrow sounds and riffs from other people: 'We are the world's biggest pinchers.'

The interview finishes with Paul talking about the future: 'The songwriting thing looks the only thing you could do at 60. I wouldn't mind being a white-haired old man writing songs – but I'd hate to be a white-haired old Beatle at the Empire Stadium playing for people.'

Day Tripper

On the same day *Rubber Soul* came out, a new single was released – their first double A side. Traditionally, the track on side A was the better song, the one with the most commercial potential, destined to get airplay and go to number one, while the B side was often just a filler. When the Beatles designated both John's 'Day Tripper' and Paul's 'We Can Work It Out' A sides, it was partly because everyone agreed both songs were strong, but perhaps also because Paul did not want his contribution to be downgraded.

'Day Tripper' begins with the enormously long double-tracked guitar riff, which had thousands of youths all over the world standing in front of the mirror pretending to play it – then you hear Paul singing 'Got a good reason'. It's an unusual, sideways, elliptical way into a song, but I still don't understand the first line – why had he a good reason to take the easy way out – or how? Did he take advantage of her availability and quickly move on, or chuck her because she was just a tease?

After the first two lines, it gets a bit clearer, though there are still ambiguities. Sexually, she was a prick teaser – which is the phrase John wanted to use but realized the suits would not allow it and it became 'big teaser'. He tried to please her, but found out she only played one-night stands. The inference here is that she had the upper hand – and he got the run-around. Then there are the druggie overtones – that she was into drugs, but only part-time, as a sort of fashion statement. In his *Playboy* interview John made it clear that this was his meaning: 'Day trippers are people who go on a day trip, right. Usually on a ferry boat or something. But it was kind of – you know, you're a weekend hippie. Get it?'

So he was mocking the Sunday hippies, who just pretended to be in the swim, right on, far out, man, people who have flowers in their hair on Sunday then go back to their nine-to-five jobs on Mondays

John dismissed it as just as anther rock'n'roll song, saying it was turned out in a hurry because they needed a single for Xmas, but the play on words is good, as is the imagery.

Some of the lines on the manuscript, in John's hand, have faded, but they are mainly the repeat lines. He appears to have begun one line with 'I tried to please her' then deleted the I at the beginning. He has also put 'Sunday Driver' in brackets for some reason, perhaps because it was going to be sung by someone else in the background.

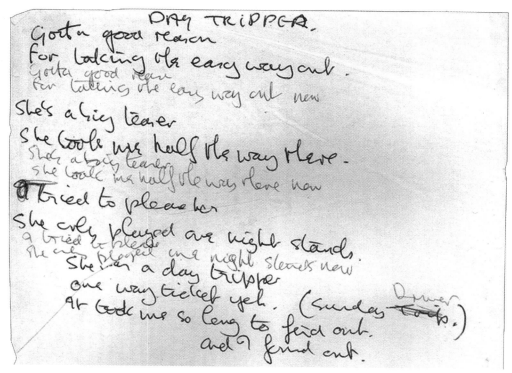

'Day Tripper' single, December 1965, in John's hand, with some lines repeated.

Got a good reason, for taking the easy way out
Got a good reason, for taking the easy way out, now

She was a day … tripper, one way ticket, yeah!
It took me so … long to find out, and I found out

She's a big teaser, she took me half the way there
She's a big teaser, she took me half the way there, now

Tried to please her, she only played one night stands
Tried to please her, she only played one night stands, now

She was a day … tripper, Sunday driver, yeah!
It took me so … long to find out, and I found out

Day tripper
Day tripper, yeah!

We Can Work It Out

This is a fascinating taste of what was to come later with 'A Day in the Life' – separate lyrics, written by each of them, then put together and made to work like a dialogue.

Paul wrote his part while visiting his father at 'Rembrandt', the house on the Wirral that Paul had bought for him. The subject is a difference of opinion with his girl, but he is trying to be positive, saying they can work it out. Nevertheless it is clearly a serious problem dividing them, one which will risk their love being gone for ever, so he wants her to see it his way.

It was inspired by a real-life situation: Jane Asher had announced that she was going to join the Bristol Old Vic theatre company, so would be moving out of London, for the time being, leaving Paul to face the prospect of staying at the Asher family home without her – just when he was about to embark on the long hard slog of putting together a new album.

Being of the post-war age – and from a Northern working-class background – Paul was probably not best pleased that his girl was intent on carving out a career, especially if it meant putting her pleasure and convenience before his. Which is odd, as his own mother held down a responsible job as a midwife. Later on, when he'd grown up and settled down as a happily married man with daughters, he would become much more in tune with our modern-day feminist attitudes.

In some ways, he was just being selfish, not thinking of her career. He was accustomed to meeting girls who were more than content to be rock-star chicks, to be arm candy at the night clubs, or stay at home – which of course Jane was not. Coming from a professional, middle-class background, she was determined to have her own career and not be an appendage.

John comes in with his middle eight and is more abrasive, both in his singing voice and his lyrics, saying that life is too short for all this fussing and fighting, warning that he will only ask her one more time. Then we return to Paul, with his sweeter voice and more reasoning, reasonable arguments.

The music swirls around the two attitudes and the two voices, ending with a sort of fairground harmonium, a sudden waltz tempo, even a tambourine in there somewhere, as if life is a rondel, a roundabout.

They worked hard for twelve hours in the studio to get 'We Can Work It Out' to sound exactly the way they wanted, adding more textures and effects than they had ever done in the past. It shows – and it paid off. It proved to be the more successful side of the single, despite the double A-side labelling of the disc.

Drive My Car

This was the first track on the album, the one that grabs and jolts everything into action, getting us away to a good start. But what does it mean? I could remember the words – at least, I thought I did, but on listening again, I realized I'd got the story all wrong. I'd thought the singer, Paul, was asking a girl to drive his car – a sexual euphemism perhaps. In fact, it's the girl who's inviting the boy to be her chauffeur, and maybe then she will love him. Role reversal – very modern, really.

The girl is a wannabe movie star, and when she's famous, he can drive her. He says he has a job, working for peanuts, but his 'prospects are good'. A nice line, sounds typical of Paul, using a period phrase, perhaps thinking of his father's job.

Then the final joke is revealed: she hasn't got a car. Beep beep yeah!

They clearly enjoyed shouting out the beep beeps, amusing themselves, and we were meant to be amused as well.

As is often the way with fun things, apparently tossed off with no effort, in reality it involved a long hard slog, taking them till well past midnight. Paul arrived with the tune but some corny words: 'You can buy me golden rings', which they had used before, and John rightly dismissed the lyric.

'We struggled for hours,' said Paul in the *Anthology* book. 'I think we struggled too long. Then it suddenly came. "Drive my Car" – and it became more ambiguous which we liked. Suddenly we were in LA cars, chauffeurs, open-top Cadillacs and it was a whole other thing.'

Perhaps it also conjured up memories of tough bitches, celebrity-mad Hollywood girls on the make, the sort they had recently met in LA, desperate to get into the movies, determined to call the shots, the sort they would never have come across in Liverpool.

Asked a girl what she wanted to be
She said baby, can't you see?
I wanna be famous, a star of the screen
But you can do something in between

Baby you can drive my car
Yes I'm gonna be a star
Baby you can drive my car
And maybe I'll love you

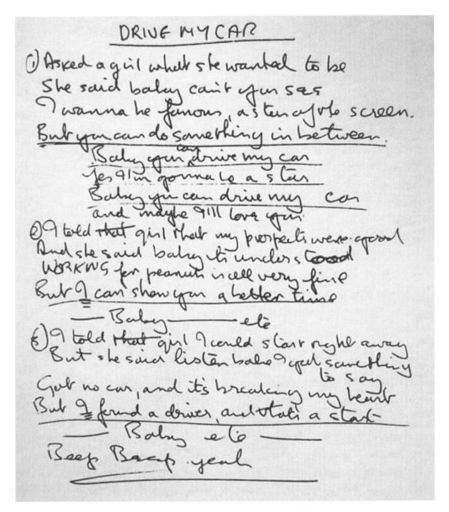

'Drive My Car', the first song on Rubber Soul, *December 1965, in Paul's hand.*

I told that girl that my prospects were good
she said baby, it's understood
Working for peanuts is all very fine
But I can show you a better time

I told that girl I can start right away
When she said listen babe I got
 something to say
I got no car and it's breaking my heart
But I've found a driver and that's a start

Baby you can drive my car
Yes I'm gonna be a star
Baby you can drive my car
And maybe I'll love you
Beep beep'm beep beep yeah
Beep beep'm beep beep yeah

Norwegian Wood

I clearly remember 'Norwegian Wood', word for word, because we gossiped endlessly about who it might be that John had an affair with – or at least a one-night stand. The rumours included a well-known female journalist (I have since asked her, more than once, and she always denies it with a smile). It could have been a certain famous actress he met on a film set, as there were strong rumours at the time, or the wife of a top photographer. Or it could simply have been an amalgam of several women, for he was still happily married to Cynthia, as far as the world could see, and therefore needed to cover his tracks.

'"Norwegian Wood" was about an affair I was having,' so John did confess later. 'I was very careful and paranoid because I didn't want my wife to know. I was trying to be sophisticated in writing about an affair but in such a smokescreen way you couldn't tell. I can't remember any specific woman it had to do with, I was writing from experience – girls, flats, things like that.'

It's mainly John's creation; he began it on a skiing holiday, but when he brought it into the studio it was still called 'This Bird Has Flown' and it didn't have much of an ending. It's probably the first of their songs where the lyrics are as important if not more important than the tune. There is no chorus, for a start, no repeat of any of the lines or verses, so you are meant to concentrate on the story being told.

It concerns a man going to a girl's flat, they drink, she shows him her room, which is done in Norwegian wood, asks him to stay, then says it's time for bed. Then she says she has to be up in the morning, though he hasn't to be. He sleeps in the bath – so he says, though it's hard to believe that happened in real life, so we take it as a joke, a way of not offending Cynthia.

That was apparently as far as he'd got when Paul helped complete the lyrics by suggesting that he lit a fire using the Norwegian wood: 'Isn't it good, Norwegian wood.'

Pine walls were very fashionable in the sixties – we had several rooms done in that way, long since stripped out – so a fashionable young woman about town would have been drawn to that style of decor. The joke about sleeping in the bath might have harked back to John's early days in a Liverpool flat, where he made visitors sleep in the bath and also burned the furniture in the fire.

A few days before *Rubber Soul* was released, Paul told the *New Musical Express*: 'We've written some funny songs – with jokes in them. We think that comedy numbers are the next thing – after protest songs.'

The jokes he had in mind were presumably the pay-off to 'Drive My Car' and the burning of the Norwegian wood. His dig at protest songs was because the Beatles, including John, were deliberately unpolitical at this stage, keeping clear of any movements or groups. Paul for example had yet to become a veggie, and enjoyed a hearty fry-up most mornings.

As with many Beatles songs, over the years many people have claimed to have had an influence. In the *Lennon Letters* (which I edited in 2012) there was a letter from John to a woman called Linda Ness. I recently heard more details of her – that she was half Norwegian, a young girl (not a girlfriend) who lived near John when young, and used to have tea at Mimi's. John kept in touch with her for some years and she gave him a wooden totem, made in Norway. She has recently put forward the theory that it might, possibly, have been the origin of the Norwegian wood, how it came into John's head. I doubt it, but a nice try.

The music is notable for the lack of drums, with John almost singing a solo, like Paul on 'Yesterday'.

Of course the big musical innovation was the use of the sitar for the first time on any Beatles record. George had become fascinated by the instrument when he heard one during the filming of *Help!* – there was a restaurant scene featuring some Indian musicians and George had a chance to muck around with their instruments. Afterwards he bought a cheap sitar and started to teach himself, though at this stage he had not progressed very far. Far enough, however, to impress John and Paul, who were eager for new sounds, and they persuaded George Martin to include it.

You Won't See Me

Another of Paul's songs inspired by Jane, written while he was still living at her London home. She had gone off to appear in *Great Expectations* at the Theatre Royal Bristol – leaving Paul full of self-pity. The song doesn't come to much of a conclusion, just repeats the same thing: she won't listen, her line is engaged when he calls her up, he can't go on. The title is good though, as you can take it literally or metaphorically.

The music has been mocked by the music experts, pointing out that it owes some of its chords to a Four Tops song that was then in the hit parade: 'It's The Same Old Song'. They haven't been keen on the soppy la-la refrain in the middle and at the end either. Personally, I rather like it, the music and the lyrics. It balances some of the previous self-pitying, as if Paul is now mocking himself for moaning, while at the same time genuinely upset.

Nowhere Man

A similar theme, but this time it's John. His is much better with cleverer lyrics, so it's a shame they put them one after the other on the album, making comparisons inevitable. They should have split them. They even contain a similar play on the verb 'see'.

The song came to John almost fully formed. After struggling without success to come up with a new song, he'd retired, fed up and miserable, as he told me in 1967: 'I'd actually stopped trying to think of something. Nothing would come. I was cheesed off and went for a lie down, having given up. Then I thought of myself as Nowhere Man – sitting in his nowhere land.'

As soon as he consciously let go, the song just seemed to come to him, summing up what he felt about himself and his life at the time: out of love with Cynthia, not knowing where he was, who he was, what to do with the rest of his life. Isn't he a bit like me and you?

There is undeniably a touch of the dirge about it, especially the rhythm and the words. Music purists have deemed it disappointing, but I think it is haunting and beautiful. It's the first Lennon–McCartney song, taking them in chronological order, not about love. There is no suggestion of a girl–boy relationship, that is not the reason he feels he's in a nowhere world. It's just him.

The manuscript, in John's hand, gives only about half of the completed lyrics. He's gone through it for some reason, putting a capital letter on Man. There's no disputing that it is John's song, but Paul remembers that when they were singing it, face to face, trying it out, John was singing the 'Nowhere Man' refrain and he would echo it, then he added to it, singing 'For nobody', which went into the lyrics. This manuscript has the verses in a slightly different order from the final version.

He's a real Nowhere Man,
Sitting in his Nowhere Land,
Making all his nowhere plans
for nobody.

Doesn't have a point of view,
Knows not where he's going to,
Isn't he a bit like you and me?

Nowhere Man please listen,
you don't know what you're missing

Nowhere Man, the world is at your
command.

Nowhere Man don't worry,
You don't know what you're missing,
Nowhere Man, the world is at your
command!

He's as blind as he can be,
Just sees what he wants to see,
Nowhere Man can you see me at all?

Nowhere Man, don't worry,
Take your time, don't hurry,
Leave it all till somebody else
lends you a hand.

He's a real Nowhere Man,
Sitting in his Nowhere Land,

Making all his nowhere plans
for nobody.
Making all his nowhere plans
for nobody.
Making all his nowhere plans
for nobody!

John's 'Nowhere Man' – with the M in man given a capital letter – from Rubber Soul, *December 1965.*

Think For Yourself

This is such a bitter, twisted, sad song by George – about someone leaving him, so he is telling her to do it, go her own way, think for herself – that it is impossible not to believe it was written about Pattie, with her threatening to leave. Which we know did eventually happen. Yes, hindsight can make us awfully clever – and we can easily get it wrong.

Yet George's explanation of how he came to write the tune is so unbelievable it could be his little joke – a bitter, sad, twisted joke. In *I Me Mine* he says of its inspiration: '"Think for Yourself" must be about "somebody" from the sound of it – but all this time later I don't quite recall who inspired that tune. Probably the government.'

Nice one, George, but you don't fool us. Perhaps he fooled himself, harbouring a subconscious fear that he was not admitting at the time or even aware of. Novelists often do that – create situations on paper, out of their imagination, which then come true.

The manuscript is in George's best handwriting, with neat capitals, so it is easy to understand. The words 'opaque' and 'rectify' didn't often appear in pop lyrics. There are some fine lines: 'the good things that we can have if we close our eyes' and 'the ruins of the life that you have in mind'. Was George now attempting poetry?

I've got a word or two
To say about the things that you do
You're telling all those lies
About the good things that we can have
If we close our eyes

Do what you want to do
And go where you're going to
think for yourself
'Cos I won't be there with you

I left you far behind
The ruins of the life that you have in mind
And though you still can't see
I know your mind's made up
You're going to cause more misery

Although your mind's opaque
Try thinking more if just for your own sake
The future still looks good
And you've got time to rectify
All the things that you should

Do what you want to do
And go where you're going to
Think For Yourself
'Cause I won't be there with you

Think For Yourself
'Cause I won't be there with you

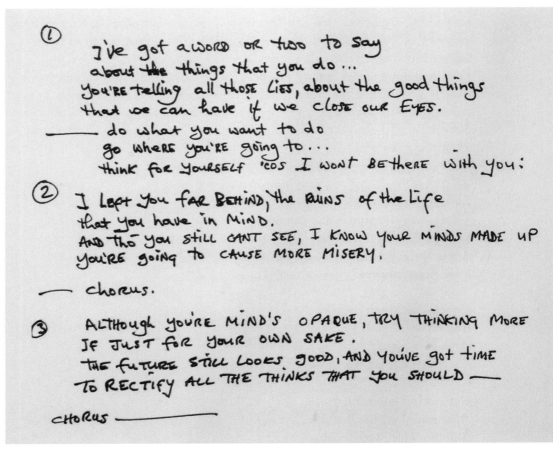

'Think For Yourself', nicely written by George, from Rubber Soul, *December 1965.*

The Word

The word in question is love – but John is not actually singing a love song. There is no boy or girl, no relationship, no sadness and heartbreak, it's all abstract, about the importance of the word love. An unusual topic for a pop song – to write it about a word.

It's heavily religious, in a gospel happy-clappy way, drawing perhaps on John and Paul's Sunday school days and church services about the Good Book, what happened in the beginning, have you heard, the word is love, have you seen the light.

What made them suddenly turn to these religious metaphors? It could well have been marijuana, smoking all those joints, or LSD, which we are told can lead to religious and spiritual visions. Peace and love, man, that's what it's all about.

The hippie generation had not yet been defined, the word hippie was not yet in widespread use, and the Summer of Love had yet to start, but in this song in 1965 John and Paul were foretelling what was to come, what a whole generation would be associated with – Love and Peace, plus drugs. It was the Beatles' first message song, though at the time it sort of seeped out, eased out, rather than hit you over the head.

'It's the marijuana period,' so John admitted later. 'It's love and peace. The word is love, right?'

The music itself seems at first to be mainly on one note – which is what Paul had been talking about in that *London Life* interview. It begins like a dirge, reminiscent of an India raga, and perhaps reflected George's new interest, but then settles down into a more conventional pop song, accessible to all.

It is mainly John's, but he and Paul completed it together at Kenwood – and having finished it, they rolled a joint to celebrate.

Instead of writing the words out quickly on any old sheet of paper so they wouldn't forget them, they found some crayons – so Paul remembered in 1997 when talking to Barry Miles – and produced an illuminated manuscript, the first time they had ever done so.* The words are in Paul's handwriting, highly decorated in a sort of psychedelic purple-red, with trees and abstract shapes. The lettering is very neat, considering they were getting high, though in the fourth line Paul wrote 'love is love' instead of 'word is love' and had to correct it. D.H. Hoek, Head of the Music Library at Northwestern, who has examined the manuscript very carefully, says that

---

* The manuscript is one of those today in Northwestern University in Evanston, Illinois.

the decorations are in fact in watercolour with some felt-pen marks – not crayons as Paul had remembered.

Say the word and you'll be free
Say the word and be like me
Say the word I'm thinking of
Have you heard the word is love?
It's so fine, It's sunshine
It's the word, love
In the beginning I misunderstood
But now I've got it, the word is good

Spread the word and you'll be free
Spread the word and be like me
Spread the word I'm thinking of
Have you heard the word is love?
It's so fine, It's sunshine
It's the word, love
Everywhere I go I hear it said
In the good and the bad books that I have read.

Now that I know what I feel must be right
I'm here to show everybody the light

Give the word a chance to say
That the word is just the way
It's the word I'm thinking of
And the only word is love
It's so fine, It's sunshine
It's the word, love

THE WORD.

① Say the word and you'll be free.
   Say the word and be like me
   Say the word I'm thinking of
   Have you heard the word is love
   Its so fine, its sunshine, its the word
                                        —love

   In the beginning
   I misunderstood
   But now I've got it
   the word is good.

   Spread the word, and you'll be free,
   Spread the word and be like me.
   Spread the word I'm thinking of
   Have you heard the word is love
        its so fine, its sunshine, its the word —love

   Everywhere I go,
   I hear it said
   in the good and the bad books
   that I have read.

① Say the word.. repeat......

   Now that I know
   what I feel must be right
   I'm here to show
   everybody the light.

   Give the word a chance to say,
   that the word is just the way,
   Its the word I'm thinking of
   and the only word is love
             its so fine, its sunshine, its the word.

'The Word', from Rubber Soul, December 1965, mainly a John song, but written out in Paul's hand, with psychedelic overtones.

Michelle

This is one of Paul's oldest tunes, written when he was still at school, the Liverpool Institute, in 1959 aged seventeen. He used to go to art college parties, through his friend John, and one of his party pieces was to pretend to be French, playing his guitar and singing in pretend French to look exotic and interesting and, so he hoped, pick up girls. French existential culture was big amongst students in the late fifties and French singers like Juliet Greco and Sacha Distel were much admired.

Six years later, in 1965, trying to get together enough new songs to fill up the *Rubber Soul* album, John reminded Paul of that tune he used to play at parties, which never had any words, not proper ones. He worked on it again, realized it must be a love ballad about a French girl, and so wanted some words that sounded, well, French.

Ivan Vaughan, one of Paul's oldest friends from school – the one who first introduced Paul to John – was visiting with his wife Jan, a French teacher, and Paul asked her for a rhyme in French for Michelle – she said Ma Belle. He then asked her to translate 'these words go together so well' into French. He later sent her a cheque, for having contributed.

When he had first played it to John, with only the chorus written, it was John who suggested the 'I love you, I love you, I love you' bit, with the accent on the word love, having been impressed by a Nina Simone song 'I Put a Spell on You' where the phrase is repeated three times – but then it's a phrase that has been used trillions of times, before and since. Listening to it again now, the roundabout rhythm of the music made me think of *La Ronde*, a French film of the fifties, very popular with students and young lovers

The use of French in an English pop lyric was most unusual, and funny in a way. It could well have ended up as a pastiche of a French accordion song, sung by a joke Frenchman with a beret and a string of onions, but Paul keeps a straight face, sticks to a simple tune, with a clear sweet voice and some great harmonies. After 'Yesterday', it is up there with his best loved, most played, most copied melodies.

The words are not memorable, they get nowhere, do little, no situation, no story, except a boy trying to woo a girl in a foreign language.

The manuscript, in Paul's hand, looks to be an early draft, before the 'I love you' middle eight and the introduction of the French words.

Incidentally, I went on the internet, accessed Dictionary.com and put in 'these are words that go together well' and in seconds the French translation came back as '*ce sont des mots cela vont ensemble bien*'. So not quite the same as Jan's. But then French people themselves can never agree on what is correct.

French. Think how today, thanks to computers, Paul could have immediately turned any old lines into any old language. Would he have gone on to use a lot more in his lyrics? I doubt it. Once was enough of an amusement.

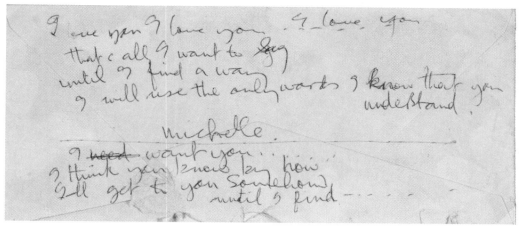

'Michelle', from Rubber Soul, *December 1965, in Paul's hand, but without the French bits.*

Michelle, ma belle
These are words that go together well
My Michelle
Michelle, ma belle
Sont les mots qui vont tres bien ensemble
Tres bien ensemble
I love you, I love you, I love you
That's all I want to say
Until I find a way
I will say the only words I know that you'll understand

Michelle, ma belle
Sont les mots qui vont tres bien ensemble
Tres bien ensemble
I need to, I need to, I need to
I need to make you see
Oh, what you mean to me
Until I do, I'm hoping you will know what I mean
I love you…

I want you, I want you, I want you
I think you know by now
I'll get to you somehow

Until I do, I'm telling you so you'll understand
Michelle, ma belle
Sont les mots qui vont tres bien ensemble
Tres bien ensemble
And I will say the only words I know that you'll understand
My Michelle

What Goes On

Another old tune resurrected at the last moment and polished up to fill the album and give Ringo a song. It had been written some years earlier by John and played to George Martin in March 1963 when they were thinking of a possible follow-up to 'Please Please Me' – but Martin declined it.

John decided to dig it out again and both Paul and Ringo helped to polish up the lyrics. Ringo, modestly, takes credit for only five words – but they include the nice phrase 'waiting for the tides of time'. The first two lines are also quite good: 'What goes on in your heart, what goes on in your mind.' But there is no development.

It is the first Beatles song in which Ringo gets a credit. On the sleeve the composer is named as Lennon–McCartney–Starkey.

It has a rockabilly feeling, which rather suits Ringo's limited singing range. In fact he sounds a bit flat, all the way through, but that adds to the charm. His pronunciation of 'tearing me apart' comes out like 'tayrin', betraying his Scouse origins.

Another example of how the Beatles, unless doing a parody or a cover version, sang in their own accents, their own voices.

Girl

'Girl' is possibly their strongest, deepest writing so far, in that it is complex, philosophical, with religious and existential overtones. John himself was rather proud of it. It was his original idea, but Paul helped out on some of the words.

At first, he appears to be leaving the girl: 'The kind of girl you want so much it makes you sorry.' Then he complains that she 'puts him down when friends are there'. He suspects she is the sort who takes pleasure from being cruel, causing pain. And finally the pay-off: 'Will she still believe it when he's dead?'

He is clearly writing about a tortured relationship, but again, he always denied he had any one girl in mind – though Cynthia later maintained that the first verse, about a girl he wants so much, was probably about her. Wishful thinking?

John explained later that, deep down, he was always waiting for an upmarket, arty intellectual sort of girl to come along – 'not someone buying Beatles records'. Which was rather cruel to Beatles fans. It turned out he was waiting for Yoko, though he didn't know it then.

'I was trying to say something or other about Christianity, which I was opposed to at the time ... the Catholic Christian concept: be tortured and then it'll be all right ... you'll attain heaven.'

The music is rich, with overtones of the *Zorba the Greek* soundtrack, George's sitar sounding a bit like a mandolin. John's voice is strong and direct, but also playful – you can hear a loud and suggestive intake of breath, magnified so it sounds like an instrument. There is also some close harmony in the background from Paul and George in which they are repeating tit tit tit tit tit, nicely mocking all the serious, intellectual sentiments.

Four months later, John returned to the theme of Christianity in his interview with Maureen Cleave, giving rise to that remark about the Beatles and Jesus ...

I'm Looking Through You

Another Paul song inspired by Jane, who had by this time departed to Bristol to pursue her acting career, leaving him wailing and wondering and rather self-obsessed, only seeing things from his point of view – but don't we all?

'It caused a few rows,' he told me in 1967. 'Jane went off and I said, OK then, leave. I'll find someone else. It was shattering to be without her. That was when I wrote, "I'm Looking Through You".'

It has some of Paul's best lines so far: simple and direct, conjuring up a situation most people have found themselves in, yet without resorting either to cliché or philosophizing. 'I'm looking through you, where did you go. I thought I knew you, what did I know.' Having dreamt up this ironic juxtaposition, he then keeps it going, aware of her lips moving, and then her voice, but nothing is clear. I can imagine him, sucking his pencil, listing other ways of supposed communication, all of them failing. Then he delivers the best line: 'Love has a nasty habit of disappearing overnight.' Sung so succinctly and clearly, enunciating every syllable.

You don't have to ponder too much about the words, or the sentiments, just move your feet. It's one I used to dance to a lot, in the old old days, when I could still move my feet …

In My Life

This originated with a long poem by John about his life – which is what Kenneth Allsop had suggested he should try. John wrote it at home at Kenwood and then put it to music, recording it on tape, then playing it back to see what it sounded like, if it was worth taking further. Fairly decent cassette recorders had come on the market and John owned about ten, which he had been messing around with for a year or two.

The lyrics describe a long bus ride through Liverpool, from his home in Menlove Avenue down to the docks, listing all the sights and sounds. It grew a bit long and boring and John went off it, thinking it was too clunky and clumsy, a bit like writing about what I did on my hols, but he liked the idea of looking back on his life, so he tightened it up, made it more universal, about someone looking back generally: the loss of childhood, the loss of close friends – presumably thinking of Stu Sutcliffe, though without naming anyone.

John was writing this at twenty-four, so on the surface it seems a bit premature to look back at a life that had hardly begun. But if you read the letter he wrote to Stu Sutcliffe in 1961, when only twenty, it's clear that even then he was somewhat philosophical and maudlin in his personal writings and ramblings, if not yet in his songs, discussing the nature of life and the universe and all that.

But then the song changes slightly, and you realize it's not some old git down memory lane, about to tell us things were better then; it is in fact a love song, about someone he loves now. He will never lose affection for people and things from the past, but he loves her more. So the song is positive, affirmative – which again is very mature.

While the words are indisputably by John, it is one of only two Beatles songs where John and Paul came into conflict over the credit. Usually, when they looked back on the Lennon–McCartney songs, there was no disagreement over what proportion they had each contributed. But in this case, Paul has a clear memory of being given John's words and then going to a Mellotron

THERE ARE PLACES I'LL REMEMBER.
ALL MY LIFE, THO' SOME HAVE CHANGED
SOME FOR BETTER
SOME FOREVER BUT NOT FOR BETTER.
SOME HAVE GONE AND SOME REMAIN.

PENNY LANE IS ONE I'M MISSING
UP CHURCH RD TO THE CLOCK TOWER.
IN THE CIRCLE OF THE ABBEY.
I HAVE SEEN SOME HAPPY HOURS.

AND THE 'BUS INTO TOWN.
THE TRAMSHEDS WITH NO TRAMS,
THE DUTCH & ST COLUMBUS

PAST THE TRAMSHEDS WITH NO TRAMS
ON THE 5 'BUS INTO TOWN
PAST THE DUTCH AND ST COLUMBUS
TO THE DOCKERS UMBRELLA THAT THEY
PULLED DOWN.

IN THE TRAMS & SPENT SOME GOOD TIMES
ALDERSHOTS WAS GOOD FOR A SUMMER
BUT IF YOU WANT TO REALLY FIND IT
REALLY WANT TO FIND IT
ALL THESE PLACES HAVE THEIR MEMORIES
SOME WITH LOVERS FORGOTTEN NEW
SOME WITH
SOME ARE DEAD + SOME ARE GLOWING.

'In My Life', from Rubber Soul, *December 1965, in John's hand, with some of the verses about Penny Lane and the tram sheds, which were never used.*

keyboard and setting it to music, inspired by the style of Smokey Robinson and the Miracles. John, however, maintained he wrote most of the music, with Paul only contributing the melody of the middle eight and some of the harmony.

'It was the first song I wrote that was consciously about my life,' John later said. 'Before, we were just writing songs à la the Everly Brothers, Buddy Holly, pop songs with no more thought to them than that – to create a sound. The words were almost irrelevant. I think this was my first major piece of work.'

The music is greatly helped by what sounds like a harpsichord, tinkling away like a Bach minuet, giving it a classical, timeless quality. This was George Martin, on a piano with the sound speeded up – his second major instrumental contribution to a Beatles song, after the string quartet on 'Yesterday'.

This manuscript, which is one John gave me, has some of the early verses of his original longer poem – or rather, lyric, as he always intended it to become a song, though it is long and complete enough to be considered poetry. It is of interest to all Beatles fans because of the second verse, about Penny Lane, which was discarded. It also includes the tram sheds with no trams, St Columba's Church and the Docker's Umbrella. The latter was a place under the overhead light railway where the dockers used to shelter from the rain. The Abbey was an old cinema. There are a lot places named, some of them not quite clear.

The discarded verses appear to read:

Penny Lane is one I'm missing
Up Church Road to the clock tower
In the circle of the Abbey
I have seen some happy hours
Past the tram sheds with no trams
On the 5 bus into town
Past the Dutch and St Columbus
To the dockers umbrella that they pulled down

In the parks I spent some good times
Calderstones was good for [jumping]
But if you want to really find me
Really want to find me
All these places have their memories
Some with loves [or lives] forgotten now
Some its . . . to be with
some are dead and some are living

While the final verse went:

There are places I remember
All my life though some have changed
Some forever not for better
Some have gone and some remain
All these places had their moments
With lovers and friends I still can recall
Some are dead and some are living
In my life I've loved them all

But of all these friends and lovers
There is no one compares with you
And these memories lose their meaning
And I think of love as something new
Though I know I'll never lose affection
For people and things that went before
I know I'll often stop and think about them
In my life I love you more

Wait

Jointly knocked into shape, head to head, as they used to do in the old days, and also jointly sung, each taking alternate verses. If it sounds like a throwback, then it was. It was recorded for the *Help!* album, written mainly by Paul perhaps with Jane in mind, when they were filming in the Bahamas, but not used. They dug it out to make up the tracks on *Rubber Soul*. The girl is being told to wait – he's coming back home. That's all there is to the lyrics. At least it makes you realize just how good, and what an advance, most of the new songs were.

If I Needed Someone

George's second song on the album and one he was quite dismissive of. 'It's like a million other songs written around the D chord. If you move your finger about you get various little melodies (and sometime you get maladies). That guitar line, or variations on it, is found in many a song and it amazes me that people still find new permutations of the same notes.'

The tune is indeed roughly all on one note, and a bit monotonous, so it's surprising that he didn't add any Indian musical instruments in the background. Perhaps he didn't feel confident enough yet with his expertise on the sitar.

In *I Me Mine* he gives us no clue to the origin of the lyrics. The guy in the song sounds rather unappealing, telling a girl he might or might not ring her up, if he had more time, and anyway he is too much in love. With Pattie, we presume.

In the manuscript he has scribbled out a few words, redoing one line and changing 'the wall' to 'my wall'.

If I needed someone to love
You're the one that I'd be thinking of
If I needed someone

If I had some more time to spend
Then I guess I'd be with you my friend
If I needed someone
Had you come some other day
Then it might not have been like this
But you see now I'm too much in love

Carve your number on my wall
And maybe you will get a call from me
If I needed someone
Ah, ah, ah, ah

Carve your number on my wall
And maybe you will get a call from me
If I needed someone

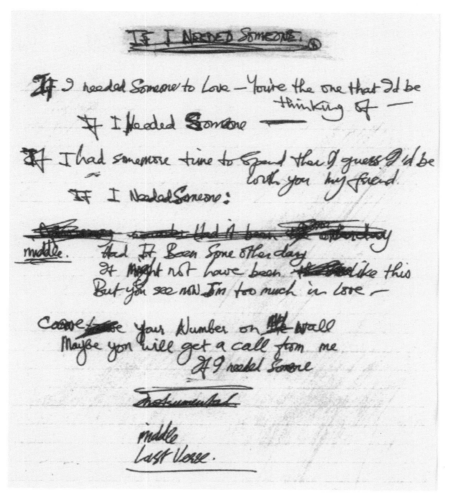

George's song 'If I Needed Someone', from Rubber Soul, *December 1965, in George's hand, with some minor corrections.*

Run For Your Life

John borrowed the main line in this song – 'I'd rather see you dead little girl than see you with another man' – lifting it from an Elvis song, 'Baby, Let's Play House', which came out in 1954. He was attracted by the intensity of that kind of love, and the jealousy that could lead him to wish someone dead. He admits in the song he is a wicked guy to think such thoughts. Which he clearly did. There was a cruel side to John, he abused Cynthia, was hurtful to women and mocked cripples. At least he was self-aware: 'I'm not always a loving person.'

But I want to be that. I want to be as loving as possible … I am a violent man who has learned not to be violent.'

I imagine the lyrics are not those he might have written once Yoko came into his life – and in fact he later seemed to regret them, saying the song was written under pressure, it was just a glib throwaway song, an example of his worst work.

The manuscript is very faint – so put your best specs on.

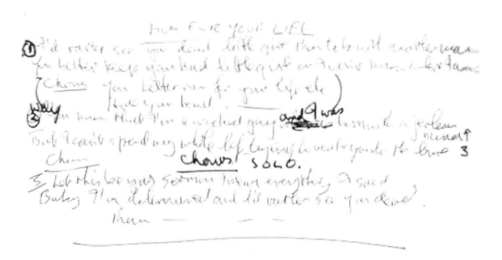

Some early verses from 'Run for Your Life', from Rubber Soul, *December 1965, in John's hand but alas a bit hard to read.*

I'd rather see you dead, little girl
Than to be with another man
You better keep your head, little girl
Or I won't know where I am

You better run for your life if you can,
    little girl
Hide your head in the sand, little girl
Catch you with another man
That's the end – ah, little girl

Well you know that I'm a wicked guy
And I was born with a jealous mind

And I can't spend my whole life
Trying just to make you toe the line

Let this be a sermon
I mean everything I've said
Baby, I'm determined
And I'd rather see you dead

You better run for your life if you can,
    little girl
Hide your head in the sand, little girl
Catch you with another man
That's the end – ah, little girl

7

REVOLVER

August 1966

Revolver was another evolution, even revolution, in that it revolved, hence the title, another jokey one. The album cover was also different from anything so far: instead of a photograph, drawings of the Beatles by Klaus Voormann, a friend from their Hamburg days, are interspersed with cut-out photos of them and other bits, very arty and psychedelic. One of their ideas for *Revolver* was to have no space between the different tracks, so that it all flowed on, one continuous sound, but EMI said no.

They were now doing so many clever things in the studio, fashioning and sculpting the sounds, that they were creating songs they could not perform, and did not perform live on stage. None of the fourteen new tracks on *Revolver* got included in their stage shows. They were fed up with touring, and this gave them one more reason to want to give up playing in public.

In 1966 when I started interviewing the Beatles, I asked whether they listened to their own music. Many creative artists can't bear to revisit their work. It depresses them, seeing how it didn't turn out they way they hoped, or depresses them in another way, wondering how they did it, whether they can manage to do it all again.

John and Paul both said they never listened to their old stuff – except as an *aide-mémoire* before a new album, to see where the were up to. 'I used to play the first four albums, one after the other,' said John, 'to see the progression musically, and it was interesting. I got up to *Revolver* and it got too many. It would be too much listening time, but you could hear the progressions, as we learnt about recording and the techniques got refined.'

Both John and Paul could not understand why anyone was surprised that they seemed to keep on progressing, wanting to do different things. It seemed to them utterly natural. In an interview with Michael Lydon, published in *Newsweek* in March 1966, Paul said:

If someone saw a picture of you taken two years ago, and said that was you, you'd say it was a load of rubbish and show them a new picture. That's how we feel about the early stuff and Rubber Soul.

There was no mystery about our growth, it was only as mysterious as a flower is mysterious. There's no more point in charting it than charting how many teeth I had as a baby and how many I have now. Nobody thought that was miraculous, except perhaps my mother. We were just growing up.

Revolver was issued in August 1966, during what turned out to be their last tour. This was their third and final USA trip, and their performance at Candlestick Park, San Francisco, on 29 August 1966 was to be their last live concert performance anywhere. Their final UK concert appearance had been in May 1966, at a *New Musical Express* event at Wembley.

From now on, they could take as long as they liked in the studio, and not have to break off to tour the world. They became a recording band, not a performing band. It also meant they were creating for a different sort of public. Instead of performing for audiences of screaming girls they were going underground, reflecting and inspiring the hippie, druggie, psychedelic, turned-on generation.

In *Revolver*, the lyrics covered subjects which would have seemed totally implausible just four years earlier: taxation, submarines, Buddhism, lonely spinsters, druggie doctors, sleep. Far-out topics and weird sounds, but *Revolver* also included some of the most beautiful songs they had written so far.

Paperback Writer

Recorded around the same time as the *Revolver* album, in April 1966, but came out before the album, in June, as a single, and set the pattern for writing about things that had nothing to do with romance or relationships. It was Paul's creation, supposedly as a result of one of his aunts suggesting they wrote a song which was not about love.

Paul's own memory is that while driving down to John's house one day, the idea came to him for a song in the form of a letter. It would begin with Dear Sir or Madam, in the classic manner, and progress from there. He had had a letter from an aspiring novelist, wanting help, and liked the sound of 'paperback writer', knowing it was something he could easily fit a rhythm to.

An author called Peter Royston Ellis believes he was the paperback writer they had in mind, as the Beatles played the backing music to a poetry reading he gave in 1960. They had also had two paperbacks written about them in 1964. *The True Story of the Beatles* by Billy Shepherd was for the fans, published by the people behind the *Beatles Monthly* magazine. The other was more upmarket: *The Beatles Progress* was written by an American journalist called Michael Braun who had accompanied them on a few of their tours. This was published by Penguin – who in those days only did paperbacks. John of course had had two books out – small, thin hardbacks at first, later reissued as paperbacks.

Paperbacks were a post-war phenomenon in the UK, but mostly they were slim volumes in comparison to the one referred to in the lyrics. A thousand pages long? Dear God, no one in their right mind would have mentioned that to a paperback publisher.

The lyrics don't in fact have a lot of logic to them. The reference to Lear was presumably Edward Lear, who never wrote novels, though John as a boy loved his nonsense poems. They're fun nonetheless, with daft things thrown in like a dirty story of a dirty man, his clinging wife and a son who reads the *Daily Mail* – which John often did, looking for inspiration. The novelist is offering all the rights, insisting it will sell millions, promising he can make it longer, change the style – that's typical of letters publishers receive even today.

The manuscript is interesting because Paul has written it out as if it is a letter – prose rather than verse, which is how lyrics are usually set out. Only when you read it do you realize it is the lyrics to the song, exactly as they were sung.

Paul, right, signing autographs before The Ed Sullivan Show *in New York, 9 February 1964.*

He signs it at the end: 'yours sincerely Ian Iachimoe'. One of Paul's jokes, apparently – what his name sounds like when played backwards.

The music itself contains a joke – which I must admit I had never spotted till I read Ian MacDonald's erudite *Revolution in the Head*. In the second chorus, George and John are not singing 'Paperback Writer' but can be heard in the background chanting 'Frère Jacques'.

'Paperback Writer', released as a single in June 1966, in Paul's hand, written out as if it really is a letter, not verses.

Paperback writer, paperback writer.
Dear Sir or Madam, will you read my book?
It took me years to write, will you take a look?
It's based on a novel by a man named Lear,
And I need a job,
So I want to be a paperback writer,
Paperback writer.

It's a dirty story of a dirty man,
And his clinging wife doesn't understand.
His son is working for the Daily Mail
It's a steady job,
But he wants to be a paperback writer,
Paperback writer.
Paperback writer, paperback writer.
It's a thousand pages, give or take a few.
I'll be writing more in a week or two.
I could make it longer if you like the style.
I can change it round,

And I want to be a paperback writer,
Paperback writer.

If you really like it you can have the rights.
It could make a million for you overnight.
If you must return it you can send it here,
But I need a break,
And I want to be a paperback writer,
Paperback writer.

Rain

I'd forgotten 'Rain', in fact I am not sure I ever listened to it properly at the time. It was the B side of 'Paperback Writer' and B-sides never got the same attention. Still not loved or known much by ordinary humming-along, Fab Four Beatles fans – but boy, the musicologists have gone to town on it over the years, seeing hidden musical depths, praising all the clever tricks, the backwards tapes, the heavy amplification, Ringo's superb drumming, saying it was at least twenty years ahead of its time. According to American musicologists Stuart Madow and Jeff Sobul in their 1992 book *The Colour of Your Dreams*, it was the Beatles 'first truly psychedelic song'.

To me, it still sounds like a dirge, with a vague Indian mono beat in the background, and a lot of assorted noises as they try out stuff to amuse themselves and give George Martin and the technicians something new to do.

John says he discovered the joy of the backwards tapes at home while enjoying himself with some herbal stimulants; he accidentally threaded a tape of the stuff they had recorded that day into his machine backwards, and out came this weird sound.

The lyrics are, on the surface, totally banal. It's about rain. You know, that wet stuff that falls down, that people are always moaning about. That's what set John off – people complaining about the rain. He then moves on to say that rain and shine are just a state of mind. How true. How very sixth-form philosophical debating society.

I can see that it could be psychedelic in that the words and music were probably influenced by herbal concoctions, but I think interpreting it as some sort of hippie bible – that John is trying to give us a message, we should rise above rain and shine, transcend good and bad, and just rise up in the air, man – is pushing it a bit.

Taxman

The first track on the album – written by George, given pride of position for once. They were kind enough to include three of his songs altogether, his biggest tally so far.

George had been incensed when he discovered how much money they were giving the taxman. In the second line of the lyrics he says 'one for you, nineteen for the taxman', but in fact the top rate in 1966 for the highest earners was nineteen shillings and sixpence in the pound (95 per cent), the highest it has ever been in the UK. Or probably anywhere.

None of the Beatles could be accused of being mercenary or money-mad, John least of all, but at various times they all did a bit of fretting and moaning about where their money was going. George, despite being the youngest (he turned twenty-three in 1966) was the first to express his anger about the government taking most of their money while they did all the work.

John helped with the lyrics, after George had rung him up, asking for ideas – another reason John was upset not to be thanked in *I Me Mine*. George says little about this song in the book: 'Taxman was when I first realized that even though we started earning money, we were actually giving most of it away in taxes. It was and is so typical. Why should this be so? Are we being punished for something we have forgotten to do?'

Brian Epstein tried a few tax-saving devices – sheltering one million with a financial wizard in a tax haven in the Bahamas. The money disappeared – and Epstein was too embarrassed and humiliated to confess it to the Beatles. He was not exactly the toughest or cleverest of businessmen, despite his public image.

George's manuscript has a discarded verse and a few bum lines which possibly John and the others persuaded him to drop, such as 'You may work hard trying to get some bread, you won't make out before your dead'. The crossings-out suggest he wasn't sure himself. Equally clumsy was the line: 'so give it to conformity'. John's input made it wittier and sharper and the finished lyrics were much better: 'If you try to sit, I'll tax your seat. If you get too cold, I'll tax the heat.'

There is one line I don't quite follow: 'Now my advice for those who die, declare the pennies on your eyes.' It sounds clever and visual, but does it mean your body parts have a value for transplant? Unlikely in 1966. (The first heart transplant was in 1967 in Cape Town.) More probably it was a reference to the custom of putting pennies on the eyelids of corpses?

There is one good joke in the finished, recorded version where you can hear the others in the background singing about Harold Wilson – who had won a landslide election for Labour in March 1966 – and also Edward Heath, leader of the Conservatives. It was the first time living folks had got a name check in a Beatles song.

They had met Harold Wilson, MP for a constituency in the Liverpool area (Huyton), who always tried to cash in on reflected glory for the global success of the Beatles. He had been Prime Minister when the Beatles received their MBEs in 1965.

Now let me tell you how it will be
There's one for you, nineteen for me
'Cos I'm the taxman, yes, I'm the
    taxman

Should five per cent appear too
    small
Be thankful I don't take it all
'Cos I'm the taxman, yeah I'm the
    taxman

If you drive a car, I'll tax the street,
If you try to sit, I'll tax your seat.
If you get too cold I'll tax the heat,
If you take a walk, I'll tax your feet.

Don't ask me what I want it for
    (ha ha Mr Wilson)
If you don't want to pay some
    more (ha ha Mr Heath)
'Cos I'm the taxman, yeah, I'm the
    taxman

Now my advice for those who die
Declare the pennies on your eyes
'Cos I'm the taxman, yeah, I'm the
    taxman
And you're working for no one
    but me.

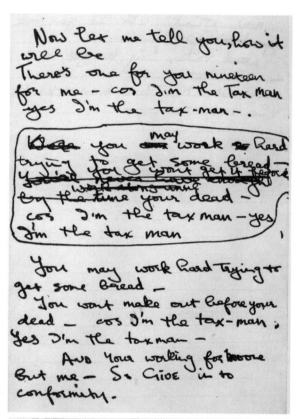

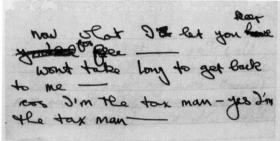

'Taxman', from Revolver, *September 1966, in George's hand, with some of the weaker lines rewritten.*

Eleanor Rigby

It was thanks to 'Eleanor Rigby' that I got to meet Paul properly. When it first came out, as a single but also on the *Revolver* album, I was so impressed by its words as well as its music, that I was determined to talk to Paul about it. I assumed, like all Beatles fans, that he must have written it, because he was the person singing it.

Being a journalist, writing a column called Atticus in *The Sunday Times*, I had a slightly better chance than most fans of actually getting to see him, though if he had written it two years earlier I might never have managed it as *The Sunday Times* did not write about pop artists, however successful, at that time.

By 1966 the chattering classes were in awe of the Beatles, and how they were creating such marvellous music without being able to read or write a note, and writing such great verses, despite not having had the benefit of a half-decent university education.

So I went to see Paul at his house in Cavendish Avenue, St John's Wood – which he still has to this day. I do like people who are consistent, who know what they like and don't like. He moved in in March 1966, having at last decided he should have a place of his own instead of using Jane's house, which he had made his home for about three years. The other three Beatles had, by this time, established themselves in deepest suburbia with lush gardens and rolling lawns, but Paul preferred to be in central London.

I remember the house as being nicely lived in, even though he had not been there long, with lots of interesting objects and paintings (over the fireplace in his main living room was a Magritte). The garden, from what I could see, was totally overgrown, left to its own devices while he decided what to do with it. It added to the bohemian feel of the place; it was very much the home of a wealthy but artistic young bachelor. There was no sign of Jane Asher, though she was still very much part of his life. In the article, I said he lived alone.

The interview followed the format popular at that time, letting the subject talk with minimum intervention, but I did manage to drag in my opinion about 'Eleanor Rigby': 'No pop song of the moment has better words or music.' Note that I referred to them as Mr McCartney and Mr Lennon. Was I being facetious, given their youth and status as pop stars? No, I was being polite and formal, as we tended to be, back in 1966.

Paul McCartney was in his new mansion in St John's Wood. He lives alone. A Mr and Mrs Kelly look after him. Nothing so formal as a housekeeper and butler. Their job, he says, is just to fit in.

The house has a huge wall and an electrically-operated black door to keep out non-Beatle life. Inside there is some carefully chosen elderly furniture. Nothing flash, affected or even expensive-looking. The dining room table was covered with a white lace tablecloth. Very working-class posh.

Mr McCartney, along with Mr Lennon, is the author of a song called 'Eleanor Rigby'. No pop song of the moment has better words or music.

'I was sitting at the piano when I thought of it. Just like Jimmy Durante. The first few bars just came to me. And I got this name in my head – Daisy Hawkins, picks up the rice in the church where a wedding has been. I don't know why.

'I can hear a whole song in one chord. In fact, I think you can hear a whole song in one note, if you listen hard enough.

'OK, so that's the Joan of Arc bit. I couldn't think of much more, so I put it away for a day. Then the name Father McCartney came to me – and all the lonely people. But I thought people would think it was supposed to be my Dad, sitting knitting his socks. Dad's a happy lad. So I went through the telephone book and I got the name McKenzie.

'I was in Bristol when I decided Daisy Hawkins wasn't a good name. I walked round looking at the shops and I saw the name Rigby. You got that? Quick pan to Bristol. I can just see this all as a Hollywood musical ...

'Then I took it down to John's house in Weybridge. We sat around, laughing, got stoned and finished it off. I thought of the backing, but it was George Martin who finished it off. I just go bash, bash on the piano. He knows what I mean.

'All our songs come out of our imagination. There was never an Eleanor Rigby. One of us might think of a song completely, and the other just adds a bit. Or we might write alternate lines. We never argue. If one of us says he doesn't like a bit, the other agrees. It just doesn't matter that much. I care about being a song writer. But I don't care passionately about each song.

'"Eleanor" is a big development as a composition. But that doesn't mean "Yellow Submarine" is bad. It was written as a commercial song, a kid's song. People have said, "Yellow Submarine? What's the significance? What's behind it?" Nothing. Kids get it straight away. I was playing with my little stepsister the other day, looking through a book about Salvador Dali. She said "Oh look, a soft watch." She accepted it. She wasn't frightened or worried. Kids have got it. It's only later they get messed up.

'I tried once to write a song under another name, just to see if it was the Lennon–McCartney bit that sold our songs. I called myself Bernard Webb – I was *a student in Paris and very unavailable for interviews. The song was "Woman", for Peter and Gordon. They made it a big-hit. Then it came out it was me. I realized that when I saw a banner at a concert saying "Long Live Bernard Webb".*

'We'd need a properly controlled experiment to find out how much our names really mean now, but I can't be bothered.

'I can't really play the piano, or read or write music. I've tried three times in my life to learn, but never kept it up for more than three weeks. The last bloke I went to was great. I'm sure he could teach me a lot. I might go back to him. It's just the notation – the way you write down notes, it doesn't look *like music to me.*

'John's now trying acting again, and George has got his passion for the sitar and all the Indian stuff. He's lucky. Like somebody's lucky who's got religion. I'm just looking for something I enjoy doing. There's no hurry. I have the time and money.

'People think we're not conceited, but we are. If you ask me if I wrote good or bad songs, I'd be thick to say bad, wouldn't I? It's true we're lucky, but we got where we are because of what we did.

'The girls waiting outside. I don't despise them. I don't think fans are humiliating themselves. I queued up at the Liverpool Empire for Wee Willie Harris's autograph. I wanted to do it. I don't think I was being stupid.

'I think we can go on as the Beatles for as long as we want to, writing songs, making records. We're still developing. I've no ambitions, just to enjoy myself. We've had all the ego bit, all about wanting to be remembered. We couldn't do any better than we've done already, could we?'

We now know, all these years later, a little more about the background to the song. Or think we do. Paul has confirmed that the name Eleanor came from the actress Eleanor Bron, who had appeared in the film *Help!*. In the eighties, a tombstone was discovered in the graveyard of St Peter's Church at Woolton, where Paul met John, marking the grave of one Eleanor Rigby. Could Paul have subconsciously stored it in his brain? Possibly, but I think it unlikely.

Pete Shotton, John's best friend, has shed more light on the subject. He was at John's house when Paul arrived with the tune completed but only half the verses done. He tried it out on John, George, Ringo and Pete, who all chipped in with suggestions. When Father McCartney was dropped – for the reason Paul gave me – Pete Shotton got out a telephone directory and found the name McKenzie. It was Ringo who suggested he was darning his socks. George came up with the line 'all the lonely people'. Paul was then stuck for an ending and Pete says that it was he who first suggested the two characters should be brought together: Eleanor, the lonely spinster, and Father McKenzie, the sad priest.

Extraordinary that a lyric with input from so many contributors turned out near perfect – not a line wasted, not a word wrong, not a corny image.

It has the simplest accompaniment – a string octet, arranged by George Martin, without any drums or guitars – which adds to the ethereal, disembodied atmosphere of the piece.

But there are so many things we still don't know. Eleanor, picking up the rice after a wedding: is she a cleaner, a guest at the wedding or just an idle visitor? Then we see Father McKenzie, another lonely person, writing a sermon which no one will hear. Why not? Is he retired, have the congregation abandoned him?

They come together when she dies. 'She died in the church': is that confirmation that she was a cleaner, dying on duty, or does it just mean she was still a member of the church? Father McKenzie leaves the grave, presumably the only person who attended the service, wiping the dirt from his hands.

She was 'buried alone with her name'. I take that to mean she was unmarried, had no family, had done nothing with her life, a nobody – but some commentators have suggested that she committed suicide.

Novelist A.S. Byatt, in a BBC talk aired in 1993, remarked on the phrase 'wearing a face that she keeps in a jar by the door'. If it had been kept by a mirror, we would immediately have thought of make-up (women often refer to putting on their face before going out), but there is no mirror mentioned, so the image becomes broader, more metaphorical.

Staring out of the window, wearing a face, she is a nobody, nobody sees her, nobody knows her. She is one of the true lonely people. When she does venture out into the world, she hides behind the face she wears, preserving her anonymity.

Was she a victim of the First or Second World War, when so many women were left alone, having lost the man they might have married? Some, more cynical, have suggested she is a prostitute – waiting for a client: that's who her face is for. The phrase 'no one was saved' has been seen as anti-Christian, anti-Catholic. Rich pickings, then, in one short song, for eager analysts.

The longest, most sustained analysis of the lyric I have read is an unpublished 29,000-word essay by Professor Colin Campbell of York University (co-author of the definitive concordance of Beatles lyrics, *Things We Said Today*, see page 5). Fascinated and mystified by the 'Eleanor Rigby' lyrics, he likens them to an opera or ballet, in which the first and third acts are there, but we are missing the second, middle act, and have to imagine it. He discusses the power of the images; the economy of expression; the enigma at the heart of the two stories; the tragedy of their lives, as in a Greek drama, balanced by the humanity of the chorus.

Campbell points out that it is the only Beatles song with a story that takes place over a period of time, and is also unique in that it is about two characters, presented separately, who are then drawn together. It's also their first song about a named individual (but only just: 'Dr Robert' was recorded ten days later), and the first Beatles song not to contain the words I, me, mine, you or your. It is a third person song – not directed at someone, like 'You've Got To Hide Your Love Away'. Fascinating stuff. Shows what you can find out if you really study the lyrics. Let's hope he gets it published.

The manuscript, now in Northwestern University, is in Paul's hand and looks like a fair copy rather than an original working version, though it was missing the last verse. There are a couple of corrections, but they appear to be simple spelling mistakes. The signature at the end is possibly in Yoko's hand, to identify it for John Cage (see pages 16–17)

'Eleanor Rigby', from Revolver, *September 1966, in Paul's hand but the signature at the end is by someone else, possibly Yoko.*

Ah, look at all the lonely people
Ah, look at all the lonely people

Eleanor Rigby, picks up the rice in the church
Where a wedding has been
Lives in a dream
Waits at the window,
Wearing the face that she keeps in a jar by the door
Who is it for?

All the lonely people
Where do they all come from?
All the lonely people
Where do they all belong?

Father McKenzie, writing the words of a sermon
That no one will hear
No one comes near
Look at him working,
Darning his socks in the night
When there's nobody there
What does he care?

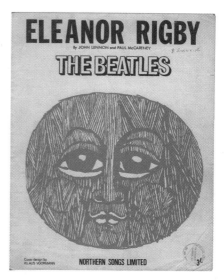

*Sheet music for 'Eleanor Rigby',
illustration by Klaus Voorman, artist
and musician, a friend of the Beatles
from Hamburg.*

All the lonely people
Where do they all come from?
All the lonely people
Where do they all belong?

Ah, look at all the lonely people
Ah, look at all the lonely people

Eleanor Rigby died in the church and was buried along with her name
Nobody came
Father McKenzie, wiping the dirt from his hands
As he walks from the grave
No one was saved

All the lonely people (Ah, look at all the lonely people)
Where do they all come from?
All the lonely people (Ah, look at all the lonely people)
Where do they all belong?

I'm Only Sleeping

When I used to go down to Kenwood and see John he was very often lying on the curved couch in his day room, half-asleep or idly reading a newspaper. I wondered why, when he had such a big house, he would huddle in what must have been the smallest room. I also wondered about the sticker on the cupboard above his head, which read SAFE AS MILK. I took it to be ironic. I never saw him drink milk.

John at home at Kenwood in his favourite room.

Paul, when he came down to Kenwood, by appointment, to work on a song, would often find John still in bed, sound asleep, and have to wake him up.

I once arrived to see John only to be informed that he had decided it was a day for not speaking. So we had lunch, not speaking. He flopped on his couch, watching children's afternoon TV, not speaking, then we had a swim in his pool, still not speaking. I was furious. All that way – to get so little out of him.

So 'I'm Only Sleeping' was true to life. He spent a lot of his days just lying around, if not in fact asleep. In the 'Jesus' interview with Maureen Cleave, she quotes him as saying that he can sleep almost indefinitely. 'Sex is the only physical thing I can be bothered with any more.'

When the idea for the song came to him, based on what he was doing, or not doing, he scribbled the first version on the back of a bill from the Post Office, being too lazy to go and find a clean piece of paper. The letter informed him he owed them twelve pounds and three shillings for a car radio bill. John was never a techie, and always had trouble remembering his own phone number or making his own calls, but being a young millionaire with a Rolls-Royce, bought in June 1965, he had acquired one of the earliest phones for use in his car.

It's a bit too obvious to say this is a druggie song, about someone who has over-indulged – which John did. I believe it really is about sleeping: the joys of it, taking your time, letting the world rush by, a neat commentary on our crazy modern lifestyle. True, 'Float upstream' could be a reference to drugs, but it is also what you do when you dream, when that marvellous drowsy feeling takes over and you feel yourself drifting away.

The words, which are sharp and succinct – not at all the mark of a lazy lyricist – can also be seen as a clear indication of his boredom, not just with life but with Cynthia.

The song took a long time to record, for they were endlessly experimenting with new sounds and effects. I had always assumed that there was a sitar being played in the background, but thanks to the musicologists I have learned that it was a backwards-played guitar. It took twelve hours to get right – for just seventeen seconds.

In John's voice I can detect the hint of an old man, singing in a strong Lancashire accent, vaguely reminiscent of George Formby. Again, that was deliberate, speeding up and slowing down the tapes to achieve the right effect.

The manuscript with the Post Office bill on the other side is clearly dated 12 April 1966, very useful for musicologists. It shows lots of changes as John worked on the lyrics. It seems to begin with the first line 'Try to sleep again. Got to get to sleep' – which he didn't use – before moving on to: 'When I waken early in the morning', which became his first line, more or less. The other lines are variations on roughly what was to come.

This manuscript is owned by Pete Shotton, John's best friend from school:

I was going to see our accountant one day, whom we both used, and John said, 'I have this bill, will you tell him about it and get him to pay it.' He gave me the bill and I turned it over and there was a song on the other side. He said, 'It doesn't matter, I'll have to write it out again on a larger piece of paper.' So I went off to the accountant, showed him the bill. He said he already had a copy, and would pay it. I shoved the bill in my suit pocket – which I never wore again for about four years. So I just kept it. There was no value in Beatles memorabilia in those days.

South-West Telephone Area, London
Telephone House
21/33 Worple Road
LONDON SW19

Telephone Manager: G. E. Brett,
ERD, BSc(Eng), AMIEE

In any reply please quote: ACA 194
Your reference:

Telephone:
TSW 1234   (switchboard)
TSW 2412   (direct line)
Telex: 21244 (TELMAN SW LDN)

1966

Dear Sir/Madam,

Radiophone 289587

May I remind you that I have not yet received payment of your radiophone bill for £12.3.0 I am sorry that we cannot allow the bill to remain unpaid indefinitely. Will you please pay it within the next seven days; unless it is paid by then we shall have no alternative but to revoke your licence and to institute legal proceedings to recover the debt. We would send you a final bill showing your total liability.

You could then only have service again if you paid your bill and we might also have to ask you for a deposit.

I hope that you will make all this unnecessary by paying your bill within the next seven days.

If you have already paid the bill please let me know straight away so that I can look into the matter.

Yours faithfully,

E. Wyllie

for. Chief Clerk

957/65(SW) (a)

Early draft (right) of 'I'm Only Sleeping', from Revolver, *September 1966, in John's hand, written on the back of a Post Office bill for £12.3s.*

Try to sleep again ~~Got to get to sleep~~,
When ~~your~~ ~~woken~~ early in the morning.
Lift ~~your~~ head stay in bed
When I wake up early in the morning
Lift my head stay in bed
~~Got to get to sleep~~ while I'm still yawning
Lift my head I'm still yawning.
~~I'm sleeping.~~

When I wake up early in the morning
Lift my head I'm still yawning
~~When I'm~~ in the middle of a dream
Stay in bed ~~float down~~ ~~the~~ stream.

Please don't know I can't go
Please don't wake no, shake me
leave me where I am I'm only sleeping.

Please don't spoil my day
I'm miles away . . .

The second manuscript of the same song, also in John's handwriting, now part of the collection housed at Northwestern University in the USA, has the title at the top and is more complete, with the three verses numbered, but some words are different from the finished version.

When I wake up early in the morning
Lift my head, I'm still yawning
When I'm in the middle of a dream
Stay in bed, float up stream (float up stream)

Please, don't wake me, no, don't shake me
Leave me where I am, I'm only sleeping

Everybody seems to think I'm lazy
I don't mind, I think they're crazy
Running everywhere at such a speed
Till they find there's no need (there's no need)

Please, don't spoil my day, I'm miles away
And after all I'm only sleeping

Keeping an eye on the world going by my window
Taking my time

Lying there and staring at the ceiling
Waiting for a sleepy feeling …

Ooh yeah

Keeping an eye on the world going by my window
Taking my time

When I wake up early in the morning
Lift my head, I'm still yawning
When I'm in the middle of a dream
Stay in bed, float up stream (float up stream)

Please, don't wake me, no, don't shake me
Leave me where I am, I'm only sleeping

Another version of John's 'I'm Only Sleeping' – now at Northwestern University, Evanston, Illinois, USA.

Love You To

This was when we all wondered what the Beatles were up to, where on earth were they going, where would it all lead. We'd heard a snatch of a funny-sounding Indian instrument on 'Norwegian Wood', then something a bit weird on 'I'm Only Sleeping'. Now we suddenly had the full-blown, right-on Indian music, played all the way through, almost like a public demonstration, a master class in the instrument, beginning with what sounded like tuning up, getting ready, practice chords, then whoosh and twang and throb throb and they were away.

George had been taking sitar lessons and at last felt confident enough to let us see where he'd got to and to share his new passion

'"Love You To" was one of the first tunes I ever wrote for the sitar,' he explained in *I Me Mine*. '"Norwegian Wood" was an accident as far as the sitar part was concerned, but this was the first song where I consciously tried to use the sitar and tabla on the basic track. I over-dubbed the guitars and vocal later.'

He got the North London Asian Music Circle into the studio to play the instruments, along with himself, so it is a pretty professional ensemble. The shock of the music – to our naïve, primitive, virgin 1966 ears, accustomed to guitar-based rock'n'roll – rather overshadowed the words. And still does. But they are pretty good.

Originally the working title of the song was 'Granny Smith' – after the apple – and George didn't decide on the final title until they were working on it in the studio. It has confused some musicologists, for the title phrase 'Love You To' does not appear anywhere in the lyrics (which makes it unusual amongst Beatles songs, along with 'Tomorrow Never Knows' and 'The Inner Light'). Personally I can't understand the confusion, for the last two lines make it perfectly clear where the title comes from: 'I'll make love to you, If you want me to.' He has just cut the lines down to three words, removing the rather bitter 'if you want me to', which would not have made such an attractive title.

George's handwriting again has a childlike, schoolboy feel to it – making him appear far less mature, less educated, and less confident than either John or Paul with their bolder handwriting. He also has to think twice about the correct spelling of 'their', as in 'all their sins'. In the line that begins 'They'll fill you in' he has deleted the first word, but it was used in the recorded version.

The lyrics seem quite short, but this is partly because he doesn't have the normal chorus, as such, just two lines repeated in the middle: 'Make love all day long, make love singing songs.' Which is a nice idea – and it can either mean making love while singing or that singing is making love.

'You don't get time to hang a sign on me' conjures up a schoolboy image, one popular in the comics we all used to read, like the *Dandy* and *Beano*, in which pompous people, like teachers or school swots, have signs hung on their backs which read 'Kick Me'. Hee hee.

'Before I'm a dead old man' is now, alas, an even sadder line than it seemed at the time – as George never lived to be old.

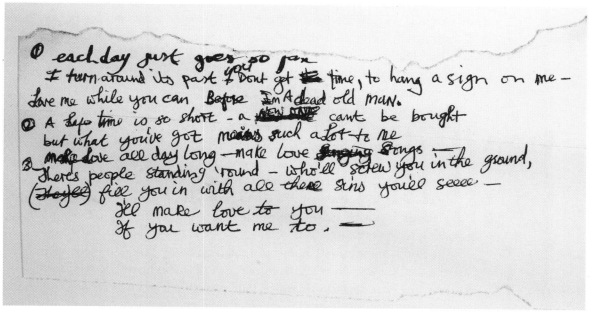

'Love You To', from Revolver, *September 1966, in George's hand – the title never actually appears in the lyrics.*

Each day just goes so fast
I turn around – it's past
You don't get time to hang a sign on me

Love me while you can
Before I'm a dead old man

A lifetime is so short
A new one can't be bought
But what you've got means such a lot
   to me

Make love all day long
Make love singing songs

There's people standing round
Who screw you in the ground
They'll fill you in with all their sins
   you'll see

I'll make love to you
If you want me to

Here, There And Everywhere

Arguably Paul's best love song. Personally, I prefer it to 'Yesterday'. It was one that he himself was very pleased with – and perhaps even more pleased that John should like it as well. He remembers how, when they were filming *Help!* the previous year, after a hard day skiing, they happened to put on a cassette of all their recent songs and when it came to 'Here, There And Everywhere', John said, 'I probably like that better than any of my songs on that tape.' That was high praise, coming from John. He could be very caustic about most things, and people, including himself.

Paul wrote it at Kenwood, John's house, when he had gone down one summer day to work, only to find that John was still asleep. So he got a cup of tea and went to sit by the pool, playing his guitar. According to some very clever experts, i.e. Ian MacDonald, he was influenced by a recent Beach Boys song, and was trying to create a similar melody.

By the time John woke up, Paul had as good as finished the tune and most of the words, but John helped finish it, making it a roughly 80–20 composition, according to Paul's estimation.

The title is a common English phrase, used many times, in many places, perhaps the best known being from the 1903 play and novel *The Scarlet Pimpernel* by Baroness Orczy, which Paul probably learned at school, or heard someone reciting. 'They seek him there, they seek him there / Those Frenchies seek him everywhere / Is he in heaven, Is he in hell / That damned elusive Pimpernel.'

In 1948, Tommy Trinder, the English comedian, starred in a new comedy musical at the London Palladium which was called *Here, There and Everywhere*. Paul was aged six at the time, so is unlikely to have been aware of it in Liverpool.

Mr MacDonald, alas, didn't think much of the lyrics; in his opinion, they 'failed to avoid sentimentality' and are 'chintzy and rather cloying'. Hmm.

It is easy to miss how clever the lyrics are. They take the three adverbs in the title, one by one, structuring the verses around Here, then There, and then Everywhere. He finishes the first line on 'here' and then begins the next line with the same word, and then repeats the same trick for the fourth and fifth lines with 'there'. This might look a bit sloppy and repetitious on paper, the sort of thing a school teacher would tell you not to do, but when sung, with all the pauses, it works well.

As for the content, despite some soppy lines, such as 'knowing that love is to share', there are some interesting expressions, for example 'to love her is to meet her everywhere'. Something lovers will understand. He presumably had

Jane in mind, at a time when their romance was apparently going well, but there is also an underlying fear that this is not true love, he is only hoping for that, knowing how good it can be.

The manuscript, in Paul's hand, has various changes: 'And if she's beside me' was originally 'As long as she's beside me'. 'Hoping I'm always there' was originally 'hoping she's always here' or possibly 'Near' or 'There'. He has stressed the first two adverbs, putting them on separate lines, underlining Here and There, indicating how he was singing those words, what the structure was in his mind.

Early version of 'Here There And Everywhere', from Revolver, *September 1966, in Paul's hand, with a few changes.*

On the reverse of the manuscript is a neatly typed-out list of Beatles events for 1966, up to the end of August. These are the arrangements and bookings Brian has made for them – which were going to be sent on to the Fan Club for them to use and inform Beatles fans. Paul was sent a copy in advance by Brian's office – and then used the back of it to write out the words for 'Here, There And Everywhere'. Perhaps he looked at the places they were due to visit on their final tours, such as Germany, Japan, Philippines and USA and thought, blimey, we're going to be here, there and everywhere …

Arrangements for the Beatles' final months of touring, June–August 1966, going here, there and everywhere, on the back of which Paul wrote the lyrics for 'Here, There and Everywhere'.

To lead a better life, I need my love to be here

Here, making each day of the year
Changing my life with a wave of her hand
Nobody can deny that there's something there

There, running my hands through her hair
Both of us thinking how good it can be
Someone is speaking but she doesn't know he's there

I want her everywhere and if she's beside me
I know I need never care
But to love her is to need her everywhere
Knowing that love is to share

Each one believing that love never dies
Watching her eyes and hoping I'm always there

I want her everywhere and if she's beside me
I know I need never care
But to love her is to need her everywhere
Knowing that love is to share

Each one believing that love never dies
Watching her eyes and hoping I'm always
    there

To be there and everywhere
Here, there and everywhere

Yellow Submarine

After all that strange Indian stuff, and love stuff – sentimental or otherwise, depending on your point of view – what fun to have … well, fun. It makes me smile even now, after all these years, to hear them enjoying themselves in the studio, making the silly noises with whistles and bells and chains, as if they are in a submarine, blowing through straws into a pan of water, shouting 'Full Steam Ahead' and 'Captain' in daft, distant voices, and then John repeating 'Sky of blue' like an echo, but in a pretend posh voice, then breaking into manic laughter. It's a perfect sing-along tune, which I feel will be sung along to forever. All over Europe you hear football crowds singing it – no doubt with their own obscene words – probably without even realizing it's a Beatles tune, thinking it's something old and traditional, like a folk song. Whenever I hear a football crowd lustily singing it, I always wonder whether Sony will bung in a copyright bill to the TV company for broadcasting it.

Paul wrote the song very quickly, lying in bed at the Asher home, having decided to write a children's song. He deliberately used short words, and short sentences, so that children would easily be able to learn it. Having written most of it, he visited the singer Donovan in his flat and played it to him. Donovan then suggested a couple of lines: 'Sky of blue, sea of green'. Not exactly earth-shattering, but they fitted nicely.

As always, the more extreme fans and madder experts are not content to take this at face value as a children's song, insisting that it is all about drug use. Well, why else would they think they're in a yellow submarine? Obvious, really.

The manuscript, covering two pages, is in Paul's hand – both pages are in the possession of Northwestern University. The pencilled signature on the first page, 'Paul McCartney', is in someone else's handwriting, added when Yoko handed the lyrics over to John Cage.

'Yellow Submarine', from Revolver, *September 1966, in Paul's hand, with comments, covering two pages. The signature at the end of the first page is not Paul's.*

On the second page you can faintly see 'John & Paul', also in someone else's hand. The words 'Disgusting!! See me' appear to be in Paul's handwriting.

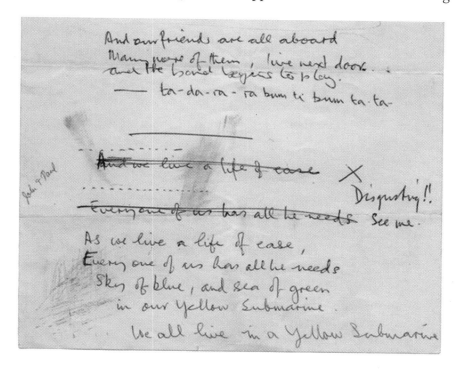

In the town where I was born,
Lived a man who sailed to sea,
And he told us of his life,
In the land of submarines,

So we sailed on to the sun,
Till we found the sea of green,
And we lived beneath the waves,
In our yellow submarine,
We all live in a yellow submarine,
yellow submarine, yellow submarine,
We all live in a yellow submarine,
yellow submarine, yellow submarine.

And our friends are all aboard,
Many more of them live next door,
And the band begins to play.

(Full speed ahead, Mr Boatswain, full
    speed ahead!
Full speed over here, sir!
All together! All together!
Aye, aye, sir, fire!
Captain! Captain!)

As we live a life of ease (life of ease)
Every one of us (every one of us) has all
    we need, (has all we need)
Sky of blue (sky of blue) and sea of
    green (sea of green)
In our yellow (In our yellow) submarine
    (submarine) (Haha!)

She Said She Said

The lyrics are an existential conversation about the nature of death and the reality of non-existence, between John and some hippie-druggie girl, or perhaps with himself, his alter ego. Any road up, not the bundle of laughs or love-ins you expect from a pop song.

The best line – 'I know what it's like to be dead' – was a pinch from Peter Fonda, the actor brother of Jane, whom John had met at a party in LA the previous year, August 1965, where they had all taken LSD. Fonda was going around saying this line, referring not to the effects of drugs but a near-death experience when he was ten, and his heart stopped beating on the operating table following an accident. Later, still in a fuddled post-LSD state, John wrote the first version of the song. Then forgot about it. A year later, working on *Revolver*, he finished it off – with George's help, rather than Paul's. Apparently John and Paul had had some sort of argument in the studio that day, which is why Paul does not appear on that track, not as a singer anyway, though he might have added a bit of bass guitar afterwards. George also recollected that John turned up at the studio with several scraps of songs, one of which began 'When I was a boy', which was welded on to 'She Said'.

It took a long time to record and the music has a jerky, staccato feeling to it, in keeping with the 'conversation', and there's an Indian influence going on in the background. According to Ian MacDonald, it is the best performance of any track on the *Revolver* album. He is thinking musically, of course. I would not be so bold.

The manuscript, which John gave me (now part of the collection in the British Library), is a very early draft and does not include the 'When I was a boy' line.

The interesting bit is in the middle, where several lines have been scribbled out. They appear to read:

> *I said who put that crap in your head*
> *— will think you are mad*
> *You know what it is to be mad*
> *And it's making me feel like my mind / head trousers were torn.*

'Crap' was changed to 'things'; thinking that she was mad was changed to him feeling mad; and the torn trousers were dropped.

His trousers being torn would have been an awful rhyme for 'never been born' and a ludicrous image. I suspect he wrote it just to fill up that line, while sucking his pen, mocking his own tortured thoughts and making himself and the others in the studio laugh.

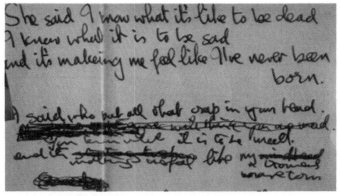

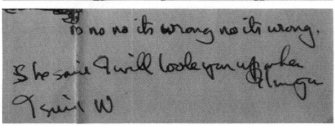

*'She Said She Said',
from* Revolver,
*September 1966, in
John's hand. 'Trousers
were torn' never
made it.*

The lyrics, while they may have been initially drafted while still
remembering or under the influence of LSD, were recollected in tranquillity
and reflect John's genuine disquiet and anguish about the world, himself and
his relationships

She said I know what it's like to be
 dead.
I know what it is to be sad
And she's making me feel like I've
 never been born.

I said Who put all those things in your
 head?
Things that make me feel that I'm mad
And you're making me feel like I've
 never been born.

She said you don't understand what I
 said
I said No, no, no, you're wrong
When I was a boy everything was right

Everything was right

I said Even though you know what you
 know
I know that I'm ready to leave
'Cos you're making me feel like I've
 never been born.'

I said Even though you know what you
 know
I know that I'm ready to leave
'Cos you're making me feel like I've
 never been born.
She said I know what it's like to be dead
I know what it is to be sad
I know what it's like to be dead

Good Day Sunshine

After all the angst and confusion with which 'She Said' finished off side one, what could be nicer than to turn over your album on your Dansette for side two and immediately have something jolly, simple and foot-tapping to hum along to, with nothing to worry about or even think about. There is no story, no development, no images – and no, it is not about drugs, though there are those who believe every song on *Revolver* is about drugs. It's a nice day and he has a nice girlfriend, end of song.

The Beatles did try to carefully balance the tracks on each album, alternating difference styles and moods and sounds, which of course is forgotten now when most people listen to their songs on downloads, in no particular order, just because they like them.

Paul wrote it one hot sunny day in 1966, while at John's house. No tricks or fancy stuff in the lyrics, but while the music appears equally simplistic, it does have some subtle references. Paul said later he had in mind the Lovin' Spoonful, a folksy, lyrical American sixties group, but listening to it now, forgetting any contemporary influences that might have been going through his head that day, I can hear echoes of old British music-hall tunes, the kind his father probably played for the whole family to sing along to at Xmas, hence the hint of a pub piano bashing away. On the word 'laugh' in the third line, I can detect Paul deliberating doing a short, flat Northern 'ah' just to amuse himself.

I have tracked down two versions of the manuscript – one written in capitals in Paul's hand, which includes the chords they were going to play and the breaks. He also has fun adding 'forte, fortas, fortissimos' like a real composer. Today it is in the collection at Northwestern University. It consists of two pages, the second, shorter page consisting of notes on how it was to be played.

The other one, also in Paul's hand, but with the title in John's hand, is owned by a private collector in California, who has kindly sent me a scan of it. He has also supplied a scan of the reverse side of the scrap of paper – which turns out to be an envelope sent to John by Miss Marguerite Libera of Connecticut. I can't quite make out the date, but it is the twenty-seventh of some month in 1966. The envelope is quite big, so she was probably sending John cuttings of some sort, or a photo to be signed. She has got his address right, apart from the spelling of Kenwood. I wonder if she ever knew that Paul picked up her envelope at John's house and used it to scribble down the words of a new song?

INTRO. (BREAKS ETC.) then GOOD DAY SUNSHINE.

① I NEED TO LAUGH, AND WHEN THE SUN IS OUT
   I'VE GOT SOMETHING I CAN LAUGH ABOUT

② I FEEL GOOD IN A SPECIAL WAY
   I'M IN LOVE AND IT'S A SUNNY DAY

CHORUS GOOD DAY SUNSHINE, ...

③ WE TAKE A WALK, THE SUN IS SHINING DOWN
   BURNS MY FEET AS THEY TOUCH THE GROUND
                        BREAK — B CHORD.
   VERSE IN B. SOLO (guitar.)

        GOOD DAY SUNSHINE (BREAKS ETC..)

④ THEN WE LIE BENEATH A SHADY TREE,
   I LOVE HER, AND SHE'S LOVING ME

   SHE FEELS GOOD, SHE'S KNOWS SHE'S LOOKING
                                     FINE.

   I'M SO PROUD TO KNOW THAT SHE IS MINE.

   GOOD DAY SUNSHINE. (FORTE FORTAS FORTISSIMOS)

              repeat — end
           Length. 2 50

INTRO. E - 16'
Good Day Sunshine.

①
②
Good Day Sunshine
③
— ④ D
B- Good Day Sunshine
⑤
⑥ Good D. S. — Good D. S. → F

'Good Day Sunshine', from Revolver, *September 1966, two pages in Paul's hand, complete with chords.*

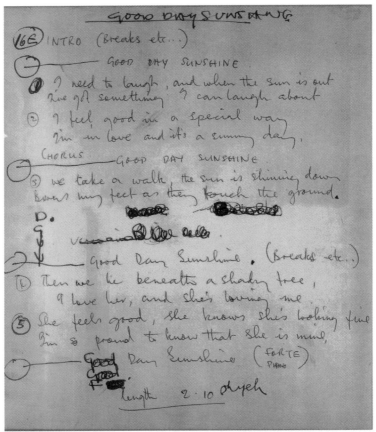

Another, earlier manuscript version of 'Good Day Sunshine', also in Paul's hand, written on the back of an envelope sent to John by an American fan.

Good day sunshine,
Good day sunshine,
Good day sunshine.
I need to laugh, and when the sun is out
I've got something I can laugh about,
I feel good, in a special way.
I'm in love and it's a sunny day.

Good day sunshine,
Good day sunshine,
Good day sunshine.
We take a walk, the sun is shining
    down,
Burns my feet as they touch the
    ground.

Good day sunshine,
Good day sunshine,
Good day sunshine.
And then we lie, beneath a shady tree,
I love her and she's loving me.
She feels good, she knows she's looking
    fine.
I'm so proud to know that she is mine.

And Your Bird Can Sing

John rubbished this song in later interviews, saying it was a 'horror' a 'throwaway' and 'fancy paper round an empty box'. He could have been playing games, so that we would reply, oh no, John, it's really good, you're putting yourself down. Or perhaps he looked back and remembered that he had done it as a trickle if not a stream of self-consciousness, to see if he could get away with it, to out-Dylan Dylan, confusing the fans and throwing in some nonsense. Why is the bird green (out of envy?)? How can a bird be broken (unless it is a toy?)?

It is their first lyric to feature deliberately rambling, incoherent psychedelic lines – but of course it contains some amusements, such as the wordplay. Firstly his bird can sing, and then she can swing – the words 'bird' and 'swing' having sixties meanings. Marianne Faithfull believes it is a reference to her – as she was Mick Jagger's bird and she could sing, so John was taking a dig at her and Mick. But it could also have been a dig by John at Paul, who was so awfully busy in the London arty scene, seeing all the wonders, that he couldn't see John. The song describes two people not communicating – not getting near each other, not seeing each other. 'You can't see me' was a metaphor John had used in the past.

The manuscript – top six and bottom seven lines in John's hand, but the middle lines look like Paul's (D.J. Hoek believes all the writing is Paul's) – is another of those in the Northwestern University collection – and it reveals that the title was originally 'You Don't Get Me' – which is the third line of the song, though he ended up using the second line instead. In the third line of the manuscript he appears to have written 'But you don't get it –' changing it to 'But you don't get me.'

The drawing is in blue biro, using the same pen as the lyrics, and it has gone a bit purple with age (don't we all). It looks a bit like a mitre, or an alien face, but is probably just a squiggle.

Paul's signature at the end is in Yoko's hand.

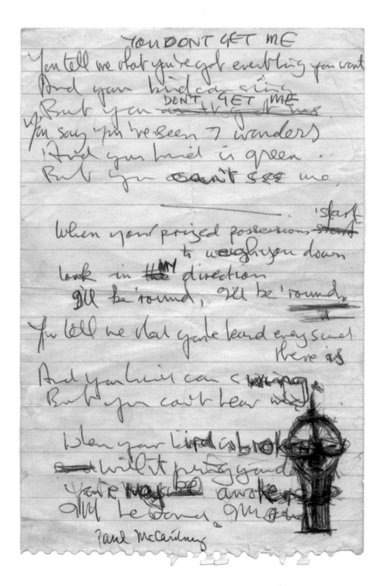

'And Your Bird Can Sing', from Revolver, *1966, top and bottom in John's hand with the middle in Paul's, shows that the song's original title was 'You Don't Get Me'.*

You tell me that you've got everything you want
And your bird can sing
But you don't get me, you don't get me

You say you've seen seven wonders and your bird is green
But you can't see me, you can't see me

When your prized possessions start to weigh you down
Look in my direction, I'll be round, I'll be round

When your bird is broken will it bring you down
You may be awoken, I'll be round, I'll be round

You tell me that you've heard every sound there is
And your bird can swing
But you can't hear me, you can't hear me

For No One

After Paul's sunny day sunshine song, this is back to a love ballad, but a sad, regretful, wistful, heartbreaking song. It appears to describe the breakup between Paul and Jane.

Paul wrote it in 1966 when he and Jane were on a skiing holiday together in Switzerland. He remembers writing this song while in the bathroom. Originally he said it wasn't really about Jane, just a relationship that was going wrong, but later he admitted it had followed an argument with Jane. The rift must have healed though. The couple subsequently got engaged (in 1968).

From a literary point of view, it is interesting that he constantly flits between the second person – 'Your day breaks' and third person: 'She wakes up'. Quite tricky, keeping a pattern without confusing the listener, and avoiding clichés. 'You see nothing' – meaning it literally and metaphorically – is, I suppose, a Lennon–McCartney cliché by now, but it's their own cliché.

The music is impeccably put together, with a wonderful French horn solo by Alan Civil, perhaps the best-known hornist of his day and Principal Horn Player with the London Philharmonic. Civil came in, was told roughly what was wanted by George Martin and Paul, composed his own bit, played and went home, earning only his session fee.

The manuscript version, again at Northwestern University (they say in

Paul's hand), shows that this too had a different title – 'Why Did It Die?' – which is more brutal and explicit than the one eventually used. The line that the original title was taken from appears halfway down the page and was cut, along with all the others which followed:

Why did it die?
You'd like to know
Cry and blame her
– you wait
You're too late
As you're deciding why the wrong one wins the end begins
And you will lose her
Why did it die
I'd like to know
Try – to save it
You want her
You need (love) her
So make her see that you believe it may work out
And one day you may need each other.

Your day breaks, your mind aches
You find that all the words of kindness
    linger on
When she no longer needs you

She wakes up, she makes up
She takes her time and doesn't feel she
    has to hurry
She no longer needs you

And in her eyes you see nothing
No sign of love behind the tears
Cried for no one
A love that should have lasted years!

You want her, you need her
And yet you don't believe her when she
    said her love is dead
You think she needs you

You stay home, she goes out
She says that long ago she knew
    someone but now he's gone
She doesn't need him

Your day breaks, your mind aches
There will be times when all the things
    she said will fill your head
You won't forget her

And in her eyes you see nothing
No sign of love behind the tears
Cried for no one
A love that should have lasted years.

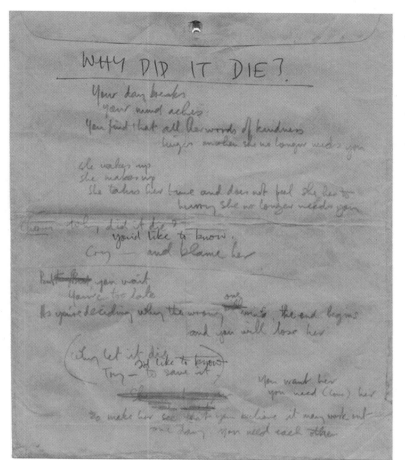

Another song, in Paul's hand, which began with a different title – 'Why Did It Die?', which became 'For No One', from Revolver, 1966.

Dr Robert

The first song overtly about drugs. It is pretty clear that Dr Robert was supplying substances in a special cup, to pick you up – but it need not have been illegal drugs. LSD – or acid, as it was usually called – was not made illegal until 1966 and along with amphetamines it was prescribed by doctors. Almost all the Beatles experts have subsequently identified a well-known New York society doctor called Dr Robert who prescribed drugs to celebrity patients. Personally I think it was more likely that John had in mind a young and trendy London dentist. It was at a private dinner party at this individual's house that John and George had their first LSD trip in 1965 – after it was slipped into their coffee disguised as a sugar lump. The reference to the National Health in the lyrics does suggest a UK setting.

John later said that he himself was Dr Robert, for he was the Beatle who carried the pills on tour in the early years.

It is a fairly mocking song about fashionable medical people who supply anything – again, a most unusual topic for a pop song. And it is witty. There is a short chorus –'Well, well, well, you're feeling fine' – where they sing in harmony like a chiming Christmas choir – making a pun on the word well.

I Want To Tell You

George's third song on the album, and the lyrics are well up to John or Paul's standards, with well-polished lines and serious subject matter. The topic is the difficulty of communicating, the games we play, and how we don't know why we feel the way we do.

Although there are no Indian instruments, there is an Indian feel to the bit of wailing at the end, and it's there in the lyrics too, with the suggestion of karma, meeting 'next time around' – i.e. in the next life – and also 'I could wait forever'. Lines like these gave a clue to the sort of Indian mysticism and philosophy George was getting into. And in due course the rest of the Beatles would follow. George, in a sense, was taking over from John as the group leader, as Indian music and thought began to dominate their lives over the next two years.

George didn't have a title for it at first, and it was filed in the studio as 'Laxton's Superb', the name of another apple, then it became 'I Don't Know' – the response George Martin got from George when he asked what it was called. It would have made a good title. In the end, it took its name from the first line.

The early manuscript, which George reproduced in *I Me Mine*, has quite a few differences from the finished song and includes some rather limp phrases, such as 'you rang me up' and 'pass the time'.

"'I Want to Tell You' is about the avalanche of thoughts that are so hard to write down or say or transmit,' writes George. He goes on to add that, if he were to write it again, he would change the line in the middle from 'it's only me, it's not my mind' and make it 'It isn't me – it is my mind'.

Then he adds a final thought: 'The mind is the thing that hops about telling us to do things and that – when what you need is to lose (forget) the mind. A passing thought.'

I want to tell you
My head is filled with things to say
When you're here
All those words, they seem to slip away

When I get near you
The games begin to drag me down
It's alright
I'll make you maybe next time around

But if I seem to act unkind
It's only me
It's not my mind
That is confusing things

I want to tell you
You rang me up, and
    I don't know why
Maybe you will be
    that one thing to
    get me by

I don't mind
I could wait forever
I've got time

Sometimes I wish I knew you well
Then I could speak my mind
And tell you
Maybe you'd understand

I want to tell you
I feel hung up, and I don't know why
I don't mind
I could wait forever
I've got time
I've got time
I've got time

'I Want To Tell You', from Revolver, 1966, an early, corrected manuscript in George's hand.

Got To Get You Into My Life

I always took this as another of Paul's love songs – about a girl he wants in his life, whom he can't do without. It has a fast, thumping beat, and Paul enjoys himself putting on his high-pitched voice when he repeats 'Got to get you into my life'. It ends with him singing the final refrain in a sort of jazz or soul improvisation, which is interesting as the Beatles, back when they were starting out at the Cavern, always said they hated jazz and the jazz fans in their Marks & Spencer pullovers – partly because the Cavern had originally been a jazz club and they were not allowed to play rock'n'roll in the early days.

Now that I have reread the words carefully, I realize there is no mention of a girl, or any female presence. So could it, shock horror, have been about drugs all along? Was that the ride he was taking, in order to see another kind of mind there? Was it a joint or suchlike that he wanted to get into his life, and not a girl?

Paul confirmed this in Barry Miles' 1997 book: 'It's actually an ode to pot, like someone else might write an ode to chocolate or claret. If anyone asks me for real advice, I would say stay straight. But in a stressful world, it really is one of the best tranquilizer drugs.'

Tomorrow Never Knows

This is their most psychedelic song, their most Indian, and so far their most influential in that it had an effect on millions of young people in America and Europe.

The title never appears in the song. It was one of Ringo's blurted-out remarks that John was forever writing down (other Ringo remarks, never used in a song, included 'slight bread' for sliced bread and 'safely beds' for safe in bed).

The first line makes it clear it is about drugs: 'Turn off your mind and float downstream'. And it is about the use of drugs to create, supposedly, a religious experience. But what the song is really about is religion and the Indian Buddhist concepts of transcendentalism and reincarnation, the need to subdue the ego and enter the void. Under LSD, people often begin to think life is all an illusion. Several influential thinkers of the time experimented with the drug, including Aldous Huxley.

Many of the references are from the Tibetan Book of the Dead. In a letter to Dr Lester Grinspoon of Harvard Medical School, written in 1979, John revealed that he had come across the Tibetan Book of the Dead after reading about it in Timothy Leary's *The Psychedelic Experience*. Leary was the American high priest of LSD and his book was a treatise on the good he thought it could do, setting people free from their minds and their bodies so that they wouldn't end up as drones for capitalist, war-mongering governments that wanted them to bomb innocent civilians with napalm in Vietnam.

The song became a feature of many stoned parties of idealistic, right-on, young men and women in the middle sixties.

The music is of course marvellous, and, yes, mind-blowing. As well as Indian instruments, like sitar and tambura, it features many specially devised and original sound effects swirling and whooshing and wailing. A lot of these they brought in from home after experimenting with backwards loops on their tape machines. John wanted it to sound like a group of chanting Tibetan monks, on the top of a mountain, and for him to be like a faint Dalai Lama in the distance – which George Martin and engineer Geoff Merrick, knowing their duties, managed to create.

However the final three lines of the lyric suggest another way of getting through life, without necessarily giving up your mind and body and entering the void – and that is to 'play the game Existence to the end'. Or the beginning of the beginning …

In an interview with *Rolling Stone* journalist Jonathan Cott, John admitted that he didn't know what he was trying to say in 'Tomorrow Never Knows': 'You just find out later. It's really like abstract art. When you have to think about it to write it, it just means you've been laboured at it. But when you just *say* it, man, it's a continuous flow. The people who analyse the songs – good on 'em – I don't mind what they do with them.'

The manuscript, in John's hand, is an early version with phrases not used in the final recording, such as 'all the colours of the earth you'll hear' and 'there's no dying'.

It was remarkable final track from a remarkable album. They'd travelled so far, it's hard to believe that only four years had passed since 'Love Me Do'. In lyrics and sounds, they had progressed so far, becoming more complex and profound, yet still with a mass audience, selling millions of records round the world. While educating themselves they had educated their audience.

Turn off your mind relax and float down stream
It is not dying, it is not dying

Lay down all thought, surrender to the void,
It is shining, it is shining.

That you may see the meaning of within
It is being, it is being

That love is all and love is everyone
It is knowing, it is knowing

That ignorance and hate may mourn the dead
It is believing, it is believing

But listen to the colour of your dreams
It is not living, it is not living

Or play the game Existence to the end
Of the beginning, of the beginning …

'Tomorrow Never Knows', the last track on Revolver, 1966, an extensive early manuscript in John's hand. The title never appears in the lyrics.

8

STRAWBERRY FIELDS FOREVER

February 1967

I went to see Brian Epstein on 26 January 1967, at his Belgravia home, to discuss my plan for a biography of the Beatles, an idea I had first put to Paul the previous month. Paul said I would have to see Brian, but he would help me write a suitable letter. Brian cancelled several times, for reasons I never knew until later.

I remember how elegant and sophisticated he was; so well-dressed, well-spoken, a man of the world. Yet at the time he was just thirty-two – two years older than me. I remember noticing two oil paintings on the wall by L.S. Lowry. But what I remember most about that meeting was 'Strawberry Fields Forever'.

He had an acetate recording of it – a sort of proof – as the record was not officially released till 17 February. Sitting back in an armchair, arms folded with fatherly pride, he waited as I listened to it.

I was stunned. Could this be the Beatles? My first thought was Stockhausen – not that I knew much about him or his music. The sounds were so avant-garde, futuristic, experimental, multi-layered that it was impossible to take in at one go, least of all the words, so I got him to play it again.

When it finished, I asked what the title meant – and he didn't know. I asked what the lyrics meant – and he didn't know that either. He had clearly not been involved in its production, and seemed slightly embarrassed by his ignorance; after all, he was their personal manager, responsible for expertly organizing their career since 1961.

He then played the other side: 'Penny Lane'. That was much easier to understand and enjoy, and as a Liverpudlian he was familiar with most places.

Afterwards he put the acetate away, saying he could not be too careful. One had already been stolen, for the recording would be worth lot of money to the pirate radio stations. I didn't believe him – it seemed far-fetched that a pirate station would pay big money, just to get the record a few days ahead of their rivals. I later discovered that one theft of an acetate had been his fault. He had brought home some young man, a sailor – butch not gay – given him drinks and pills and tried to get him into bed. The sailor had then beaten Brian up and left – taking the acetate with him. Overwhelmed by humiliation and guilt, Brian then took more pills and went into a deep depression, cancelling everything for a few days – including two appointments with me – until he could face the world. The Beatles were aware that he was gay, but they knew none of the details of his personal life.

During that first meeting, Brian suggested a clause in the contract neither I nor my agent had mentioned. He said he would give no access to the Beatles to any other writer for two years after my book came out. It came out in October 1968; two years later, in 1970, the Beatles had disbanded. So mine was to be the one and only authorized biography of the Beatles, though I had no idea of it at the time. How lucky was that?

Although I was astounded by 'Strawberry Fields', I rather wondered what some of the fans would make of it. It was yet another tremendous leap forward for the Beatles, when they'd already made so many in the last two years. How fortunate I would be – if the book came to pass, if we didn't all fall out, if the project didn't get cancelled – to witness firsthand the Beatles at home and in the studio, making more music like this, making yet further progress.

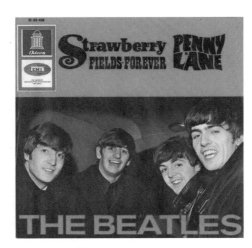

Strawberry Fields Forever

John wrote the song in Spain in September 1966, while filming *How I Won the War*. Once the touring had stopped, and the public performances were coming to an end, each of them was free to do their own thing until they assembled together in the studio for the next record.

They had been thinking of a concept album about their childhood and Liverpool, as the unused verses of 'In My Life' indicated, but it was never completed.

Now, far from home, stuck out in Almeria, John began thinking back to his childhood when he used to visit the nearby Salvation Army home, Strawberry Field (without the s), a gothic mansion with a large overgrown garden. He loved going to the annual fête or breaking in and playing there with his friends Pete Shotton and Ivan Vaughan, climbing the trees, imagining he was in an *Alice in Wonderland* magic world. 'As soon as we could hear the Salvation Army band playing,' so his Aunt Mimi told me, 'John would jump up and down shouting, "Mimi, come on, we're going to be late."'

His random childhood memories got mixed up and fused with drug-related images and influences – tune in, take you down, nothing is real. John was always conscious of the feelings of displacement and disorientation he had experienced as a child – or told himself he had. He was also aware of his own habit of thinking or saying one thing, then the next moment the opposite, believing it each time. It's getting hard, but it all works out, it doesn't matter much, it's all wrong, I think I know, yes, I think I disagree. Two of the best lines are: 'Nothing is real and nothing to get hung about' and 'Living is easy with eyes closed, misunderstanding all you see.'

The earliest known demo of the sung, done by John on a tape recorder in Almeria, had no chorus and only one verse which began, 'There's no one on my wavelength, I mean it's either too high or too low.' Wavelength was later changed to tree.

In 1980, he explained that he had felt different all his life, which is what he was saying with the phrase 'No one I think is in my tree'. At the same time he felt he was too shy and self-doubting – or a genius. 'I mean

John and George in the Apple studio, 1969.

it must be high or low.' The phrase 'nothing to get hung about' suggests not having any hang-ups, but also hanging from a tree possibly, remembering Aunt Mimi telling him not to climb over the wall and play there, and John replying, 'They can't hang you for it.'

The song sums up everything about the Beatles at this stage: introspection, disorientation, self-doubt, all wrapped up in beautiful, original, multi-layered, disturbing music. Even if you take away the musical sounds and trimmings, it is still a fine song.

John always considered it one of his best – along with 'I Am The Walrus', 'Help!', 'In My Life' and 'Across The Universe'. He reckoned the lyrics to all of those were pretty good. 'The best lyrics stand alone. They don't have to have a melody.' John always thought he was a poet. 'Except I am not educated.'

'Strawberry Fields' became the most analysed of all the Beatles songs they had done so far, with the experts attempting to unravel how every sound was made – identifying the trumpets and cellos, maracas and slide guitar, explaining the electronic wizardry and background sounds. It took the Beatles an unprecedented amount of time – fifty-five recording hours in all, spread over five weeks – to get it to their satisfaction: a sign of their power but also their perseverance.

The music press were a bit confused by it. In the *New Musical Express* on 11 February 1967, Derek Johnson wrote that it was 'certainly the most unusual and way out single the Beatles have yet produced – both in lyrical content and scoring. I don't really know what to make of it.' But he did find it 'completely fascinating' and more spellbinding every time he played it.

'Strawberry Fields' was their first single since 'Please Please Me' in January 1963 not to go straight to number 1 in the UK. It got stuck at number 2 – kept out of the top spot by Engelbert Humperdinck's 'Release Me'. Ringo said he was relieved – it took away the pressure.

The manuscript, which I believe is the only copy that has ever turned up, given to me by John, has only twelve lines, several of them slightly different from the final version, but you can see his thought process, writing one thing, then commenting on it in his mind, as if thinking, er, I disagree.

I can't quite make out what that scribbled-out first line was originally, before he inserts 'I think in my tree'. But it does look like that line he had sung on the tape – 'There's no one on my wavelength'. At this stage, in these lines, 'Strawberry Fields' is not mentioned.

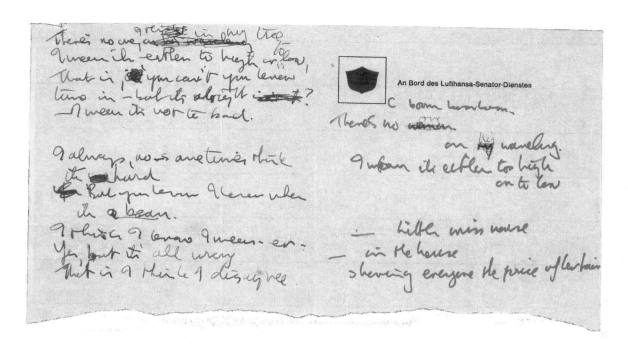

'Strawberry Fields' single, January 1967, early version written by John on Lufthansa airline notepaper, with no reference to Strawberry Fields.

Let me take you down
'Cos I'm going to Strawberry Fields
Nothing is real
And nothing to get hung about
Strawberry Fields forever

Living is easy with eyes closed
Misunderstanding all you see
It's getting hard to be someone
But it all works out
It doesn't matter much to me

No one I think is in my tree
I mean it must be high or low
That is you know you can't tune it

But it's all right
That is I think it's not too bad

Always, no, sometimes, think it's me
But you know I know when it's a dream
I think I know I mean a 'Yes'
But it's all wrong
That is I think I disagree

Let me take you down
'Cos I'm going to Strawberry Fields
Nothing is real
And nothing to get hung about
Strawberry Fields forever

Penny Lane

The other side of the 'Strawberry Fields' single – and the other side of the Beatles. This is Paul, writing at his piano in his music room in his new house, taking the same subject of childhood memories, but treating it openly, straightforwardly, cheekily, cheerfully, cleverly – in fact very like Paul himself. No hang-ups here – his memories are fun: blue suburban skies, nice images, nice people.

The musical arrangement is just as clever and rich as 'Strawberry Fields', though not as confusing, with the use of top-class trumpets, flutes, and oboes, along with bells and other appropriate noises.

John's preoccupation with loss, anger and disorientation in his childhood is often put down to the death of his mother when he was fifteen, but Paul also lost his mother, equally tragically, at the age of fourteen – and yet I have never heard him say that it made him angry, depressed, screwed up, or affected his outlook on life and his subsequent behaviour.

In the original version of 'In My Life' (page 131), written in John's hand, there are some unused verses which list places remembered, including Penny Lane. Both John and Paul had Penny Lane in their life – John living very near it and Paul singing in the local church choir at St Barnabas. It was also where Paul's dad took him and brother Michael to have their hair cut.

Penny Lane is not a lane, as such. 'Lane' conjures up the image of a quiet country byway, which it originally was, but the Liverpool version today is a busy, rather featureless thoroughfare. The name is used to refer to the immediate neighbourhood, as well as the road itself. In reality, the only attractive thing about it is the name – which I am sure appealed to Paul. It sounds made-up, like a street in a children's picture story, and that is how the lyrics read; it becomes a mythical place where the sun always shines with stock characters like a barber, a fireman, a poppy seller. The name Strawberry Fields is equally sylvan and picture-bookish. Weren't they lucky, having real but fictional-sounding places from their childhood.

The places mentioned in Penny Lane are on the whole genuine – there was a barber, a fire station, a roundabout – but the little additions, like the fireman with an hourglass in his pocket, sound more surreal. We also have pouring rain with blue skies, which sounds rather unlikely. So Paul could do opposites as well as John. And the barber did not have photographs of every head 'he's had the pleasure to know' – but photos of different hairstyles. Lyrical licence.

There are a couple of sexual innuendos that were put in, so Paul said, to amuse the smuttier Liverpool teenagers. 'Finger pie' was a local term, referring to the female genitalia area, and there is slight smirk around the word 'machine' and keeping it clean. There is also a suggestion that the fireman has some dodgy habits. All good clean schoolboy fun.

The narrative structure of the lyrics is lightly done. There is a slight development, in that we go back to the barber, fireman and the banker, but seen from an outside observer, telling us about it in the third person. There is no I, no first-person memories. 'Meanwhile back' is an amusing device, making it clear it is a story, a fictional, stylized childhood place. The pretty nurse selling poppies feels she is in a play – she is anyway. He could have gone on to suggest we are all in a play, as John and George might have done, but avoided it.

In the USA, where there is no tradition of artificial poppies being sold to commemorate the 1918 Armistice, there was some consternation when fans misheard the words and wondered why the nurse was selling puppies from a tray.

The manuscript of 'Penny Lane' has turned up in several bits and pieces, now owned by different collectors. In both, Paul has written 'In Penny Lane' but dropped the 'In' when he came to sing it. They contain a few odd lines never used, such as one about the barber: 'It was easy not to go – he was very slow'. A good line, so it's surprising it wasn't used.

Penny Lane – there is a barber showing photographs
Of every head he's had the pleasure to know
And all the people that come and go
Stop and say hello

On the corner is a banker with a motorcar
The little children laugh at him behind his
  back
And the banker never wears a mac
In the pouring rain …
Very strange

Penny Lane is in my ears and in my eyes
There beneath the blue suburban skies
I sit, and meanwhile back

In Penny Lane there is a fireman with an
  hourglass
And in his pocket is a portrait of the Queen.
He likes to keep his fire engine clean
It's a clean machine

Sheet music for 'Penny Lane', on the reverse of 'Strawberry Fields' single, January 1967.

Penny Lane is in my ears and in my eyes
Four of fish and finger pies
In summer, meanwhile back

Behind the shelter in the middle of a roundabout
A pretty nurse is selling poppies from a tray
And though she feels as if she's in a play
She is anyway

Penny Lane the barber shaves another customer
We see the banker sitting waiting for a trim
Then the fireman rushes in
From the pouring rain …
Very strange

Penny Lane is in my ears and in my eyes
There beneath the blue suburban skies
I sit, and meanwhile back
Penny Lane is in my ears and in my eyes
There beneath the blue suburban skies …
Penny Lane.

Two versions of 'Penny Lane', both in Paul's hand. The third line on the right never made it.

Both 'Strawberry Fields' and 'Penny Lane' were given A-side status on the single. Initially the two songs were intended to be part of the new album they were about to start work on, but they decided the themes didn't quite fit in. However the two songs did go well together, making it the best single they ever did – which is why it deserves a chapter on its own.

These were the first Beatles songs to name real places. In the general run of British pop music, it was most unusual to hear a British location mentioned – or at least a location outside of London. Yet we all sang about places in America that none of us had ever visited and most probably never would, like Chicago, New Orleans, California, Massachusetts, New York New York.

Today, both Strawberry Fields and Penny Lane have taken on the status of mythical magical places. In New York, Strawberry Fields is the memorial garden in Central Park dedicated to John, near the building where he was shot. Penny Lane has also turned itself into a shrine of sorts, with a Penny Lane wine bar featuring photos of the Beatles. The barber's shop, originally Mr Bioletti's Barber Shop, is now unisex and called Tony Slavin, but it too features Beatles memorabilia. Tourists take photos of each other standing outside, just as they do on the Abbey Road pedestrian crossing in London.

There is a modern ironic use of the names Penny Lane and Strawberry Fields at Guantánamo Bay in Cuba, where in 2014 the American CIA detention camp were still holding suspected terrorists. One of the prison houses was known as Penny Lane and is next door to Strawberry Fields. The latter was named first, after the last word in its title – Forever.

The record came out at a time when social and cultural class barriers in Britain seemed to be on the verge of being broken down. Didn't matter where you came from, even if it was a provincial place like Liverpool, you could still succeed and find fulfilment. We had just won the World Cup, our fashions and designs, films and art and popular music were being enjoyed around the world. Oh, being alive was heaven, back in 1967. That's honestly how it felt.

George Martin has said that he considers 'Strawberry Fields'/'Penny Lane' their best record – meaning best single. Looking back now, it still seems to sum up that era – and the Beatles in general. There was the psychedelic, futuristic, drug-inspired, mysterious words and weird musical arrangement of 'Strawberry Fields' juxtaposed with the fun and accessible words and music of 'Penny Lane'. There was something for everyone, avant-garde or traditional, intellectual or otherwise, young and old, rich or poor, to enjoy, think about or just admire and hum and dance along to.

The record showed us the differences between John and Paul – which we had hitherto only suspected. It seemed to confirm that John saw music as a vehicle for thought whereas Paul saw it as a matter of mood and melody.

Not always true, of course, as John could do love songs and Paul could do angst. But as a generalization, it seemed to stack up. Melody flows from Paul, out of every pore; musically, he is the more naturally gifted. John was interested in words, much more than Paul. But there again, each could do both.

The two songs illustrated the sort of subject matter they had gravitated towards. John always said that his best subject was himself. Once he realized he could write about himself, instead of boy–girl, blue moon love, that was what he concentrated on: 'I'm not interested in writing third party songs,' he told *Playboy* in 1980. 'I like to write about me, 'cos I know me.'

Paul could and did write about his feelings, but even then he usually disguised them, preferring in his lyrics to go for narrative, a story, a setting, little vignettes, as in 'Penny Lane', using mainly the third person. He also loved nostalgia, pastiche, parodies of former forms of music.

Paul was the hard worker who beavered away, seeing it through rather than leaving things half done, the way John tended to. George Martin used to say that Paul came into the studio with fixed ideas, knowing how he wanted the song to sound. With John, it had to be dragged out of him, he didn't quite know his own mind, or couldn't express it as clearly as Paul.

Hence it was a great partnership, each producing different sorts of songs but at the same time able to inspire the other, help them improve. It was a competition, sibling rivalry, to impress the other. Which had worked brilliantly. So far.

But had the Beatles reached their zenith with 'Strawberry Fields' and 'Penny Lane'? That was a thought that came into my head as I started work on their biography. Was it possible that the fans of Engelbert Humperdinck had got it right, the ones who kept his record at number 1 for six weeks? Honestly, some people, eh?

The NME *chart for 8 March 1967 with Engelbert still topping the Beatles – shame.*

NEW MUSICAL EXPRESS *

NME TOP 30

(Wednesday, March 8, 1967)

LAST WEEK	THIS WEEK		WEEKS IN CHART	HIGHEST POSITION
1	1	RELEASE ME .... Engelbert Humperdinck (Decca)	6	1
3	2	PENNY LANE/STRAWBERRY FIELDS FOREVER ...... Beatles (Parlophone)	3	2
2	3	THIS IS MY SONG .... Petula Clark (Pye)	5	1
4	4	HERE COMES MY BABY ......Tremeloes (CBS)	6	4
5	5	EDELWEISS .... Vince Hill (Columbia)	5	5
6	6	ON A CAROUSEL .... Hollies (Parlophone)	4	6
11	7	DETROIT CITY .... Tom Jones (Decca)	4	7
8	8	SNOOPY V. THE RED BARON .. Royal Guardsmen (Stateside)	7	6
12	9	THERE'S A KIND OF HUSH ....Herman's Hermits (Columbia)	4	9
15	10	GEORGY GIRL .... Seekers (Columbia)	3	10
7	11	I'M A BELIEVER .... Monkees (RCA)	10	1
9	12	MELLOW YELLOW .... Donovan (Pye)	5	9
10	13	PEEK-A-BOO ... New Vaudeville Band (Fontana)	6	8
30	14	THIS IS MY SONG ..... Harry Secombe (Philips)	2	14
16	15	GIVE IT TO ME .... Troggs (Page One)	4	15
14	16	I WON'T COME IN WHILE HE'S THERE ... Jim Reeves (RCA)	6	11
17	17	IT TAKES TWO .. Marvin Gaye and Kim Weston (Tamla-Motown)	7	16
	18	MEMORIES ARE MADE OF THIS Val Doonican (Decca)	1	18
13	19	LET'S SPEND THE NIGHT TOGETHER . Rolling Stones (Decca)	8	2
22	20	I'LL TRY ANYTHING ... Dusty Springfield (Philips)	2	20
	21	I CAN'T MAKE IT .... Small Faces (Decca)	1	21

9

SGT. PEPPER'S LONELY HEARTS CLUB BAND

June 1967

Every day, in every way, on every album since *With The Beatles* in 1963, they seemed to be getting better, or at least different, moving on, or at least moving sideways, and of course sometimes deliberately backwards, but *Sgt. Pepper* turned out to be a multi-media, multi-level giant leap forward.

Take the album cover: endlessly voted the best cover ever, it was the first to have all the lyrics of the songs printed on the rear cover – which was a blessing. By this time, we all wanted to know the words. With most songs, most singers, you can easily mishear or misinterpret, as Dylan did, so it was handy to see every word written down, and spelled correctly.

Professor Colin Campbell, who compiled that concordance of the lyrics, had to listen to every word on every record, over and over, and write them down, exactly as he heard them, because he could not trust the several printed versions of lyrics to get all the words correct – until the *Sgt. Pepper* album came along and made his research much easier.

It was a gatefold album, which meant it opened like a book, rather than consisting of a single sleeve. Inside one pocket was the album, and in the other was a stiff cardboard sheet with cut-outs of Sergeant Pepper, his moustache, badges, stripes, picture and stand-up sign. The cover photograph, now such an iconic image, showed thirty-nine heroic or famous figures.

I remember being present for the photo shoot and seeing one figure they had been persuaded to abandon at the last moment: a full-size Hitler. I was surprised it got as far as the studio. Jesus was chucked out much earlier.

I like to think that including Albert Stubbins was my idea. At Paul's one day, I heard them discussing the figures they might have and I said surely they should have one famous footballer, even though I knew that not one of them had been regular football fans as a boy, or ever played football. John thought hard and chose Albert Stubbins, who had played for Liverpool in the fifties just because he had always thought Albert Stubbins was a funny name.

As we were leaving Paul's house, he asked me to bring any interesting looking object that could be added to the photographic set. From his mantelpiece I picked up a little silvery statue thing that looked like a sputnik – apparently some award he had been given – which I plonked down at the front in the middle of the word Beatles, which was spelled out in flowers. Study the front cover carefully and you can just see it, between the L and E. I've boasted about that for decades.

Photo session evening. Carol Rusell there first, suowing drawings
for Apple. their nre organisation. Paul liked the, then discussed
neon sign, made suggested aout colouretc. Tea - ham and eggs.
Robert Fraser
Neil arrived and Exi, all in car to pick up George, then to
Michael Copper's studio in Flood street. There Ringo, John, Pete
Blake, wife Jan Howarth, Cooper and three assistant, Miles and girl.
Huge studio. Back line of life sizem,ccut out famous figures -
Huxley, Ghandi, Bud and Lou, Marilyn , Bettey David, Issy Bond, Tommy
Handley, s veral gurus, Einstein, Karl Marx, El is. WC Fields

Sgnt Peppn Cover

15

Albert -tubbings - ex Liverpool footballer , Terry Southern, etc etc.
At the side of the stiid was standing Hitler - they been persudaed no
to have him. Nor Jesus either, Last time mentioned Jesus, look:
what happened,
At the right side, huge wax model of Sonny Liston and four
xxx waxmode s of Beatles - all from Madame Tussueads. At t e right
old woman with child on knee and coybody, all stuffed - by Jan
Howart.
In front, stood Beatles - dressed in fantisc coloured
ornate iniforms, with a big drumsin f ront pianted on 'Sgnt
Peppers Lonely Heart Ikub s Band."
In front of them , a grassy knows - with false grass, but
real flowers planted in it. A line of pink hyacnith spell out
Beatles.

Cover is to have that pic on front. Insidem doubke page
-spread, big drawing by Dutch cdpple of wired fairy tale
land. Txyxx Also a xxx badge, printed words of all song
a toy - those things on a strong you pull. Then inside
next cover - the record itself. Most expesnive rec
covere ever?   Nov - April £25,000 . 1st co

My scruffy, badly typed, misspelt notes, written straight after going from Paul's house to the photo session for the Sgt. Pepper *cover, 30 March 1967. Hitler was there but not included.*

The music, of course, was what it was and is all about, along with the fact that the songs were arranged in a special way, the conceit being that they were a band giving a concert. It became known as the first ever concept album, copied since by many other singers and artists.

It was a bit of a con, the so-called concept idea. There is in fact not much connection between the songs. There was nothing really to differentiate it from a traditional album made up of a collection of tunes, played one after the other. But it did originate with an overall concept: the Beatles would pretend to be another group, to submerge their individual personalities as Beatles – which they were all beginning to find a bit of a burden and a bore, especially George and John. Instead, they would be an Edwardian-style brass band giving a concert; the kind of band they'd seen giving Sunday concerts in the local park during the fifties, when they were growing up. Only they'd be bringing it into the modern age, and giving it psychedelic overtones.

There are several pastiche songs, performed tongue-in-cheek, affectionately mocking styles from an earlier age, and some nice period references in the lyrics: 'guaranteed to raise a smile ... may I inquire discreetly'. Ringo is at one stage introduced as Billy Shears, but aside from dressing up for the photograph and promo material, they didn't keep up their alter egos and soon ignored them. But who cared. It turned out to be the most wonderful, innovative, brilliant, imaginative album they had done. Perhaps anyone had ever done, until then.

Sitting in Abbey Road, during the making of *Sgt. Pepper*, I did used to wonder how George Martin and his technicians must have felt, being made to sit silently behind their glass wall, twiddling their thumbs, while John and Paul messed around down below in the bowels of the studio, still working on the tune, insisting on going endlessly over the same stuff, which really they should have finalized before they had ever come into the studio. As of course they had done in their early days.

It took them almost five months in the studio, at a cost of some £25,000 – compared with one day in the studio at a cost of £400 for their first album, *Please Please Me*. They had reached the point where they were the complete boss of their own brand, so they could spend whatever it took without asking anyone's permission. Now that they had stopped touring and performing in live concerts, they could put all their energy and time into the art and craft of creating recorded music in a studio.

There is still some argument about where the name Sergeant Pepper came from. The story I like to believe, and which I was told at the time, while they were still making it, is that the words originated with Mal Evans, their roadie. During a meal he misheard someone's request for salt and pepper as Sergeant Pepper.

Omnibus titles were in vogue, with groups choosing fanciful names like the Incredible String Band and Jefferson Airplane, and trendy fashion shops in London called Granny Takes a Trip and I Was Lord Kitchener's Valet. Take an old-fashioned-sounding name, pair it with a modern, psychedelic design and you were at the height of fashion.

From what I saw, the driving force for the whole album, including the cover design, was Paul, who seemed to have taken on the lead role, having the final say on most decisions. This was partly because he was the only one living in the centre of London, handy for the West End and EMI Studios in Abbey Road, and so many meetings with designers and others took place at his house. I was never aware of Brian Epstein being involved with the production at all.

Another interesting aspect was that there wasn't a single love song, certainly not a lovey-dovey, or unrequited love song. All their albums, even *Rubber Soul* and *Revolver*, had included at least one song about lurve. *Sgt. Pepper* had no love songs – unless you count lusting after a traffic warden in her uniform . . .

Sgt. Pepper's Lonely Hearts Club Band

Paul introduces us to the band, and hopes we will enjoy the show, to cheers and applause from the audience, then they hear the brass band play, very loudly and proudly. They are told they are 'a lovely audience – we'd like to take you home with us', which is a good joke.

One of the things about the Beatles when they first appeared on stage was that they did not tell the audience they were lovely – a phoney tradition that went back decades and was very irritating and patronizing. When a fifties singer got up in his shiny suit and fake America accent, he invariably began by trying to ingratiate himself with the audience by saying he was thrilled to be in Hicksville, or wherever, and they were all lovely. Still goes on today.

The manuscript is in Paul's hand, as the main begetter of *Sgt. Pepper*. The third and fourth lines didn't make it: 'He showed them how to please a crowd, the men's leader has made them very proud.'

There is also a sketch, in Paul's hand (sold at Sotheby's in December 1982), which shows the band members in stylish Edwardian costumes, with droopy moustaches – which at the time they had in real life anyway. They are in a period living room with photographs and trophies on the wall – an early sketch of what became the cover. Paul, in some ways, is and was a better artist and draughtsman than John, in that he could do likenesses and draw to scale, though he was perhaps less imaginative and original than John – and less messy.

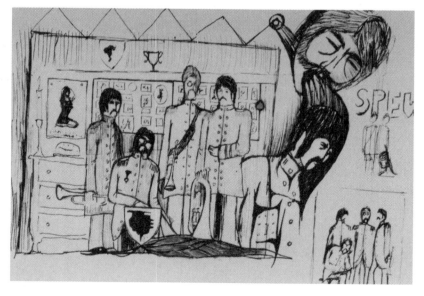

Drawing by Paul for the Sgt. Pepper *cover, showing that he had a pretty good artistic hand.*

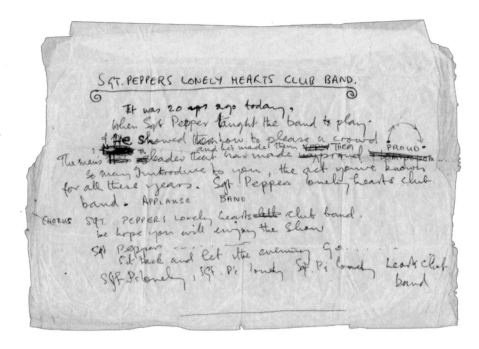

Early version of the Sgt. Pepper *title track in Paul's hand, with lines three and four which were not used.*

It was twenty years ago today,
Sgt. Pepper taught the band to play
They've been going in and out of style
But they're guaranteed to raise a smile
So may I introduce to you
The act you've known for all these years
Sgt. Pepper's Lonely Hearts Club Band
We're Sgt. Pepper's Lonely Hearts
    Club Band
We hope you will enjoy the show
Sgt. Pepper's Lonely Hearts Club Band
Sit back and let the evening go
Sgt. Pepper's lonely, Sgt. Pepper's
    lonely
Sgt. Pepper's Lonely Hearts Club Band

It's wonderful to be here
It's certainly a thrill
You're such a lovely audience
We'd like to take you home with us
We'd love to take you home
I don't really want to stop the show
But I thought that you might like to
    know
That the singer's going to sing a song
And he wants you all to sing along
So let me introduce to you
The one and only Billy Shears
And Sgt. Pepper's Lonely Hearts Club
    Band

With A Little Help From My Friends

This was one of the songs I witnessed being created, writing down what I observed happening from my 1968 biography (see below). I didn't know, while watching, where it was going, whether it would be used or not. They had done some initial work on it, calling it at that stage 'Bad Finger Boogie', and now needed to complete it. The idea was to come up with a Ringo song, like 'Yellow Submarine', one for the kiddies, and one which would suit Ringo's limited range. They were under pressure to finish it – and Ringo had been 'ordered', he would be turning up at the studio later that evening to record whatever it was they had created – yet I don't remember any panic. It was mostly a laugh. But in between doing daft things, they kept returning to the matter in hand, knowing they had to solve the problems they had set themselves. Their subconscious was at work, even while doing apparently disconnected things.

It was a method they had used for some years – messing around together, very often with a little audience of friends around that they could use as a sounding board, though the audience knew not to interrupt unless their opinion was asked, which it very often was. Some of those present would come away thinking, hey, I helped on that line, that word was mine – which was pleasing, but I am sure that both Paul and John had already considered most possibilities, turning rhymes over and over in their heads, and were simply wanting a reaction. What was interesting was that they seemed to know instinctively when a suggestion would work, sensing that it would fit in with what was already floating around in their minds.

'With A Little Help From My Friends'

In mid–March 1967 they were getting towards the end of the Sergeant Pepper album. They were halfway through a song for Ringo, a Ringo sort of song, which they'd begun the day before.

At two o'clock in the afternoon John arrived at Paul's house in St John's Wood. They both went up to Paul's workroom at the top of the house. It is a narrow, rectangular room, full of stereophonic equipment and amplifiers. There is a large triptych of Jane Asher on the wall and a large silver piece of sculpture by Paolozzi, shaped like a fireplace with Dalek heads on top.

John started playing his guitar and Paul started banging on his piano. For a couple of hours they both banged away. Each seemed to be in a trance until the other came up with something good, then he would pluck it out of a mass of noises and try it himself. They'd already established the tune the previous afternoon, a gentle lilting tune, and its name, 'With A Little Help From My Friends'. Now they were trying to polish up the melody and think of some words to go with it.

'Are you afraid when you turn out the light,' sang John. Paul sang it after him and nodded that it was good. John said they could use that idea for all the verses, if they could think of some more questions on those lines.

'Do you believe in love at first sight,' sang John. 'No,' he said, stopping singing. 'it hasn't got the right number of syllables. What do you think? Can we split it up and have a pause to give it an extra syllable?' John then sang the line, breaking it in the middle: 'Do you believe – ugh – in love at first sight.'

'How about,' said Paul, 'Do you believe in a love at first sight.' John sang it over and accepted it. In singing it, he added the next line, 'Yes, I'm certain it happens all the time.'

They both then sang the two lines to themselves, la-la-ing all the other lines. Apart from this, all they had was the chorus: 'I'll get by with a little help from my friends.' John found himself singing 'would you believe', which he thought was better.

Then they changed the order, singing the two lines 'Would you believe in a love at first sight / Yes I'm certain it happens all the time' before going on to 'Are you afraid when you turn out the light,' but they still had to la-la the fourth line, which they couldn't think of.

It was now about five o'clock. Cynthia, John's wife, arrived wearing sunglasses, accompanied by Terry Doran, one of their (and Brian Epstein's) old Liverpool friends. John and Paul kept on playing. Cyn picked up a paperback book and starting reading. Terry produced a magazine about horoscopes. John and Paul were singing their three lines over and over again, searching for a fourth.

'What's a rhyme for time?' said John. 'Yes, I'm certain it happens all the time. It's got to rhyme with that line.'

'How about "I just feel fine",' suggested Cyn.

'No,' said John. 'You never use the word just. It's meaningless. It's a fill-in word.'

John sang 'I know it's mine,' but nobody took much notice. It didn't make much sense, coming after 'Are you afraid when you turn out the light'. Somebody said it sounded obscene.

Terry asked me what my birthday was. I said January seventh. Paul stopped playing, although it had looked as if he was completely concentrating on the song, and said, 'Hey, that's our kid's birthday as well.' He listened while Terry read out the horoscope. Then he went back to doodling on the piano.

In the middle of the doodling, Paul suddenly started to play 'Can't Buy Me Love'. John joined in, singing it very loud, laughing and shouting. Then Paul began another song on the piano, 'Tequila'. They both joined in again, shouting and laughing even louder. Terry and Cyn went on reading.

'Remember in Germany?' said John. 'We used to shout out anything.' They played the song again. This time John shouted out a different thing in each pause in the music. 'Knickers' and 'Duke of Edinburgh' and 'tit' and 'Hitler'.

They both stopped all the shouting and larking around as suddenly as they'd begun it. They went back, very quietly, to the song they were supposed to be working on. 'What do you see when you turn out the light,' sang John, trying slightly new words to their existing line, leaving out 'afraid'. Then he followed it with another line, 'I can't tell you, but I know it's mine.' By slightly rewording it, he'd made it fit in.

Paul said yes, that would do. He wrote down the finished four lines on a sheet of exercise paper propped in front of him on his piano. They now had one whole verse, as well as the chorus. Paul got up and wandered round the room. John moved to the piano.

'How about a piece of amazing cake from Basingstoke?' said Paul, taking down a piece of rock-hard cake from a shelf. 'It'll do for a trifle,' said John. Paul made a face. Terry and Cynthia were still quietly reading. Paul got a sitar from a corner and sat down and started to tune it, shushing John to keep quiet for a minute. John sat still at the piano, looking blankly out of the window. Outside in the front courtyard of Paul's house, the eyes and foreheads of six girls could just be seen peering over the front wall. Then they dropped, exhausted, on to the pavement beyond. A few minutes later they appeared again, hanging on till their strength gave way.

John peered vacantly into space through his round wire spectacles. Then he began to play a hymn on the piano, singing words he was making up as he went along.

'Backs to the wall, if you want to see His face.'

Then he seemed to jump in the air and started banging out a hearty rugby song. 'Let's write a rugby song eh?' No one listened to him. Paul had got his sitar tuned and was playing some chords on it, the same ones over and over again. He got up again and wandered round the room. John picked up the sitar this time, but he couldn't get comfortable with it. Paul told him that he had to sit on the floor with his legs crossed and place it in the bowl of his foot. Paul said George did it that way; it felt uncomfortable at first, but after a few centuries you got used to it. John tried it, gave up, and placed the sitar against a chair.

Paul then went back to his guitar and started to sing and play a very slow, beautiful song about a foolish man sitting on the hill. John listened to it quietly, staring blankly out of the window, almost as if he weren't listening. Paul sang it many times, la-la-ing words he hadn't thought of yet. When at last he finished, John said he better write the words down or he'd forget them. Paul said it was okay. He wouldn't forget them. It was the first time Paul had played it for John. There was no discussion.

They then lit a marijuana cigarette, sharing it between them. It was getting near seven o'clock, almost time to go round the corner to the EMI recording studios. They decided to phone Ringo, to tell him his song was finished – which it wasn't – and that they would do it that evening. John picked up the phone. After a lot of playing around, he finally got through, but it was busy. 'If I hold on, does that mean I eventually get through?'

'No, you have to hang up,' said Paul.

In my description of the writing process that evening, John criticizes Cynthia for suggesting 'just', which he says is a non-word, a fill-in word. In the event, he broke his own rule – which he had done anyway in the past – with the line 'I just need someone to love'. But it's a good rule, and shows that he did have rules when it came to vocabulary, even when he ignored them.

They were well aware at the time of the sexual connotation of 'I know it's mine' and also of the double meaning of the phrase 'I get high with a little help from my friends'. The drug reference was deliberate, to amuse their friends, and most fans. It was a song about pot, something all four of them looked upon as a friend – but only if you wanted to read it that way. Up to you.

I wasn't really aware at the time how clever they had become at using their real-life dialogue: one of them saying a line, trying it out, and the other replying. They then incorporated this repartee into the lyrics. In the song, in the second verse, there is a question and answer session, with Ringo asking the questions and the others singing their response. It gives the lyric a narrative and progression, stops it from being too sad, too pathetic. Ringo could have sounded like Billy No Mates moaning on, but instead his friends are offering helpful comments.

The manuscript is in Paul's hand with 'Bad Finger Boogie', the original title, in brackets at the top. It also features a different second line: 'would you throw a tomatoe at me' which Ringo objected to, saying it reminded him of the days when people did throw things at him. This might have been in his Butlins holiday camp days or possibly when he first took over from Pete Best as drummer, and the Pete Best fans were very upset. Or more recently when Beatles fans threw Jelly Babies which Ringo, sitting down, found hard to avoid.

What would you think if I sang out of tune,
would you stand up and walk out on me?
Lend me your ears and I'll sing you a song,
and I'll try not to sing out of key.
Oh, I get by with a little help from my friends,
Mm, I get high with a little help from my friends,
Mm, I'm gonna try with a little help from my friends.

What do I do when my love is away?
(Does it worry you to be alone?)
How do I feel by the end of the day?
(Are you sad because you're on your own?)
No, I get by with a little help from my friends,
Mm, I get high with a little help from my friends,
Mm, I'm gonna to try with a little help from my friends.

'With A Little Help From My Friends', from Sgt. Pepper, *January 1967. An earlier title, 'Bad Finger Boogie', is in brackets and in the second line, a tomato is being thrown, which did not appeal to Ringo.*

(Do you need anybody?)
I need somebody to love.
(Could it be anybody?)
Yes, I want somebody to love.

(Would you believe in a love at first sight?)
Yes I'm certain that it happens all the time.
(What do you see when you turn out the light?)

I can't tell you, but I know it's mine.
Oh, I get by with a little help from my friends,
Mm, I'm gonna try with a little help from my friends,
Oh, I get high with a little help from my friends,
Yes I get by with a little help from my friends,
with a little help from my friends.

Lucy In The Sky With Diamonds

I think by now most pop pickers know that it does not stand for LSD – which was the rumour back in 1967. John denied it enough times, but that did not stop the rumour-mongers. The original idea came when his son Julian, aged four, brought a drawing home and John asked him what it was, what the shapes meant. Julian said it was Lucy, a girl in his class, and she was in the sky and those were diamonds. Lucy O'Donnell, also aged four, did not discover she had been immortalized in a song until she was aged thirteen. (She died in 2009, aged forty-six, having suffered from lupus and other autoimmune system diseases.)

That doesn't mean to say that the images in the song were not drug-induced, as John was still taking a lot of LSD at home, but it's equally possible that he drew on childhood memories of *Alice in Wonderland*, in which Alice gets taken on a rowing boat by the Queen – who turns into a sheep. There is also a possible *Goon Show* connection. According to Spike Milligan, a friend of John's at one time, they used to talk about 'plasticine ties'.

The verbal and visual images are surreal but straightforward, in the sense that you can picture them dreaming up daft or unlikely juxtapositions which would be amusing for a child, such as trees made of tangerines, marmalade skies, marshmallow pies, hee hee. Paul, on a visit to John, helped him finish off the verses and was responsible for 'newspaper taxis', which I used to think meant taxis carrying newspapers but was actually a reference to taxis made out of newspaper.

The images, I assume, are also the sort of thing that flit through the minds of people on drugs, when weird things appear to happen, when you find yourselves in strange places. But they also happen to ordinary people in ordinary dreams as well. Asked about the last line, the girl waiting at a turnstile with kaleidoscope eyes, John later said it was Yoko, though he didn't know it at the time. So the song could have been called 'Yoko In The Sky With Diamonds', giving us the initials YSD, which no one could have objected to.

Three versions of the manuscript are known – with parts in the hand of both Paul and John, but with no important differences, apart from the order of the verses. One version (opposite, top left), now owned by a Californian collector, is in John's hand and has the line 'with plasticine porters looking-glass eyes' with the word ties inserted above 'eyes'. It also has a drawing, another version of the cover image of the Sergeant Pepper Band, with a trophy beside them and two rocking-horse people. At the bottom, in different handwriting, possibly Paul's, it reads 'Wednesday morning . . .', the beginning, we now know, of a later song. The version opposite is in John's hand but the last five lines are in Paul's.

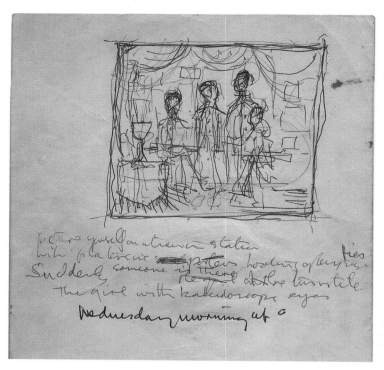

Another sketch, possibly by Paul, for the Sgt. Pepper *cover – but the four lines below it are John's early handwritten lyrics for 'Lucy In The Sky With Diamonds'. 'Wednesday morning at …' is in Paul's hand, plus a longer version of 'Lucy' by John.*

'Lucy In The Sky With Diamonds', from Sgt. Pepper, *January 1967, in John's hand.*

Picture yourself in a boat on a river,
With tangerine trees and marmalade skies.
Somebody calls you, you answer quite slowly,

A girl with kaleidoscope eyes.

Cellophane flowers of yellow and green,
Towering over your head.
Look for the girl with the sun in her eyes,
And she's gone.

Lucy in the sky with diamonds,
Lucy in the sky with diamonds,
Lucy in the sky with diamonds,
Ah … Ah …

Follow her down to a bridge by a fountain,
Where rocking horse people eat marshmallow pies.
Everyone smiles as you drift past the flowers,
That grow so incredibly high.

Newspaper taxis appear on the shore,
Waiting to take you away.
Climb in the back with your head in the clouds,
And you're gone.

Picture yourself on a train in a station,
With plasticine porters with looking glass ties.
Suddenly someone is there at the turnstile,
The girl with kaleidoscope eyes.

Getting Better

'Getting Better' was another song I witnessed from its early creation – and wrote about in the biography. I didn't go into the details of John's contribution to the lyrics, which were very important, starting with a caustic 'can't get much worse'. He turned an upbeat song into a confessional, admitting he had been cruel and mean to his woman and beaten her up (which was true, as Cynthia later revealed), but he was trying to do better, so in a way the song does end optimistically. In the description I didn't mention I was there, all the time, but wrote it like a fly on the wall – which was what I was trying to be.

Another afternoon it was the first afternoon of spring – like spring, and Paul went for a walk with his dog Martha. John still hadn't arrived for the latest work on Sergeant Pepper.

He pushed Martha into his Aston Martin and got in beside her and started the car, but it wouldn't start. He gave it a few bangs, hoping that would do it, then he gave up and got out of the Aston Martin and into his black-windowed Mini Cooper. He revved up first time. His housekeeper man opened the large dark green doors and he shot through, catching all the fans by surprise. He was away before they realized he'd come out. He drove to Primrose Hill, where he parked the car and left it without locking it. He never locks his cars.

Martha ran around and the sun came out. Paul thought it really was spring at last. 'It's getting better,' he said to himself. He meant the weather, but the phrase made him smile because it was one of Jimmie Nicol's phrases, one they used to mock all the time in Australia. When Ringo was once ill and unable to play, Jimmie Nicol deputized for him on part of their Australian tour. Every time one of them asked Jimmie how he was getting on, if he was liking it and was he managing okay, all he ever replied was 'It's getting better.'

That day at two o'clock, when John came around to write a new song, Paul suggested: 'Let's do a song called "It's Getting Better".' So they got going, both playing, singing, improvising, and messing around. When the tune was at last taking shape, Paul said, 'You've got to admit, it is getting better.'

'Did you say, "You've got to admit, it's getting better"?'

Then John sang that as well. So it went on till two in the morning. People came to see Paul, some by appointment. They were left waiting downstairs, reading, or were sent away. John and Paul stopped once for a meal, a quick fry-up.

The next evening, Paul and John went to the recording studio. Paul played the new song on the piano, la-la-ing the accompaniment or banging in tune to his words, to give the others an idea of what it sounded like. Ringo and George said they liked it; so did George Martin.

The first stage in the layer-cake system they now use in recording songs was to get the backing recorded on one track. They discussed what the general sound would be like and what sort of instruments to use. They also chatted about other things. When they got bored they went off and played on their own on any instruments lying around. There was an electronic piano in the corner of the studio, left over from someone else's recording session. Someone doodled on it and the group decided to use it.

Ringo sat at his drums and played what he thought would be a good drum backing, with Paul singing the song into his ear. Because of the noise, Paul had to shout in Ringo's ear as he explained something. After about two hours of trying out little bits and pieces, they had the elements of a backing. George Martin and two studio technicians, who'd been sitting around just waiting, went up into their soundproof glass-front control room, where they continued to sit around and wait for the Beatles to get themselves organized.

Neil and Mal got the instruments and microphones arranged in one corner of the studio and the four of them at last started to sing and play 'It's Getting Better'. Ringo looked a bit lost, sitting slightly apart on his own, surrounded by his drums. The other three had their heads together over one microphone.

They played the song over about 10 times. All that was being recorded, up in the soundproof box, were the instruments, not the voices. From time to time Paul said, 'Once more, let's try it this way,' or 'Let's have less bass,' or 'More drums.' By midnight they had recorded the backing.

The next day John and George assembled at Paul's house. Ringo wasn't there. They were just going to do the singing track for 'It's Getting Better' and he wouldn't be needed. Ivan Vaughan, the school friend of John and Paul, was also at Paul's house. At seven thirty they all moved round to EMI where George Martin, like a very understanding housemaster, was ready and waiting for them.

A technician played the backing for 'It's Getting Better' they'd recorded the night before. It was played over and over again. George Harrison and Ivan went off to chat in a corner, but Paul and John listened carefully. Paul instructed the technician which levers to press, telling him what he wanted, how it should be done, which bits he liked best. George Martin looked on, giving advice where necessary. John stared into space.

Dick James, the Beatles' song publisher, arrived wearing a camel coat. He said hello to them all, very jolly and breezy. He made a joke about there being no truth in the rumour that EMI was buying Northern Songs. He listened to the backing of 'It's Getting Better' and showed no expression. Then they played him one of their other songs, about the girl leaving home. George Martin said this was the one that almost made him cry. Dick James listened and said yes, it was very good. He could do with more of them. 'You mean you don't like the freak-out stuff?' Dick James said no, no, he didn't mean that. Then he left.

They played 'It's Getting Better' for what seemed the hundredth time, but Paul said he wasn't happy about it. They better get Ringo in and they would do it all again. Someone went to ring for Ringo.

Peter Brown arrived. He'd just returned from a trip to America. He gave them some new American LPs, which they all jumped on. They played him 'She's Leaving Home' and a few other of the Sergeant Pepper songs, already recorded. Then they played him the backing track of 'It's Getting Better'. As it was being played, Paul talked to one of the technicians and told him to try a slightly different sound mix. The technician did so, and Paul said that was much better. It would do. They didn't need to bring Ringo in now after all.

'And we've just ordered Ringo on toast,' said John. But Ringo was cancelled in time and the studio was made ready to record the sound track, the voices. As it was being set up by Neil, Mal brought in tea and orange juice on a tray. Paul let his tea go cold while he played with an oscillating box he'd found in a corner. By playing around with the switches, he managed to produce six different noises. He said to one of the sound engineers that if someone could produce oscillating boxes with the sounds controlled and in order, it would be a new electronic instrument.

They were ready at last. The three of them held their heads round one microphone and sang 'It's Getting Better' while up in the control box George Martin and his two assistants got it all down on the track. The three Beatles were singing, not playing, but through headphones strapped to their ears they could hear the backing track. They were simply singing to their already recorded accompaniment.

In the studio itself, all that could be heard were the unaccompanied, unelectrified voices of the Beatles singing, without any backing. It all sounded flat and off key. They ran through the song about four times and John said he didn't feel well. He could do with some fresh air. Someone went to open the back door of the studio. There was the sound of loud banging and cheering on the other side. The door began to move slightly inward under the strain of a gang of fans who'd somehow managed to get inside the building.

George Martin came down from his box and told John it would be better to go up on the roof and get some air, rather than go outside. 'How's John?' Paul asked into the microphone to George Martin up in the control box.

'He's looking at the stars,' said George Martin.

'You mean Vince Hill?' said Paul. He and George started singing 'Edelweiss' and laughing. Then John came back.

In the corner of the studios, Mal and Neil and Ivan, the friend, couldn't hear the jokes over the headphones. They'd finished their tea. Ivan was writing a letter to his mother. Neil was filling in his diary. He'd only started it two weeks earlier. He said he should have started one about five years ago.

A man in a purple shirt called Norman arrived; he used to be one of their recording engineers and now had a group of his own, The Pink Floyd. Very politely he asked George Martin if his boys could possibly pop in to see the Beatles at work. George smiled unhelpfully. Norman said perhaps he should ask John personally, as a favour. George Martin said no, that wouldn't work. If by chance he and his boys popped in about eleven o'clock, he might just be able to see what he could do.

They did pop in around eleven, and exchanged a few half-hearted hellos. The Beatles were still going through the singing of 'It's Getting Better' for what now seemed the thousandth time. By two o'clock they had it, at least to a stage that didn't make them unhappy.

I mentioned in my account of the evening that John felt ill and went up on the roof – but I was not aware at the time of the reason, nor was George Martin, who suggested John should go out on the roof to get some fresh air. John was suffering the ill effects of having taken too much LSD earlier in the day. It wasn't something they normally did when they were working, or even about to start working. In the circumstances, going on the roof was a pretty dangerous move – still under the influence, he might well have decided he could fly.

The manuscript, in Paul's hand, is on a piece of notepaper, a flier from the Roundhouse in Chalk Farm, North London, not far from Paul's house, where a rave was about to be held.

He has included in the lyrics, at the end of the second and third lines, in brackets, 'now I can't complain', which on the record you can hear John singing, but these words are not included in the lyrics printed on the album sleeve. Note also the odd Ah and Oh written out, though these sound spontaneous on the record.

It's getting better all the time
I used to get mad at my school (No, I can't complain)
The teachers who taught me weren't cool (No, I can't complain)
You're holding me down
Turning me round
Filling me up with your rules

I've got to admit it's getting better (Better)
It's a little better all the time (It can't get no worse)
I have to admit it's getting better (better)
It's getting better
Since you've been mine

Me used to be a angry young man
Me hiding me head in the sand
You gave me the word, I finally heard
I'm doing the best that I can

I've got to admit it's getting better (Better)
A little better all the time (It can't get no worse)
I have to admit it's getting better (Better)
It's getting better
Since you've been mine

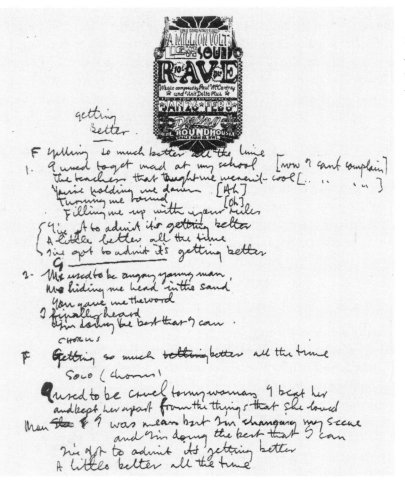

'Getting Better', from Sgt. Pepper, *January 1967, in Paul's hand on notepaper for a Roundhouse Rave.*

Getting so much better all the time!

I used to be cruel to my woman
I beat her and kept her apart from the things that she loved
Man, I was mean but I'm changing my scene
And I'm doing the best that I can (ooh)

I admit it's getting better
A little better all the time (It can't get no worse)
Yes, I admit it's getting better, it's getting better
Since you've been mine

Getting so much better all the time

Fixing A Hole

Usually Beatles songs were investigated for hidden meanings about drugs – but in this case, the opposite happened. Most commentators decided that the song was about a real hole in a real roof – the one on the remote cottage Paul had bought in Scotland in June 1966, which needed fixing. The timing appeared right, but in 1997, during an interview with Barry Miles, Paul admitted that it began as another ode to pot (not heroin, despite the use of the word 'fix'), the drug that got him out of everyday worries and allowed his mind to explore. And it was written not in Scotland but at his new house in Cavendish Avenue, where he was by this time living alone, though still officially with Jane Asher.

The analogy of fixing a hole in a roof/a hole in the mind is an attractive one, and he was well aware of all the double meanings. He was beginning to feel oppressed by his relationship with Jane and by the Beatles' financial and legal affairs which were becoming a burden. There's a sense here of him longing to be free to experiment more – with life, the arts, and yes drugs and stimulants, and not worry about silly people telling him what he should or should not do, that he is right even if he is wrong. It sounds very like John – which just goes to show that Paul could do moody, personal stuff. The lyrics appealed greatly to hippies everywhere.

The manuscript in Paul's hand has one rather interesting difference from the finished version. At the end of the second verse and then repeated as the final line, he has written 'flying around in a world it is dying to know', which was not used, but is a good line.

At the end, he or someone has written Suddenly-on-Sea – which I think must have been a play on words – for Suddenly I See. Back to Lennon–McCartney's fondness for things being seen or not seen, or seen through.

I'm fixing a hole where the rain gets in
And stops my mind from wondering
Where it will go

I'm filling the cracks that ran through the door
And kept my mind from wondering
Where it will go

And it really doesn't matter if I'm wrong I'm right
Where I belong I'm right
Where I belong.

a song to be done, on the sheet lie below.

1. I'm fixing a hole where the rain gets in.
    and stops my mind from wandering
    where it will go — Instrumental echo.

2. I'm filling the cracks that ~~ran~~ RAN through the door
    And kept my mind from wandering
    where it will go
    flying around in a world it is dying to know

SO I'm painting my room in the colourful way,
    And when my mind is wandering,
    There I will go, ——————

And I ~~#~~ really doesn't matter if I'm wrong I'm right
                    where I belong, I'm right
~~See~~ the people standing there, ~~who~~ disagree   where I belong
    and never win + wonder why they don't get in
                        my door.

    I'm taking the time for a number of things
    that weren't important yesterday
            And I still go ——————

SOLO
    ——————

    It makes very little difference if I'm wrong or right
                        where I belong, I'm right
        where I belong.
    Silly people ~~run around~~ and worry me
    ~~and~~ they never ask me why they don't get past the door
        I'm fixing a hole where the rain gets in,
        and stops my mind from wandering
            where it will go
            flying around in a world it is dying
                        to know

                SUDDENLY — ON-SEA

*'Fixing A Hole',
from* Sgt. Pepper,
*January 1967, in
Paul's hand. Was
Suddenly-on-Sea
a joke version of
Suddenly I See?*

See the people standing there
who disagree and never win
And wonder why they don't get in my door

I'm painting my room in a colourful way
And when my mind is wandering
There I will go

Silly people run around they worry me
And never ask me why they don't get past my door
I'm taking the time for a number of things
That weren't important yesterday
And I still go

I'm fixing a hole where the rain gets in
And stops my mind from wandering
Where it will go

She's Leaving Home

Usually John was the one to draw inspiration from a newspaper story, but this time it was Paul, reading a story in the *Daily Mail* on 27 February 1967 about a girl, Melanie Coe, who had run away from home at the age of seventeen. In the account, her parents were quoted as saying they couldn't understand it as they had given her everything. It was that last line which inspired Paul: the clash of the generation gap, the misunderstanding between parents and their children.

There were quite a few stories of this sort at the time, both in the UK and the USA, as an older generation brought up in the more restrictive post-war era, began finding that their sixties teenagers did not aspire to a life devoted to a boring job with a secure pension, or a marriage to someone their parents considered suitable; instead they wanted to go off on the hippie trail to California or Soho and Carnaby Street and find themselves.

Paul's narrative, with John's help – imagining the scene, and what the parents might be saying when they discovered their daughter had gone – turned out to be pretty near the truth. Melanie herself later admitted that she had been given a car, a diamond ring, a mink coat, but she had felt stifled as an only child in her North London home. 'Living alone for so many years' as Paul had imagined it. She had in fact met Paul and the Beatles three years earlier when she appeared on a TV pop show, *Ready Steady Go!*, as one of the dancers – but none of the Beatles remembered her.

The lyrics are well crafted, creating a genuine narrative, poignant and moving without teetering into sentimentality, painting a picture of society known to many people at the time – and throughout time. Paul sings it in the third person, describing what is happening, then John comes in with a refrain in the background as the parents, and the two are skilfully blended together. John probably had the image of Aunt Mimi in his head when helping with the words, all her reprimands and self-righteous homilies about never thinking of herself.

In the song, it turns out the girl has gone off to meet a man from the motor trade. At the time, this was assumed to have referred to Terry Doran, the Beatles' friend, who sold expensive motor cars, but Paul has said he was not thinking of anyone in particular. He just liked singing 'a man from the motor trade', which conjured up a suitably sleazy image. In real life, Melanie had met a man from a casino – which would have done just as well.

The musical arrangement, using a cello, violins and harp, was for the first time not the work of George Martin. He was busy working on a Cilla Black recording. Paul was in a hurry, couldn't wait, and so he instructed and hired another arranger, Mike Leander, which did not please George Martin. None of the other Beatles played on the record – it is just Paul, with some extra vocals from John.

The manuscript, in Paul's hand, was sold at Sotheby's in August 1982, with the proceeds going to a children's hospital.

A-level girl dumps car and vanishes

By DAILY MAIL REPORTER

THE FATHER of 17-year-old Melanie Coe, the schoolgirl who seemed to have everything, spent yesterday searching for her in London and Brighton.

Melanie had her own car, an Austin 1100. It was left, unlocked, outside her home when she vanished.

She had a wardrobe full of clothes. She took only those she was wearing—a cinnamon trouser suit and black patent leather shoes.

She left her cheque book and drew no money from her account.

Melanie, who has long blonde hair and is 5ft. 1in. tall, was studying for her A-level examinations. She planned to go to university or drama school.

She has been missing from her home at Amhurst Park, Stamford Hill, N., for a week.

Search

Her father, businessman Mr. John Coe, said yesterday: "I cannot imagine why she should run away. She has everything here. She is very keen on clothes but she left them all, even her fur coat.

"We have spoken to her friends and visited the places where she goes, but there is no trace of her. I only wish she would telephone us."

Melanie is a pupil at Skinner's Grammar School, Stamford Hill.

MELANIE COE . . . PICTURED THE DAY SHE VANISHED

The Daily Mail *story from 27 February 1967, which sparked off 'She's Leaving Home'.*

Wednesday morning at five o'clock as the day begins
Silently closing her bedroom door
Leaving the note that she hoped would say more
She goes downstairs to the kitchen clutching her handkerchief
Quietly turning the backdoor key
Stepping outside she is free.

She (We gave her most of our lives)
is leaving (Sacrificed most of our lives)
home (We gave her everything money could buy)
She's leaving home after living alone
For so many years. Bye, bye.

Father snores as his wife gets into her dressing gown
Picks up the letter that's lying there
Standing alone at the top of the stairs
She breaks down and cries to her husband Daddy our baby's gone
Why would she treat us so thoughtlessly
How could she do this to me?

She (We never thought of ourselves)
is leaving (Never a thought for ourselves)
home (We struggled hard all our lives to get by)
She's leaving home after living alone
For so many years. Bye, bye.

Friday morning at nine o'clock she is far away
Waiting to keep the appointment she made
Meeting a man from the motor trade.

She (What did we do that was wrong)
is leaving (We didn't know it was wrong)
home (Fun is the one thing that money can't buy)
Something inside that was always denied
For so many years. Bye, bye
She's leaving home. Bye, bye

Being For The Benefit Of Mr Kite!

Inspired by a Victorian circus poster that John had acquired in an antiques shop in Sevenoaks, Kent, while they were filming a promotional video for 'Strawberry Fields' in January 1967. Almost every line in the song was lifted, word for word. (The circus could presumably have charged a copyright fee if the song had been done earlier, but the poster is dated 1843 and such copyright normally runs out in seventy years.)

'Being for the Benefit of Mr Kite' appears in large letters on the poster, along with 'Mr Henderson', 'Pablo Fanque', 'hoops', 'trampoline' and a 'Hogshead of real fire'. On the poster, the horse is called Zanthus, which they were probably unsure how to pronounce, so they changed its name to Henry.

The poster was hanging on John's wall when Paul arrived for a writing session. John had already started putting it to music – and together they finished it off. George Martin added all the swirling fairground noises, as suggested by John.

They cleverly twisted their tongues round all the phrases and some complicated names, even managing quite a few rhymes, only adding the odd modern phrase such as 'what a scene'. It finished the first side of the album with a period flavour, just in case we had forgotten we were supposed to be listening to Sergeant Pepper's Edwardian band.

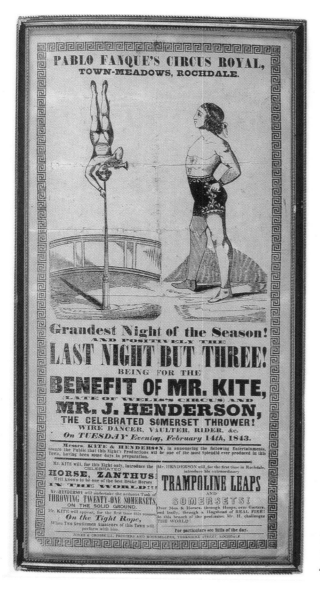

In 1967, when I interviewed him for the biography, John rather dismissed the song, saying he was just going through the motions, there was no real work, but by 1980, when talking to *Playboy*, he had decided it was rather beautiful. 'The song is pure, like a painting, a pure watercolour.'

The manuscript, in John's hand, is written in capitals, presumably so that other people in the studio would be able to read it. It has been nicely decorated at the top, to give it a poster feeling.

The original 1843 poster which inspired 'Being For The Benefit Of Mr Kite!' from which most of the lyrics were lifted.

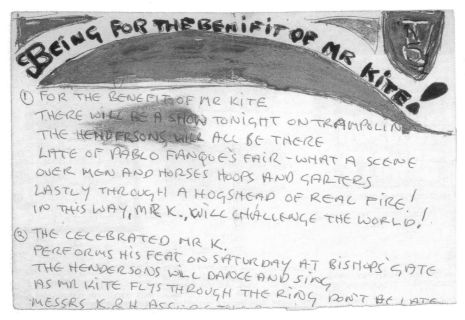

For the benefit of Mr Kite
there will be a show tonight on trampoline.
The Hendersons will all be there
late of Pablo Fanque's Fair – what a scene
Over men and horses hoops and garters
lastly through a hogshead of real fire!
In this way Mr K. will challenge the world!

The celebrated Mr K.
performs his feat on Saturday at Bishopsgate
the Hendersons will dance and sing
as Mr Kite flies through the ring don't be late
Messrs K. and H. assure the public
their production will be second to none
and of course Henry The Horse dances the waltz!

The band begins at ten to six
when Mr K. performs his tricks without a sound
and Mr H. will demonstrate
Ten somersaults he'll undertake on solid ground.
Having been some days in preparation
a splendid time is guaranteed for all
and tonight Mr Kite is topping the bill

Within You, Without You

Well, what a shock this was. We knew the Beatles were now into Indian music and playing some funny instrument called the sitar, or at least George was, but we didn't really know he was so far into Indian philosophy.

The tune came to George after a dinner in Hampstead at the home of Klaus Voormann, one of their artistic friends from the Hamburg years. He did the drawings for *Revolver* and was the bass guitarist for the Manfred Mann group. George was pottering around on a pedal harmonium when he started the tune, then he began putting a few words to it, based on the dinnertime conversation – 'We were talking …' Sounds as if it was a typically hippie, cosmically conscious sixties dinner party. George was extremely serious at this stage, devoting all his time to studying Indian music and religion. When visiting him it was hard to get him to talk about much else. He practised the sitar for three hours a day and was teaching himself Indian script, so that he could write down what the Indian musicians had to play.

The best line, and the title line, came later – about life going on within you and without you, supposedly taken from a book about Buddhism which his sister-in-law, Jenny Boyd, had been reading. George immediately saw the double meaning in the word 'without' – either outside you in the world, or when you have gone.

The other lyrics veer between the simplistic – 'you're really only very small' – and the fairly profound 'people who gain the world and lose their soul', a warning expressed in many religions, though he rather ruins it by adding the finger-waving 'are you one of them?' The message, put simply, is to love one another because we are all one. How true. Some people mocked at the time, but George was young and sincere and trying so hard to understand something beyond himself.

'The words are always a hang-up for me,' he told me at the time of the *Sgt. Pepper* album. 'I'm not very poetic. But I don't take it seriously. It's just a joke, personal joke. It's great if someone else likes it.'

The lyrics are good – the best song he had written so far. The saving grace is at the end – when after the last chords you can hear laughter. This was George's own idea, sending himself up, showing he was self-aware, though still taking it all very seriously.

In *I Me Mine* George explains that he wrote it after he had got into meditation. Looking back, the bit he liked best was the instrumental solo in the middle.

None of the other Beatles took part in the recording, it was just George and some Indian musicians plus Neil, their roadie, banging a few instruments when required.

The manuscript is in George's hand. He has added a little grave with a cross on it after the phrase 'pass away'. There are some other scribbles, in unknown hands, such as 'Long Thin Heart', which could be a good title for something. 'Double Bedouin' sounds a like a bad pun. 'White collar workers and Polo neck skivers' could have been some of the people being criticized during the dinner party.

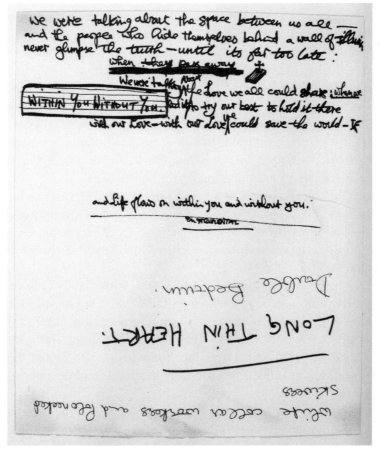

'Within You, Without You', from Sgt. Pepper, January 1967, in George's hand, with some notes, possibly for other songs or lines.

We were talking – about the space
between us all
And the people – who hide themselves
behind a wall of illusion
Never glimpse the truth – then it's far too
Late – when they pass away.
We were talking – about the love we all
could share – when we find it

to try our best to hold it there – with our love
With our love – we could save the world –
if they only knew.

Try to realize it's all within yourself
no one else can make you change
And to see you're really only very small,
and life flows on within you and without you.

We were talking – about the love that's
gone so cold and the people,
who gain the world and lose their soul –
they don't know – they can't see – are you
one of them?
When you've seen beyond yourself –
then you may find peace of mind, is
waiting there –
And the time will come when you see
we're all one,
and life flows on within you and without you.

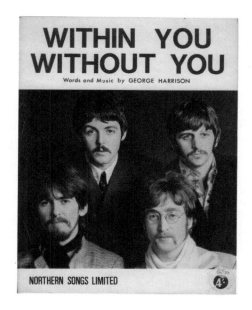

When I'm Sixty-Four

And now for something that could not have been more different, dragging us
back to the notion of an old-fashioned band. The song was old in every sense
– one of Paul's earliest songs, written when he was living in Forthlin Road
and banging out the tune on his father's old piano (which he still has at his
home). He thinks he might have been as young as sixteen when he first played
the song. If so, it shows remarkable maturity for one so young, capturing
the sounds and rhythm of a 1920s music-hall number, though of course his
father had played that sort. He also managed to capture the period flavour in
the words 'indicate precisely what you mean to say', while making jokes and
puns. Writing a postcard 'stating point of view' is witty, as is 'mending a fuse,
when your lights have gone'. It's also interesting that the idea of being old and
needing someone to look after him should have come into the thoughts of
someone who was only fifteen.

Paul used to play it on stage in the Quarrymen and early Beatles days
to fill in between their rock'n'roll numbers when the amps failed. Recording

something which was a pastiche, and would mostly amuse parents rather than their teenage fans, presumably did not occur to them till much later.

It's a fun song – but the melodies and arrangements are well crafted, as are the words. You can tell it's meant to be fun as Paul affects a pre-war George Formby, Lancashire music-hall accent. He also rolls his r's in the Scottish fashion on the phrase 'on your knee'. I like the grandchildren being called Vera, Chuck and Dave – and I like his voice singing it.

Back in the sixties, once the Beatles were into their stride and gave up covering American songs like 'Twist And Shout', I liked the fact that they tended to sing in their own accent – one of their many attractions. In *The Colour of Your Dreams*, Stuart Madow and Jeff Sobul say that it was only in 1967, when they first listened to 'When I'm Sixty-Four', that it struck them the Beatles were singing in an English accent. 'Rarely did an accent show up in any British Invasion group's vocals. Most often there was an American accent or none at all.' And the words that struck them as very British? Vera, Chuck and Dave: 'Paul slips into his British accent, especially on the name Chuck.' I suppose they did not realize that 'chuck' is a Northern term of endearment, like darling or dear, hence Paul was singing it in his own accent, whereas of course in the USA Chuck is a common first name. But it was interesting to see Americans spotting and being aware of British accents – which, when songs are sung, are usually hard to detect.

By chance, Paul's father Jim turned sixty-four in 1967 when the song finally came out – and I happened to be staying with him that weekend, in his home in the Wirral, where he was living with his new wife Angie. (Paul and brother Michael seemed less than keen on their stepmother; history later repeated itself when Paul became a widower and got remarried to Heather Mills, which did not exactly thrill his own children.) While I was there, Jim received an acetate of the record, sent by Paul, and we played it all evening, me and Angie dancing round and round the room. I was young then. Jim was so pleased – just his sort of music.

The manuscript, in Paul's hand, seems to have got wet at some time, and the ink has run in places. At the end, the line which had originally read 'yours sincerely, waiting for you', got crossed out and became 'wasting away', which is more graphic.

When I get older losing my hair,
Many years from now,
Will you still be sending me a Valentine
Birthday greetings bottle of wine.

If I'd been out till quarter to three
Would you lock the door.
Will you still need me, will you still
    feed me,
When I'm sixty-four.

'When I'm Sixty-Four',
from Sgt. Pepper,
January 1967, in Paul's
hand, with some changes
and damp patches.

When I get older losing my hair,
Many years from now
Will you still be sending me a Valentine
Birthday Greetings bottle of wine,
If I'd been out till quarter to three
Would you lock the door
Will you still need me, will you still feed me,
When I'm sixty four.

Middles. - - - - - - - - -
You'll be older too,
And if you say the word, I could stay with you

I could be handy, mending a fuse
When your lights have gone.
You can knit a sweater by the fireside
Sunday mornings. go for a ride
Doing the garden, digging the weeds
Who could ask for more?
Will you still need me, etc. . . . . .

Mid. Every summer we can rent a cottage.
in the Isle of Wight, if its not too dear.
We shall scrimp and save
. . . Grandchildren on your knee
Vera, Chuck and Dave
- - - - - - - -
Send me a postcard, drop me a line,
Stating point of view
Indicate precisely what you meant to say
wasting away
Yours sincerely mine for ever more . . .
send me your answer fill in a form
etc . . .

oo oo oo oo oo oo oo oooo
You'll be older too, (ah ah ah ah ah)
And if you say the word,
I could stay with you.

I could be handy, mending a fuse
When your lights have gone.
You can knit a sweater by the fireside
Sunday morning go for a ride.

Doing the garden, digging the weeds,
Who could ask for more.
Will you still need me, will you still feed me,
When I'm sixty-four.

Every summer we can rent a cottage
In the Isle of Wight, if it's not too dear
We shall scrimp and save
Grandchildren on your knee
Vera, Chuck and Dave

Send me a postcard, drop me a line,
Stating point of view
Indicate precisely what you mean to say
Yours sincerely, wasting away.

Give me your answer, fill in a form
Mine for evermore
Will you still need me, will you still feed me,
When I'm sixty-four.

Lovely Rita

Fun followed by fun, what could be nicer? Another pastiche, honky-tonk song from Paul. John could not, or would not, have written such a song about an ordinary boring person like a secretary or traffic warden, doing their boring job, which is presumably what he meant when he once said he did not do third-party songs. Is this perhaps why at the very end of the record you can hear John saying 'Leave it'?

Ordinary people are of course universal, and have universal feelings and problems, like getting to sixty-four and wondering if they will be needed.

'Lovely Rita' was not yet universal, being a new and modern phenomenon. Paul was amused when he learned that in the USA they were known as meter maids rather than traffic wardens. He needed a woman's name that rhymed with meter, hence Rita.

At first it was going to be an anti-warden song, as they had quickly become hate figures. It would have made for an easy bit of authority-bashing, but Paul liked the sexy overtones of the word 'maid'. He imagined some boy asking her out, hoping to tow her heart away, having dinner with her – for which she paid – then trying to get off with her on her sofa.

There was no specific Rita, but he had been fined by meter maids several times for illegal parking (which was hardly surprising, as he was very cavalier about his cars, forever leaving them parked, unlocked, in silly places). A meter maid who had fined him in St John's Wood, near his house, and with whom Paul had chatted about her name – which was Meta Davis – later came forward to claim that she had inspired the song, but Paul had no memory of her.

There are two manuscript versions, one of which (below) is in the hand of Neil Aspinall, their roadie. 'In her cap, she looked so stunning' got changed to 'looked much older'. There are also six lines on the opposite side of the page, not part of the Rita lyrics: 'I'm real, in a world that is turning to grey … I'm grey in a world that is turning to night.' Was this intended to be a new song?

The other manuscript is mainly in Paul's hand and contains some different lines, such as 'filling in a ticket with her little blue pen'. At the bottom of the left-hand page, the last line appears to be an attempt at a pun on her name – 'go to meter', i.e. go to meet her.

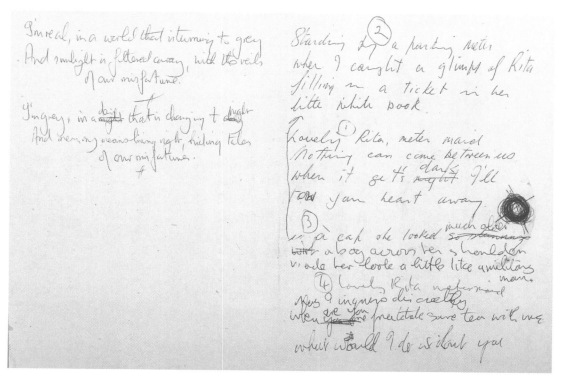

'Lovely Rita' from Sgt. Pepper, *January 1967, possibly in the hand of Mal Evans or Neil Aspinall, their two roadies, with corrections by Paul. On the left-hand side are lyrics for another, unknown song.*

Lovely Rita meter maid.
Lovely Rita meter maid.

Lovely Rita meter maid,
nothing can come between us,
when it gets dark I'll tow your heart
    away.

Standing by a parking meter,
when I caught a glimpse of Rita,
filling in a ticket in her little white
    book.

In a cap she looked much older,
and the bag across her shoulder
made her look a little like a military
    man.

Lovely Rita meter maid,

may I inquire discreetly,
when are you free
to take some tea with me?

Took her out and tried to win her,
had a laugh and over dinner,
told her I would really like to see her
    again.
Got the bill and Rita paid it,
took her home I nearly made it,
sitting on the sofa with a sister or two.

Oh, lovely Rita meter maid,
where would I be without you?
Give us a wink and make me think of
    you.

Lovely Rita meter maid.

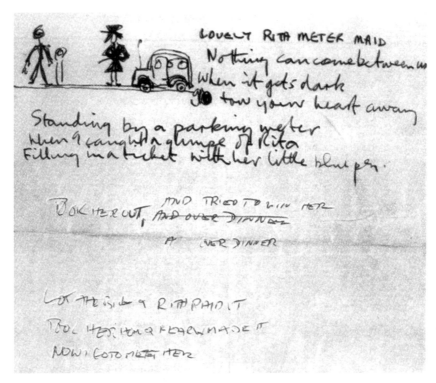

*Illustrated lyrics for
'Lovely Rita',
mainly in Paul's
hand, with some
lines in capitals,
possibly Mal's hand,
not used.*

Good Morning, Good Morning

John rather dismissed this song when I asked him about it as we sat in his little room at Kenwood with the TV blaring away. 'I often sit at the piano working at songs, with the telly on low in the background. If I'm a bit low and not getting much done, then words on the telly come through. That's when I heard "Good Morning, Good Morning" – it was a cornflakes advertisement.'

The words of the jingle went 'Good morning, good morning. The best to you each morning. Sunshine breakfast. Kellogg's Corn Flakes. Crisp and full of fun.' In John's version there is also a reference to *Meet the Wife*, a popular TV show at the time.

Later, in his interview with *Playboy*, John was even more self-critical, calling it a throwaway song and garbage.

It is a bit of a hotchpotch of found phrases and clichés, veering between being nasty and cynical about the treadmill workaday world, then he adds, 'but it's OK'. Paul thought it was John reacting against his own boring life and empty marriage and having nothing to do. The line 'go to a show, you hope she goes' possibly refers to Yoko, whom he had met (in November 1966 at the Indica Gallery) but not yet got involved with. That didn't happen until May 1968.

The record begins with a cock crowing, as it is morning, and ends on a cacophony of animal noises. One of the perks of being at Abbey Road, EMI's studios, with its long history, extensive facilities and multitude of instruments and devices lying around, not to mention an impressive sound archive, was that almost any odd noise they wanted could be found fairly quickly and tacked on.

The final noises included cockerels, birds, dogs, cows, a fox being chased, lions, horses, sheep. They were supposedly deliberately arranged in order, with John insisting that each one was capable of eating or frightening the one before. I can't say I spotted that at the time – or now. But they're great sound effects.

The manuscript, in John's hand, has a few crossings out, but is no different from the recorded song.

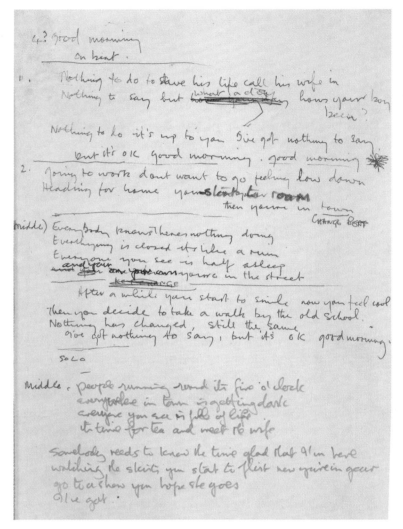

'Good Morning, Good Morning', from Sgt. Pepper, *January 1967, in two inks, Paul in blue and John in green.*

Nothing to do to save his life call his wife in
Nothing to say but what a day, how's your boy been
Nothing to do it's up to you,
I've got nothing to say but it's OK
Good morning, good morning

Going to work don't want to go feeling low down
Heading for home you start to roam then you're in town
Everybody knows there's nothing doing
Everything is closed it's like a ruin

Everyone you see is half asleep
And you're on your own, you're in the street
Good morning, good morning …

After a while you start to smile, now you feel cool
Then you decide to take a walk by the old school
Nothing has changed, it's still the same
I've got nothing to say but it's OK.
Good morning, good morning …

People running round it's five o'clock,
Everywhere in town it's getting dark,
Everyone you see is full of life,
It's time for tea and meet the wife

Somebody needs to know the time, glad that I'm here
Watching the skirts you start to flirt now you're in gear
Go to a show you hope she goes
I've got nothing to say, but it's OK
Good morning, good morning …

A Day In The Life

After the reprise of the Sgt. Pepper theme tune, telling us we are getting near the end, we have a real end – probably the most cataclysmic, orgasmic, crashing, vibrating, shuddering, juddering, shattering, echoing end in the whole of popular music. 'A Day In The Life' is often considered their greatest ever song, the best produced, most inventive, most moving. Little wonder it gets played at so many funerals all over the world and has been described as pop music's version of *The Waste Land*.

And yet it came out of two little scraps of songs, which were not connected, not related, leaving George Martin with the task of somehow fitting them together, instrumentally.

John's contribution to the lyrics was the major part – writing the beginning and the end, with Paul filling the sandwich in the middle.

Once again it was a case of John lying around at home, fairly aimless, reading the papers, scribbling notes, tinkling on the piano, picking up on three stories – two from the newspapers, and one from his own life. One was about the death of someone they knew vaguely – Tara Browne, an Irish socialite around town and member of the Guinness family, whose death was reported in the *Daily Mail* on 17 January 1967. He had been driving his sports car and smashed into a parked vehicle, killing himself – possibly high on drugs, though this was not stated. He was not in fact in the House of Lords but was the son of a lord. 'Tara didn't blow his mind out, but it was in my mind when I was writing that verse,' John told me.

In the same paper was a small story, really just a filler, about there being four thousand potholes in Blackburn, Lancashire – which begs the question: who counted them? It amused John to imagine how big the holes would be, what sort of space they would take up – and he came up with the idea of the Albert Hall. He had been looking for something to rhyme with 'rather small' and Terry Doran, his friend from the motor trade, suggested 'Albert Hall'.

The bit from his own life is a reference to the film he had recently appeared in: *How I Won the War*. It is not clear from the lyrics whether people turned away after watching it, shocked by the horror of war, or if he is returning to the motor accident at this point.

The scrap of a song that Paul came into the session with was even smaller: a memory of his school days, back in the fifties, about him getting up, combing his hair, running for the bus. Just nine lines, getting nowhere, with no narrative or development – and of course no connection with the lyrics John had written.

The references to drugs – with John singing 'I'd love to turn you on' and Paul having a smoke and going into a dream – resulted in the BBC banning the song.

The BBC's Director of Sound Broadcasting, Frank Gillard, wrote personally to Sir Joseph Lockwood of EMI, on 23 May 1967.

'I never thought the day would come when we would have to put a ban on an EMI record, but sadly that is what has happened over this track. We have listened to it over and over again with great care and we cannot avoid coming to the conclusion that the words "I'd love to turn you on" followed by that mounting montage of sound, could have a rather sinister meaning.'

He had to take account of the interpretation many young people would put upon it. '"Turned on" is a phrase currently in vogue in the jargon of drug addicts,' as he helpfully explained.

The music has been endlessly analysed, the crescendos taken to pieces, the instruments catalogued and identified. For the final recording the musicians – almost a complete orchestra – wore formal evening dress, with the addition of some novelty noses, and the recording was captured by seven hand-held cameras. They knew at the time, as so much thought and love and attention had gone into its creation, that 'A Day In The Life' was a big event. Which it has remained.

The manuscripts, one side in joined-up writing and the other on the reverse in caps, are both in John's hand (without the inclusion of Paul's verse, so they are incomplete lyrics). Both have minor one-word differences from the final version. It looks as if an early version of the line 'a crowd of people turned away' was 'a crowd of people stared and stared'.

'A Day In The Life', the final track on Sgt. Pepper, *January 1967, in John's hand, with minor changes.*

It was first sold at auction in 1992, when it was said to have come from the estate of Mal Evans, for the record sum of $100,000. In 2010 it was sold at Sotheby's in New York for $1.2 million, which remains the highest price paid for a Beatles lyric.

'A Day In The Life', in John's capitals, again without Paul's 'woke up, got out of bed' contribution.

I read the news today oh boy
About a lucky man who made the grade
And though the news was rather sad
Well I just had to laugh
I saw the photograph
He blew his mind out in a car
He didn't notice that the lights had changed
A crowd of people stood and stared
They'd seen his face before
Nobody was really sure
If he was from the House of Lords.

I saw a film today oh boy
The English Army had just won the war
A crowd of people turned away
but I just had to look
Having read the book
I'd love to turn you on

Woke up, got out of bed,
Dragged a comb across my head
Found my way downstairs and drank a cup,
And looking up I noticed I was late.
Found my coat and grabbed my hat
Made the bus in seconds flat
Found my way upstairs and had a smoke,
and somebody spoke and I went into a dream

I read the news today oh boy
Four thousand holes in Blackburn, Lancashire
And though the holes were rather small
They had to count them all
Now they know how many holes it takes to fill the Albert Hall.
I'd love to turn you on

Sgt. Pepper is still regarded by many as their greatest album – while others think it has dated. It does have some marvellous, inventive, reflective, disturbing, witty words and music. And a shattering ending, the sort of pop song we had never heard before.

It marked yet another massive stage in their development and Paul's ascension to the role of dominant influence. John had as good as given up being the boss or the leader, now that he was sitting around all day at home in suburbia, relying for inspiration on mundane domestic activities such as watching TV, reading the newspapers, or lifting lyrics from circus posters.

Brian Epstein, meanwhile, had all but disappeared from their creative life. Two months after the album was released, on 27 August 1967, Brian was found dead. He was only thirty-two.

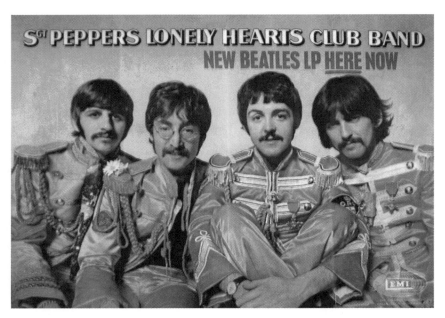

Sgt. Pepper *flyer, January 1967, for the retail trade, now highly collectable.*

10

MAGICAL MYSTERY TOUR

1967–1968

After the exertions and excitements and success of *Sgt. Pepper*, they didn't release another full-length new album for a whole year. Nevertheless they were highly productive when they did get together, working on two film projects (*Magical Mystery Tour* and then *Yellow Submarine*) that needed new songs and also a handful of singles.

Magical Mystery Tour was the first and most interesting project, in that it had some good songs and it also looked as if it would take them in a totally new direction. It didn't quite go to plan, but I remember all the enthusiasm and ideas that went into it and the anticipation and excitement when we were shown it for the first time.

The Beatles decided to throw a private *Magical Mystery Tour* party for friends and family, which was held at the Royal Lancaster Hotel on 21 December 1967. We had been told to come in costumes, which had me moaning about having to spend money renting clothes. My wife and I went as a Girl Guide and Boy Scout, wearing ill-fitting stuff borrowed from some kids in our street. Everyone else wore really expensive costumes. Paul and Jane Asher came as a Pearly King and Queen and looked ever so loving and sweet. Four days later, on Christmas Day 1967, they announced their engagement. John was dressed as a Teddy Boy and looked menacing in his leather jacket, drainpipe trousers, brothel-creepers with his hair greased back in a duck's arse (DA, in polite circles). At the same time, he seemed rather distant, switched off, not much interested – which was how he had been during most of the filming. Later he tried to disown the film, saying it was all Paul's doing, he was just dragged along, which was more or less true.

For a year, they had been putting off doing a third Beatles film, then on a flight back from the USA with Jane, Paul came up with the idea of doing an hour-long TV film in which they would all get on a bus, shoot stuff, see what happens. It would be mysterious in as much as no one would know where they were going. And magical, in that they could do whatever they wanted.

The 'Mystery Tour' notion harked back to their childhood; in the fifties, few working-class families had a car, so bus and train companies would run excursions to popular destinations, sometimes keeping the destination secret to add to the excitement. Growing up in Carlisle, as I did, you always ended up in the Lake District, so it was never much of a mystery. It was still a good day out though; the dads would take a crate of beer on board and everyone would sing on the way home.

The other element in Paul's mind, which sparked off the idea, was hearing about a group of West Coast hippies, led by author Ken Kesey, who toured in a psychedelically painted coach.

Having come up with the idea, another six months went by before Paul began to flesh it out, by which time Brian Epstein was dead. With no manager to calm them down or provide back-up, they set off on the jaunt with little planning, no real script, taking along some character actors whom they admired (there were no auditions; they simply invited them to come along).

Paul, in his naïvety, thought they could just turn up at Shepperton Studios to shoot the big scenes – not realizing such places have to be booked months if not years in advance. In the end, they had to mock it up in an old airfield in Kent.

When it came to the editing, Paul set aside two weeks – but in the event it took eleven, hacking ten hours of film down to sixty minutes.

I used to visit him in an editing studio in Old Compton Street, Soho, up some stairs above a dodgy club. Outside there was often a drunken old tramp with carnations behind his ears who did a funny dance on the pavement. Paul was amused and would invite him upstairs – which led to more delays as they couldn't get rid of him. His party piece was 'Bless 'Em All', with obscene words substituted.

At the time, watching Paul directing the film – which in essence he did – and then editing it, I thought it amazing that this young lad, with no training in film technique, was working it all out for himself, doing it his way. They'd done the same thing with music: composing songs without being able to read or write a note of music, and making records before they had any studio experience. This was their philosophy: you could do these things, if you really wanted. There was no need to follow the rules or be bossed around. A very modern concept. Of course, it helped that by this time they were multi-millionaires who had already made their mark in the music business.

The film was sold to the BBC for £10,000 and broadcast on Boxing Day, shoe-horned between a Petula Clark show and a Norman Wisdom film. It was well and truly slaughtered by the critics. The *Daily Express* declared it 'blatant rubbish'. Paul went on *The David Frost Show* next day to apologize, saying he had goofed, which I thought was slightly craven.

I think one reason for the criticism was that, after five years of Beatlemania, worldwide adulation, being hailed as the best-known people on the planet, bla-

bla, many in the media were looking for a chance to take them down a peg or two, especially when they appeared to be condoning drugs.

They should have worked harder on the script beforehand, planned all the scenes in advance, but the idea was to make it spontaneous, provide family amusement over the festive season. As a Beatles fan, then and now, I enjoyed it. It was a modest, short film, done on a budget. I couldn't see why the clever-clogs critics were so beastly.

The BBC's internal Audience Research Report for Tuesday, 26 December 1967 reported that 25 per cent of the population of the UK had watched it – but alas the majority had not enjoyed it. Comments from viewers included: 'The biggest waste of public money since the Ground Nut Scheme', 'A load of RUBBISH. We have made better home movies ourselves', 'I found it unspeakably tiresome and not the least bit funny – but perhaps this is "sick" humour in which case I am emphatically not "with it".' However, the songs were said to be the only redeeming feature.

The songs, such as 'I Am The Walrus', have survived the test of time (despite Russell Brand mucking it up at the 2012 London Olympics). The way the songs were shot as self-contained little rock videos was ahead of its time. Over the decades, the film has acquired a bit of a cult following. It has improved with age, as we all do, tra la …

Magical Mystery Tour

Six of the numbers from the film came out in the UK as a double EP, which was accompanied by a twenty-eight-page booklet with stills from the film, the lyrics of five* of the songs and a synopsis of the plot, written and drawn as a children's comic. It was a neat little production.

'Magical Mystery Tour', the introductory number, didn't really have much in the way of lyrics. More a list of clichés and exhortations, inviting punters to join the tour. And that was how the lyrics were first written, with Paul asking anyone around to shout out likely lines. They had tried to buy some mystery tour posters, so they could get the genuine words, but when Mal Evans was sent out on an expedition to find some, he came back empty-handed. It seemed there weren't any mystery bus tours any more, at least in London and the South. So this first track is really just a list, telling you to roll up, make a reservation, satisfaction guaranteed, with Sergeant Pepper-type brass band music. I described the recording of the song in the biography.

---

* NB five songs, not six. One of the tracks, 'Flying', was an instrumental.

When the Beatles arrived at the EMI studios at seven thirty one evening to record 'Magical Mystery Tour', all they had was the title and a few bars of the music.

There was the usual crowd of fans waiting for them as they went in. Not screaming. Just quiet and contrite, like humble subjects subdued by the Presence. As they went in, one girl very shyly gave George a button badge that said 'GEORGE FOR P. M.'

'Why wouldn't Paul McCartney want you?' said John to George.

Paul played the opening bars of 'Magical Mystery Tour' on the piano, showing the others how it would go. He gestured a lot with his hands and shouted Flash, Flash, saying it would be like a commercial. John was wearing an orange cardigan, purple velvet trousers, and a sporran. He opened the sporran and took out some pot, which he lit, then passed around. They all had a drag. Someone shouted that Anthony, John's chauffeur, wanted him on the phone.

They leaned round the piano while Paul was playing, going over and over the opening. Paul told Mal to write down the order of how they would do the song. In a very slow schoolboy hand, Mal wrote down the title and got ready for Paul's instructions. Paul said Trumpets, yes they'd have some trumpets at the beginning, a sort of fanfare, to go with 'Roll Up, Roll Up, for the Magical Mystery Tour.' Mal had better write that line down as well, as it was the only line they had. Paul told Mal to write down DAE, the first three chords of the song. Mal sucked his pencil, waiting for more of Paul's inspired words, but nothing came.

The instruments were then set up and they got ready to record the backing, which as usual was to be the first track they would do. John came back and asked Mal if he'd got in touch with Terry yet. Mal said he couldn't get through to him. John said it was his job to get through. Just keep on until he did.

It took a couple of hours to work out the first backing track and get it recorded. After it was done, Paul went up to see George Martin in the control room. Paul had the track played back to him, again and again. Below, in the studio, while Paul got the technicians to do things upstairs, George got a set of crayons out of his sheepskin painted waistcoat jacket and started to draw a picture.

Ringo stared into space, smoking, looking very unhappy, which is his natural expression when he's not talking. John was at the piano, sometimes playing quietly, other times jumping up, pretending to be a spastic, or thumping out loud corny tunes. No one was watching him. He smiled fiendishly to himself through his spectacles, like a Japanese gnome. Neil was reading a pile of occult weeklies which they'd all been thumbing through earlier in the evening. Mal had disappeared.

Paul was at last satisfied with the sound of the first track. He came back down and said he thought they could now add a few more things to it.

Mal reappeared carrying a big brown paper bag full of socks, all in bright self-colours. He passed the bag to John first. He grabbed it in great delight. He chose several pairs of orange terry-towelling socks, then passed the bag around for the others to have a dip. The night before he had said, just in passing, 'Socks, Mal.'

After the socks had been handed out, Paul asked Mal if he'd managed to get any real mystery-tour posters. Mal said he had been round the bus stations all day looking for them. But he couldn't find any. They had hoped that some real posters would have given them some ideas for the words of the song. Instead they all tried again to think of some good words apart from 'Roll up, roll up,' which was still all they had.

As they shouted ideas, Mal wrote them all down. 'Reservation,' 'Invitation,' 'Trip of a lifetime,' 'Satisfaction guaranteed.' But they soon got fed up. They decided they would just sing any words that came into their heads, just to see what happened. So they did.

When they'd finished that, Paul decided that on the next track he would add a bit of bass to the backing. He put on the headphones, so he could hear what they'd done so far, and strapped on his bass guitar. After that he said they should add even more instruments. All of them, Paul, Ringo, John, George, Neil, and Mal, then picked up any old instruments that were lying around – maracas, bells, tambourines. They put on head-phones and banged and played to the music.

By two o'clock they had recorded a basic backing and had layered onto it a bass track, a lot of shouting and disjointed words and some percussion instruments. The 'Magical Mystery Tour' was then forgotten about for almost six months.

Your Mother Should Know

Having recorded the introductory song, they then took a break for about four months, before recording the second track. This one doesn't have much in the way of lyrics either, apart from inviting everyone to get up and dance to a song your mother should know. Musically, there is no middle eight, the whole thing consists of a chorus – and very nice it is too, a pastiche of the sort of songs Paul's family used to sing and dance to around the piano at Christmas time. It looked good in the accompanying film with the four Beatles in white suits descending a staircase to be joined by a team of dancers. Even John seemed to be enjoying himself.

Paul wrote it in Cavendish Avenue at a time when some of his relations were staying with him, playing it on a harmonium while they listened in the next room. It's Paul having one foot in real life, able to be psychedelic and multi-layered and use Indian instruments, and the other foot in the past, able to commune with all generations.

I Am The Walrus

John's contribution to *Magical Mystery Tour* could not be more different – another of the stream-of-consciousness nonsense he wrote in his poems and letters, stuff that he never thought, back in 1962, he would ever get away with in a pop song. And yet it is in some ways just as nostalgic as Paul's efforts.

Many of the lines are straight pinches from his childhood, all of them still totally familiar to me, though probably not to most people under the age of fifty. In British school playgrounds in the fifties, we used to recite a poem that went 'yellow matter custard'; another playground favourite was 'umpa umpa, stick it up your jumpa', which John can be heard chanting at the end of the song. Other influences are clearly Edward Lear's nonsense and *Alice in Wonderland*.

I was with John when the first stirrings of the song came to him. It was the day I arrived to find he wasn't talking, but while we were swimming in the pool the sound of a police car sparked off a rhythm in his head. He later started putting words to the rythmn: 'Mist-er Cit-ee police-man sitting pretty'. In 1968 he told interviewer Jonathan Cott about it: 'I had this idea of doing a song that was a police siren, but it didn't work in the end [sings like a siren] 'I-am-he-as-you-are-he-as …' You couldn't really sing the police siren.'

He ended up with three scraps of songs which were eventually put together and the lyrics completed. According to Pete Shotton, it was the arrival of a letter from Quarry Bank schoolboy Stephen Bailey telling him that the lyrics to *Sgt. Pepper* were now being analysed by school teachers and academics, that prompted John to include some of the dafter phrases in 'I Am The Walrus': 'Let the fuckers work that one out' so he said to Pete.

The words have indeed been heavily analysed over the years. The reference to pigs in a sty has led some to interpret it as an anti-capitalist rant, which John said was never his intention. Others have claimed it is anti-education, because he mocks the 'expert texperts' who made snide remarks while he was crying by asking who is the joker now, i.e. who's having the last laugh. That was one of John's pet themes: he always felt his teachers were against him and did not recognize his brilliance.

But even nonsense words have to come from somewhere, there must have been a thought process that threw them up. John admitted that he was thinking of Allen Ginsberg when he wrote 'elementary penguin singing Hare Krishna', as Ginsberg used to chant it at his performances.

While John was working on the final version, before going into the recording studio, I misheard the line 'waiting for the man to come'. It sounded to me like 'waiting for the van to come', which I told him was a phrase from my school days, when someone thought to be potty or mad would be told that a van would come and take them away. John liked the image and so changed man into van.

Some words are made up, such as crabalocker, which sounds connected with fishwife. I like the idea 'how they snied'; was he picturing pigs making snide comments? Semolina and pilchards were foods from the fifties that we all hated.

The walrus came from Lewis Carroll's 'The Walrus and the Carpenter' – though John at the time had not realized that the walrus was the bad guy, so it should have been 'I am the carpenter'.

I only recently heard of a possible explanation for the eggmen. Eric Burdon, leader of the Animals, with whom John had shared a few wild parties, supposedly enjoyed breaking an egg on the naked body of a girl.

The music caught the surrealist feeling of the words, with a swirling crescendo of sounds, from rock to classical orchestra music, a chorus of backing singers and backdrop of people talking.

The manuscript, in John's hand, has some changes: 'pornographic policeman' became' pornographic priestess', 'through a dead dog's eye' became 'from a dead dog's eye' and 'you been a lucky girl, you let your knickers down' became 'you been a naughty girl'. It was not officially banned by the BBC, for they allowed the song to be included in the Magical Mystery Tour film, but on November 27th 1967, the Controller of BBC1 issued an internal memo saying it contained "a very offensive passage" and the record itself could not be played on radio or TV, which included programmes such as *Top of the Pops* and *Juke Box Jury*. 'Other possible outlets are similarly blocked off.'

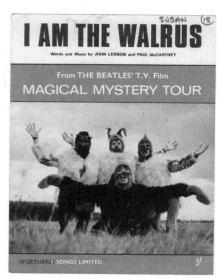

I am he
as you are he
as you are me
and we are all together.
See how they run
like pigs from a gun
see how they fly. I'm crying.

Sitting on a cornflake, waiting for the
   van to come.
Corporation tee-shirt, stupid bloody
   Tuesday,
man, you been a naughty boy, you let

your face grow long.
I am the eggman, oh, they are the eggmen –
Oh, I am the walrus GOO GOO G'JOOB.

Mr City, policeman sitting pretty little policemen in a row,
see how they fly
like Lucy in the sky
see how they run. I'm crying – I'm crying.
I'm crying – I'm crying.

Yellow matter custard dripping from a dead dog's eye.
Crabalocker fishwife, pornographic priestess,
Boy, you been a naughty girl you let your knickers down.
I am the eggman, oh, they are the eggmen –
Oh, I am the walrus, GOO GOO G'JOOB.

Sitting in an English garden waiting for the sun,
if the sun don't come, you get a tan from
standing in the English rain.
I am the eggman, oh, they are the eggmen –
Oh, I am the walrus, G'JOOB, G'GOO, G'JOOB …

Expert texpert choking smokers,
Don't you think the joker laughs at you? Ha ha ha!
See how they smile
like pigs in a sty,
see how they snied. I'm crying.

Semolina pilchard, climbing up the Eiffel Tower.
Elementary penguin singing Hare Krishna
man, you should have seen them
kicking Edgar Allan Poe.
I am the eggman, oh, they are the eggmen. –
Oh, I am the walrus GOO GOO GOO JOOB
GOO GOO GOO JOOB GOO GOO
GOOOOOOOOOJOOOOOOOOOB.

I am he as you are he as you are me and we are all together.
see how they run like pigs from a gun
see how they fly. – I'm crying.

Sitting on a cornflake, waiting for the van to come.
corporation teashirt stupid bloody tuesday man you
been a naughty boy you let your face grow long
I am the eggman – they are the eggmen –
I am the walrus – Goo Goo Joob.

Mr city policeman sitting pretty little policeman
see how they fly like lucy in the sky,
see how they run. – I'm crying – I'm crying I'm crying.
yellow matter custard, through a dead dog's eye
crabalocker fishwife pornographic policeman boy
you been a lucky girl you let your knickers down
I am the eggman – they are the eggmen
I am the walrus – Goo Goo Joob.
        Sitting in an english garden
        waiting for the sun
        if you get a tan from
        don't the english rain.

*'I Am The Walrus',
from the* Magical
Mystery Tour *EP,
December 1967, in
John's hand. The
'lucky girl you let your
knickers down', seven
lines from the end,
became 'naughty girl'.
And I should think
so, too.*

The Fool On The Hill

This was the song I heard Paul playing to John while they were working on 'With A Little Help From My Friends'. Paul has since said he might have been thinking of a maharishi – but he could not have been thinking of Maharishi Mahesh Yogi, as they did not meet him until August 1967 and the song, with most of the words, had been written in March. So it was a guru figure in general that had come into his mind, a foolish savant, the sort who sits on a hill or in a cave and people think he is either very wise or very foolish. Paul, looking back, remembered that he enjoyed singing 'perfectly still'. Another example of how composers, like novelists, are often sparked off or fall in love with a particular word or phrase.

Alistair Taylor, a friend of theirs who worked at NEMS, remembers walking with Paul one morning at daybreak on Primrose Hill and coming across a man who one minute seemed to be there and the next disappeared – which fascinated Paul, making him wonder who the man had been. The music, complete with flutes and fairground roundabout noises, does have a spinning, ethereal quality to it.

The lyrics are well worked – the idea of a man with a thousand voices whom nobody hears, with eyes in his head that see the world spinning round. But he gives us no clue to the fool's identity.

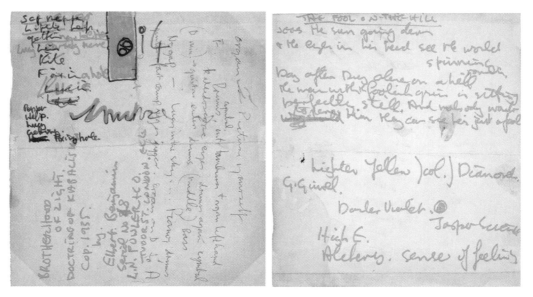

'The Fool On The Hill', from Magical Mystery Tour, *with the reverse side (left) containing a* line-up for Sgt. Pepper, *and other notes and lists. The orange handwriting appears to be John's and the blue Paul's.*

In the first manuscript (one of mine, now in the British Library), there are only the first few lines, but on the reverse are some interesting notes, such as a list of *Sgt. Pepper* titles. I shalll leave the experts to work out the rest. In the second – on Hotel Negresco notepaper – the fool is sitting perfectly still, then gets changed to 'keeping perfectly still'.

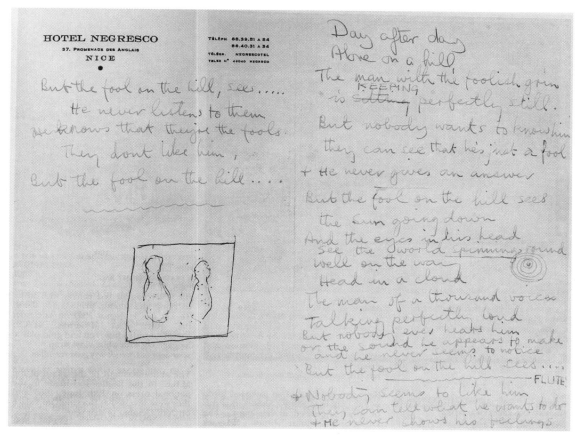

Day after day, alone on a hill,
The man with the foolish grin is keeping perfectly still
But nobody wants to know him,
They can see that he's just a fool,
And he never gives an answer,

But the fool on the hill sees the sun going down,
And the eyes in his head see the world spinning round.

Well on the way, head in a cloud,
The man of a thousand voices talking perfectly loud

Another version of 'The Fool on the Hill', written on hotel notepaper from Nice, mainly in Paul's hand.

But nobody ever hears him,
or the sound he appears to make,
and he never seems to notice,

And nobody seems to like him,
they can tell what he wants to do,
and he never shows his feelings,

Oh, oh,
'Round and 'round and 'round.

He never listens to them,
He knows that they're the fools
They don't like him,

The fool on the hill sees the sun going down,
And the eyes in his head see the world spinning 'round.

Ooh,
'Round and 'round and 'round

Blue Jay Way

George wrote this in Los Angeles, having just arrived. The Beatles' friend
and one-time PR Derek Taylor, who was then working in LA as a publicist,
was supposed to meet him but he'd got lost in the fog. So while he waited for
Derek to arrive, George amused himself by sitting at a small Hammond organ
and writing a song. 'By the time I got there, the song was practically intact,'
said Derek later. 'At the time I felt very bad, being two hours late.'

Some people have imagined that George was making a complicated pun
out of 'don't be long'/'don't belong' – i.e. don't take part in society – and that the
phrase 'lost their way' meant lost their way in life, not just on a foggy road. But
there were no messages. The lyrics are about what they say they are about.

I used to have the original manuscript, which George let me have while
I was doing the biography, but some years later he asked for it back in order
to include it in his book *I Me Mine*. There are an extra four lines at the end,
beginning 'When I see you at the door' presumably part of the original, which
were not used in the recorded version.

There's a fog upon L. A.
And my friends have lost their way
We'll be over soon they said
Now they've lost themselves instead.

Please don't be long
Please don't you be very long
Please don't be long
For I may be asleep

well it may go to show
And I told them where to go
Ask a policeman on the street
There's so many there to
    meet.

Please don't be long
Please don't you be very long
Please don't be long
For I may be asleep.

Now it's past my bed I know
And I'd really like to go
Soon will be the break of day
Sitting here in Blue Jay Way.

Please don't be long
Please don't you be very long
Please don't be long

'Blue Jay Way', from Magical Mystery Tour, *in George's hand – with four extra lines at the end, not used.*

All You Need Is Love

Before *Magical Mystery Tour* came out, they produced a single in July 1967 which was their contribution to a landmark in television history. The Beatles had been approached by the BBC to take part in the biggest live television programme ever, a global event linking twenty-six countries, with contributions from Europe, the Americas, Africa, Japan and Australia. Technologically, it was a massive undertaking, especially at that time. As a publicity tool, with global reach, it was also a good move for the Beatles, though they didn't really need it, considering they were known throughout the world already. Brian Epstein, who was still alive at the time (he died a month later) certainly thought so. After a long absence from the recording studio he suddenly appeared in publicity shots taken at rehearsals for the programme, sitting adoringly with his boys.

John also thought it was a good idea. He liked the challenge of creating a simple song with words and music that would be easily understood by all nationalities, all cultures. And he liked the idea of creating a slogan, a song with a simple message.

Both John and Paul went off to think of suitable ideas – but it was John's 'All You Need Is Love' that surfaced first and was chosen.

The global TV broadcast was aired live on 25 June 1967, with the Beatles in colourful clothes surrounded by their celebrity friends, including Mick Jagger, Marianne Faithfull and Eric Clapton, who all joined in with the chorus and held up balloons and placards. The broadcast was transmitted in black and white – this was, after all, 1967 – so the full effect of the colourful clobber was rather wasted.

On a personal note, most references books that list the personal guests of the Beatles present include moi. When I first saw this, I rushed to my diary for 25 June 1967 and for some reason it was blank. In the months before and afterwards, I have lots of entries for Abbey Road, or Paul's house, indicating I was watching them compose and record, but nothing for that evening. So was I there? The awful thing is, I really can't remember. I have looked for myself on the video, but quite a lot of people at that time looked like me. I now imagine I was there, because the event is so well known. Or perhaps I was just at the rehearsals.

George Martin did a great job on the musical special effects, beginning with the 'Marseillaise', to give it an international flavour, and it ends with bursts of 'Greensleeves', 'In the Mood' and 'She Loves You'. It's a jolly, rousing, happy-clappy cheerful song with a good, catchy title – but what about the lyrics? Hmm. There is a lot of repetition of 'All you need is love', plus eight clever-sounding lines where John gets carried away with the notion that there's nothing/nobody/nowhere you can't sing/make/see/be. Paul later said there were some lines in the lyrics he did not understand – presumably one of those lines. Is it true there's nothing you can make that can't be made? Science is continually discovering things we didn't know – though I suppose you could say that God knew about them all the time, being awfully clever. And is there nowhere you can be you where you were not meant to be? I suppose so, if you believe in Fate.

All the same, the basic message is clear: you can do anything you want, if you want to – a philosophy which is still very fashionable today. And of course love conquers everything, love is what matters, love is all, etc, which was the Beatles message in 'The Word' and elsewhere.

I once asked John about the title, 'All You Need Is Love', and he pointed out a detail I had overlooked: it can be taken in two ways. At one level it means that love is the most important thing in the world, but it can also mean that love is the one thing you are lacking, the thing you haven't got.

The love in 'All You Need Is Love' is a different, more universal, abstract concept than the love in 'She Loves You' and most of their early songs.

The manuscript is a neat version in John's hand of those 'There's nothing you can do …' lines, which he used as a crib in the studio. Perhaps in case he got the negatives in the wrong place. It was sold at auction in 2005 for $1 million.

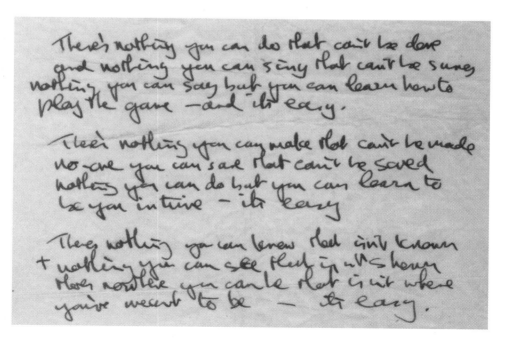

'All You Need Is Love' single, July 1967, in John's awfully neat handwriting. All you need to buy it now would be $1 million, plus …

Love, Love, Love.

There's nothing you can do that can't be done.
Nothing you can sing that can't be sung.
Nothing you can say but you can learn how to play the game.
And it's easy.

Nothing you can make that can't be made.
No one you can save that can't be saved.
Nothing you can do but you can learn how to be you in time.
It's easy.

All you need is love.
All you need is love.
All you need is love, love.
Love is all you need.

Nothing you can know that isn't known.
Nothing you can see that isn't shown.
Nowhere you can be that isn't where you're meant to be.
It's easy.

All you need is love (All together, now!)
All you need is love. (Everybody!)
All you need is love, love.
Love is all you need (love is all you need)
(love is all you need) (love is all you need)
(love is all you need) Yesterday (love is all you need)
(love is all you need) (love is all you need)

Yee-hai!
Oh yeah!
love is all you need, love is all you need, love is all you need,
    love is all you need, oh yeah oh hell yea! love is all you need
    love is all you need love is all you need.

Baby You're A Rich Man

This was the B side of 'All You Need Is Love', released 7 July 1967. It didn't appear on the *Yellow Submarine* LP (as 'All You Need Is Love' did). It is a bit of a mess and shows signs of over-confidence and under-achievement.

It began as two different songs that then got lumped together. John was responsible for 'How does it feel to be one of the beautiful people', while Paul's contribution was 'Baby you're a rich man'. Two different and incomplete sets of verses, with not much to connect them, and neither John nor Paul really worked hard enough to improve them.

The Beautiful People, self-titled, were the affluent Californian hippies with beads and flowers, supposedly all doped up in San Francisco's Haight Ashbury district, who were being written about in all the newspapers. A week or so before the recording, John was present at The 14-Hour Technicolor Dream, an all-night festival held at Alexandra Palace in north London, where Britain's version of the Beautiful People turned up, tuned in, turned on. John, presumably, was mocking the use of the phrase, and their lifestyle – but the hippies loved the song.

Paul is thought to have been mocking Brian Epstein with 'Baby you're a rich man', as their manager had made a lot of money out of them. His line 'what a thing to do' must be one of the weakest he had ever written. The reference to a natural E is not to drugs, but the musical key – and also a pun on 'naturally'.

The first manuscript – in Mal Evans's hand – includes one line in John's final verse which wasn't used: 'How do you like to be free'.

The second manuscript – in capitals and different inks with lots of patterns – is in Paul's hand and is much more interesting, despite a few blotches and ink stains. (It is in private hands in the USA and the collector says it has never been seen before.) This version has three lines at the end which were never used: 'How do you like being free? / Happy to be that way / Changing your tune to another.'

How does it feel to be	How does it feel to be
One of the beautiful people.	One of the beautiful people.
Now that you know who you are	How often have you been there.
What do you want to be?	Often enough to know.
And have you travelled very far?	What did you see, when you were there.
Far as the eye can see.	Nothing that doesn't show.

Baby you're a rich man,
Baby you're a rich man,
Baby you're a rich man too.
You keep all your money in a big brown
   bag inside a zoo.
What a thing to do.
Baby you're a rich man,
Baby you're a rich man,

Baby you're a rich man too.

How does it feel to be
One of the beautiful people
Tuned to a natural E
Happy to be that way.
Now that you've found another key
What are you going to play

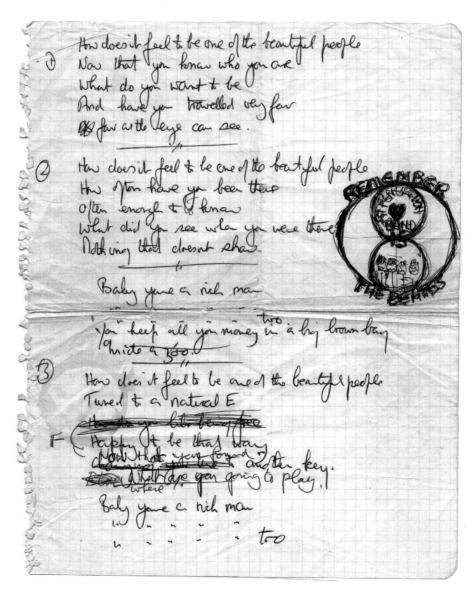

'Baby You're A Rich Man',
the B side of 'All You
Need Is Love', July 1967,
in Mal's handwriting,
includes lines not used.

'Baby You're A Rich Man', a decorated, colourful but rather inky version in Paul's hand.

Hello, Goodbye

This track was completed after the *Magical Mystery Tour*. It was not used in the film but went on the other side of 'I Am The Walrus'. Officially it was the A side, which did not please John.

It was composed as a sort of verbal exercise. Alistair Taylor remembers Paul playing it and asking him to shout out the opposite of whatever word or phrase he sang – stop and go, yes and no, hello and goodbye. The song proved very popular and stayed at number 1 in the US and UK for many weeks.

The phrase you can hear them chanting at the end – 'Hela hey aloha' – is a Hawaiian greeting and was used as a chorus in the *Magical Mystery Tour* film.

Paul has said that he was trying to illustrate duality, that things in life come in opposites, but that he personally always takes the positive side.

Lady Madonna

Paul came from an Irish Catholic family on his mother's side. Growing up in Liverpool he was surrounded by similar families, so the image and significance of the Madonna was well known to him. In this case, he has transferred it to all women, an ode to the load that women have to bare.

He has given slightly different versions of the origin of the title. In one he says that he was thinking of the Virgin Mary, which moved on to working-class women in Liverpool, then on to women everywhere. In another interview he has said that it was inspired by an issue of *National Geographic* featuring a photograph of a Polynesian woman with a child at her breast and the caption 'Mountain Madonna'.

Again the music harks back to another era, this time to fifties, boogie-woogie music – a change from all the recent psychedelic or Indian sounds. One of the tunes in his head when he started was 'Bad Penny Blues', as played by Humphrey Lyttleton. To get the right jazzy background, he hired Ronnie Scott and three other well-known saxophonists for the session. It is also a bit of a rocker. One of the many people who did a cover version was Fats Domino.

I don't remember the lyrics being hailed as feminist at the time, yet in some ways it is, protesting at the lot of women, wondering how they manage to make ends meet, listing the never-ending daily chores.

Some cynics have suggested that in this Lady Madonna is a prostitute, hence the mystery of how she finds the money to pay the rent, arriving somewhere on a Friday without a suitcase – but I am sure the Friday-morning arrival does not refer to Lady Madonna but her useless fellow, finally turning up. There is a neat pun on the use of the word 'run': when referring to a child tying his bootlace, it means normal running, but when it comes to the stockings that need mending, it means a ladder, a tear in the fabric.

It was only many years later that Paul realized, in going through the days of the week in the lyrics, that he had missed one – Saturday. And on a strictly fascinating factual note, the days of the week that receive the most mentions in Beatles lyrics are: Sunday (5), Monday and Tuesday (3), Wednesday and Friday (2) Thursday and Saturday (1). (Not counting same lines repeated in same song.)

'Lady Madonna' in Paul's handwriting, with some splodges.

Lady Madonna children at your feet
wonder how you manage to make ends meet.
Who finds the money, when you pay the rent
Did you think that money was heaven sent?
Friday night arrives without a suitcase
Sunday morning creeping like a nun
Monday's child has learned to tie his bootlace.
See how they run.
Lady Madonna baby at your breast
wonder how you manage to feed the rest.
See how they run.
Lady Madonna lying on the bed
listen to the music playing in your head.
Tuesday afternoon is never ending
Wednesday morning papers didn't come
Thursday night your stockings needed mending.
See how they run.
Lady Madonna at your feet
wonder how you manage to make ends meet.

The Inner Light

'The Inner Light' was the B side of 'Lady Madonna', released on 15 March 1968.
It was the first time a song written by George had appeared on a Beatles single
in the UK.

After 'Within You Without You', Juan Mascaro, a Sanskrit lecturer at
Cambridge University, wrote to George suggesting he should write a song
using the words from a holy book by Tao Te Ching, which he had translated.
Its theme of searching for inner light greatly appealed to George, who was still
searching for his own inner truths. In the original, the words were 'Without
going out of my door I can know the ways of heaven'. George changed it to:
'Without going out of my door, I can know all things on earth.' But in essence,
he used all the lines, though Mascaro was not credited as the lyricist on the
single.

In *I Me Mine* George reveals the background, and thanks Mascaro. He
sounds regretful that the song didn't catch on: 'I think the song went unnoticed
by most people as I was getting a bit out of it as far as Western popular music
was concerned, at that period.'

The manuscript, in George's hand, is written in capitals, the better to be understood. At the end, he has written 'Yeah – Yeah – Yeah' which I take to be a bit of self-mockery, poking fun at his seriousness.

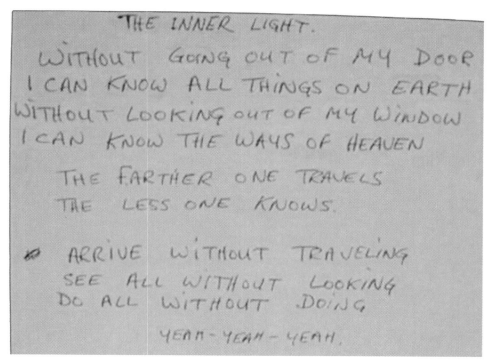

'The Inner Light', George's first Beatles single, the B side of 'Lady Madonna', March 1968, in George's hand – including his satirical 'Yeah Yeah Yeah' at the end.

Without going out of my door
I can know all things on earth
Without looking out of my window
I can know the ways of heaven

The farther one travels
The less one knows
The less one really knows

Without going out of your door
You can know all things on earth

Without looking out of your window
You can know the ways of heaven

The farther one travels
The less one knows
The less one really knows

Arrive without travelling
See all without looking
Do all without doing

Hey Jude

This began as 'Hey Jules' – meaning Julian, John's five-year-old son. Paul was driving down to see Julian and his mother, Cynthia, after John had left them for Yoko and divorce was imminent. He found himself humming along to 'Hey Jules' and then came the lines 'don't make it bad, take a sad song and make it better'.

It was typical of Paul to care about Julian. He has always had a rapport with kids, of any age, and could play with them and amuse them – unlike John, who found it harder to connect, apart from drawing with them. When Paul, along with Linda and her daughter Heather, visited us for a holiday in Portugal in 1968, my own children were constantly clamouring to play with Paul, be with him, climb all over him.

When he first played the song to John, Paul was a bit embarrassed by the line 'the movement you need is on your shoulder', as it was just a fill-in line, till he thought of something better, but John said no, it's great, go for it. Personally, I am still not sure what that line means, and probably Paul didn't either. He feared it might suggest a parrot. The best explanation is that on your shoulder is your head, and the movement is to nod, thus saying yes to the world.

In fact John got it into his head that the song was really about him – encouraging him to go off with Yoko, because of the lines 'you have found her, now go and get her' and 'you're waiting for someone to perform with'.

The verses get more complicated as they go on, progressing from a simple encouragement to cheer up, don't make it worse, then to accept things, not let people down, go out and meet the world, moving on from personal advice to guidance in general.

So while the verses repay a more careful reading, over recent years the tune itself has taken a bit of a hammering. At seven minutes and nine seconds long – a marathon, as singles went – it featured an orchestra of thirty-six classical musicians as well as the Beatles themselves. It was incredibly successful all over the world when it first came out as a single in August 1968, selling five million copies in six months, and staying at number 1 in the USA for nine weeks. It was soon being sung at public gatherings ranging from national events, pop concerts to football matches. Alas, it has become rather a cliché, in the UK anyway, with Paul being mocked for always seeming to sing it at some public event, leading and encouraging the whole audience in going 'na na na na …'

If you are listening in the flesh – and I have recently heard Paul perform it at the O2 Arena in London – it is hard not to join in and enjoy it with everyone else. But I have to admit that, if it comes on the radio when I'm at home, I usually turn off before the interminable na na nas get started.

Julian did not realize the song was about him till he was about eleven or twelve. Now, whenever he hears it by chance, in a bar or public place, he says it still makes him shiver. He managed to buy a copy of the manuscript – with Paul's instructions on it – when it was sold at auction in 1996 for $40,000. But several versions of the manuscript have since appeared – some of the verses in the handwriting of Mal Evans.

This manuscript in Paul's hand has a couple of variations. In the twelfth line he is undecided between making his life or his world a little colder. Two lines on, 'She had found you now make it better' became 'You have found her now go and get her.' For some reason, the last eight lines are missing. Did he struggle to come up with them, leaving it until they were in the studio? Or were they written on another page?

'Hey Jude' single, August 1968, in Paul's hand. Eight lines from the end, he is undecided about whether his life or his world will be a little colder.

Hey Jude, don't make it bad
Take a sad song and make it better
Remember to let her into your heart
Then you can start to make it better

Hey Jude, don't be afraid
You were made to go out and get her
The minute you let her under your skin
Then you begin to make it better

And anytime you feel the pain, hey Jude, refrain
Don't carry the world upon your shoulders
For well you know that it's a fool who plays it cool
By making his world a little colder
Nah nah nah nah nah nah nah nah nah

Hey Jude, don't let me down
she had found you, now make it better
Remember to let her into your heart
Then you can start to make it better

So let it out and let it in, hey Jude, begin
You're waiting for someone to perform with
And don't you know that it's just you, hey Jude, you'll do

The movement you need is on your shoulder
Nah nahnah nah nah nah nah nah nah yeah

Hey Jude, don't make it bad
Take a sad song and make it better
Remember to let her under your skin
Then you'll begin to make it
Better better better better better better, oh
Nah nah nah nah nah nah, nah nah nah, hey Jude, etc

Revolution

The first version of 'Revolution' to be released was on the B side of 'Hey Jude'. There were two released versions in all. John wrestled with it for a long time, musically and lyrically, aided and abetted by Yoko, his new best friend, and with not a lot of help from Paul, who appears not to have been so keen on it.

The lyrics were attacked by the extreme left who did not agree with John's view that destruction – i.e. violent action – was not the answer, nor going around carrying photos of Chairman Mao. And if they were wanting money, they would have to wait. After he started speaking out about the Vietnam War and working with Yoko for peace, loads of organizations and action groups began asking him for donations. He did, however, give a lot of money away, and attended several rallies.

The final message of the song, that it was 'going to be alright' also infuriated die-hard revolutionaries who felt John had sold out and was just another rich pop star.

John himself seems to have been ambivalent about what he actually thought. He was against the Vietnam War, and against war in general, but he was also against violent action, which upset the revolutionaries, particularly in the USA. On the single version – which is a fairly fast rocker – he asked to be counted out when it came to destruction. On the album version, which is slower, the lyrics of 'Revolution 1' are identical except for one additional word: he states his position as both 'out/in'. ('Revolution 9', was a long, mainly instrumental number, with no real lyrics, so does not concern us here.)

The manuscript is half typed and half written in John's hand. It includes the line that caused a lot of ill feeling in the underground press when the single was released: 'Don't you know that you can count me out.'

You say you want a revolution
Well, you know
We all want to change the world
You tell me that it's evolution
Well, you know
We all want to change the world
But when you talk about destruction
Don't you know you can count me out

Don't you know it's gonna be alright
Alright, alright

You say you got a real solution
Well, you know
We don't love to see the plan
You ask me for a contribution
Well, you know
We're doing what we can
But if you want money for people with
   minds that hate
Well, all I can tell you is brother you
   have to wait

You say you want a revolution
Well, you know we all want to change the world
Tell tell me that it's evolution
Well, you know we all want to change the world
But when you talk about destruction
Don't you know that you can count me out

Don't you know it's going to be alright. etc.

You say you got a real solution
Well, you know we'd all love to see the plan
You ask me for a contribution
Well, you know we're all doing what we can
But if you want money for people with minds that hate
Well, all I can tell you is brother you have to wait

Don't you know it's going to be alright, etc.

'Revolution', the B side of 'Hey Jude', August 1968. The handwriting is John's and the typing could be, as he could type, but not usually as neatly as this. In line six he clearly says 'count me out'. In a later recording he became ambivalent, making it 'count me out-in'.

Don't you know it's gonna be alright
Alright, alright, al…

You say you'll change the constitution
Well you know
We all want to change your head
You tell me it's the institution
Well you know

You better free your mind instead
But if you go carrying pictures of
   Chairman Mao
You ain't going to make it with anyone
   anyhow

Don't you know it's gonna be alright
Alright, alright

11

THE WHITE ALBUM

November 1968

The Beatles with Maharishi on the train in 1967: (left to right) Hunter Davies, Paul, Ringo, John, Maharishi, George.

The Beatles had first met Maharishi Mahesh Yogi at the Hilton Hotel in London on 24 August 1967. The next day they went off to Bangor in North Wales to meet him again. I went up with them on the train – sitting with the four Beatles in their colourful finery, along with Mick Jagger and Marianne Faithfull. They been given their mantra by the Maharishi and joined in his Transcendental Meditation meetings. It was this same weekend, while we were still in Bangor, that news came through of the death in London of Brian Epstein. Not suicide – although he had made an earlier attempt – but an accidental overdose of drugs.

While Brian had ceased to play a vital role in their lives, they had lost someone who had in some senses been a spiritual leader, who had always believed in them and loved them, guided them at a vital stage in their development. In the Maharishi they found, for a while, another spiritual leader. Of a different sort.

In February 1968 all four of the Beatles, plus wives and, in the case of Paul, his fiancée Jane Asher, went out to India. At this stage, although John had met Yoko, he was still officially with Cynthia, and she accompanied him. They all went to stay and study at Rishikesh, away from the media circus that had surrounded them for the last five years.

It brought them together, whereas in London various petty squabbles had been tearing them apart, and it removed them from boring business meetings and worries. It also reduced their individual egos, as they were supposed to be thinking of higher things. It confirmed George as the most influential figure, as he was the most knowledgeable and devoted and spiritual. But probably the greatest effect of the Indian trip was in their music.

They had a lot of free time to play and think and be with each other, and the result was that they returned to their former methods of songwriting – instead of being holed up in their individual mansions or stuck in a studio with a deadline and the latest electronic wizardry, they were able to sit around with their acoustic guitars, making music.

Ringo and his wife Maureen returned first – he missed some of the essentials of his life back at home, such as baked beans. John wrote him a postcard: 'Just a little vibration from India. We've got about two LPs worth of songs now so get your drums out.'

Two LPs! That suggested something in the region of thirty songs, since the standard LP at that time had about fourteen songs. All that, in just the few weeks they had been in India? It turned out not to be an exaggeration. John and Paul, while out in India,* had indeed worked on at least thirty new songs. Not all of these appeared on their next record – probably about half made it – and not all were completed, but they came home very excited, keen to start work again and knock their new creations into shape. They decided to keep it fairly simple, not as elaborate or as way-out as some of their songs on *Sgt. Pepper*. A return, in many ways, to simple songwriting.

The album – their ninth, and the first to appear on their own Apple Records label - turned out to be a whopper. They had so many ideas, so many songs, that it became a double album – two whole records, with twenty-eight new songs in all. It took them almost six months to record – from May to October 1968 – and during this time various difficulties began to emerge between the four of them. Sources of conflict included Yoko's influence over John, and problems with Apple, their new company, and all its various bits (some of them fairly mad and eccentric). Even the normally placid George

---

* In the end, Paul stayed six weeks, John and George about two months.

Martin began to get fed up with them and their demands.

The album was at first going to be called 'A Doll's House', until they discovered another rock group, Family, were calling their latest album *Music in a Doll's House* (it came out while the Beatles were still recording).

After all that jazzy, snazzy, busy, fizzy, colourful packaging of *Sgt. Pepper*, the album cover this time was minimalistic – all white, front and back, with no photos, no printed lettering. A blank cover, in fact. Each record was numbered, like a collector's edition. (The numbers stopped in 1969 – the highest known number being 3,116,706.)

The album was actually called *The Beatles*, but this was so discreet, embossed so subtlety, that it was easy to miss. Most people, then and now, called it *The White Album* or perhaps *The Double White Album*. Referring to it as *The Beatles*, its official title, was too confusing.

Tucked inside the sleeve was a large sheet with photos on one side, including one of John in bed with Yoko. By the time the album came out – on 22 November 1968 – John had left Cynthia and was living with Yoko. They were also making records together, *Two Virgins* being the first, as well as becoming involved in various other excitements of an artistic nature.

The other side of the sheet contained all the words of all the lyrics, a practice they'd started on *Sgt. Pepper*. Hurrah for that. Such a help, then and now, for all fans and for all lyricalists. Is there such a word? Definitely a species.

Back In The USSR

It still makes me smile, after all these years, one of the wittiest songs they ever did. The fun – well, I think it's funny – is that it sounds just like an American rock song, sung in an American accent, but it's about the USSR. Which of course does not exist now, so young people today might not get it. It's a pastiche, in both words and in music: not an easy trick to pull off.

It was one of fifteen songs that Paul wrote in Rishikesh, and was inspired by a suggestion from Mike Love of the Beach Boys, so he has claimed (Mike was also in India, along with the singer Donovan). The idea was to do a version of Chuck Berry's 'Back in the USA' but set it all in the USSR. There were also hints of the Beach Boys own song 'Surfin' USA'.

Some right-wingers in the USA did not get the joke. Russia was their deadly enemy, backing the baddies in the Vietnam War, and thousands were being killed, so the Beatles were accused of being Communists. These right-wingers did not seem to realize that in the USSR, the Fab Four were considered by the Communist Party as being capitalist lackeys.

When I visited the USSR in 1988, still under Communism, every young person I met knew the words of every song – and of course one of their faves was 'Back in the USSR', getting the jokes many Americans had missed. (I discovered that they had all read my biography of the band as well – not officially but in dissident samizdat versions, duplicated and passed around.) Today, the Russians remain passionate Beatles fans. There have recently been academics, in the USA and the USSR, who have written learned articles arguing that it was the influence of the Beatles that helped bring down the USSR.

'Back In The USSR', from The White Album *(officially* The Beatles*), November 1968, in Paul's hand.*

The record starts with a sound of an aeroplane, which was a bit confusing, for the first number on a brand-new album when you didn't know what was coming. This was to let us know our Russki hero was arriving back from the USA, looking forward to the delights of Ukraine and Moscow girls. It was a change to have a song that mentioned Russian places as opposed to the endless references to California. 'Georgia's always on my mind' still works, in both the USA and Russian worlds, though the reference to BOAC (a British airline which eventually landed for good) is now meaningless.

During the recording session, Paul and Ringo fell out. Ringo had increasingly felt he was being marginalized, ever since the touring stopped and their work became entirely studio based. On this occasion he got upset when Paul criticized his drumming. He said he was leaving the Beatles, and went off on holiday on Peter Sellers' yacht in the Med. Paul therefore played drums and piano on 'Back In The USSR' as well as singing. He might even have made the aeroplane noises – he is multi-talented.

Ringo did come back, two weeks later, and found his drum kit wreathed in flowers and a banner saying Welcome Back.

The manuscript has turned up in two versions. One is in capitals written by Mal, and one in Paul's flowing handwriting, both clean versions, except for a couple of corrections.

Flew in from Miami Beach BOAC
Didn't get to bed last night
On the way the paper bag was on my
    knee
Man, I had a dreadful flight
I'm back in the USSR
You don't know how lucky you are, boy
Back in the USSR

Been away so long I hardly knew the
    place
Gee, it's good to be back home
Leave it till tomorrow to unpack my
    case
Honey disconnect the phone
I'm back in the USSR
You don't know how lucky you are, boy
Back in the US

Back in the US
Back in the USSR
Well the Ukraine girls really knock
    me out
They leave the west behind
And Moscow girls make me sing and
    shout
That Georgia's always on my my my my
    my my my my mind
Oh, come on
Hu hey hu, hey, ah, yeah
Yeah, yeah, yeah
I'm back in the USSR
You don't know how lucky you are, boys
Back in the USSR

Oh, show me round your snow peaked
Mountains way down south
Take me to your daddy's farm
Let me hear your balalaika's ringing out
Come and keep your comrade warm
I'm back in the USSR
Hey, you don't know how lucky you are, boy
Back in the USSR

FLEWIN FROM MIAMI BEACH BOAC
DIDNT GET TO BED LAST NIGHT
ON THE WAY THE PAPER BAG WAS ON MY KNEE
MAN I HAD A DREADFUL FLIGHT
I'M BACK IN THE USSR
YOU DON'T KNOW HOW LUCKY YOU ARE BOY
BACK IN THE USSR.

BEEN AWAY SO LONG I HARDLY KNEW THE PLACE
GEE IT'S GOOD TO BE BACK HOME
LEAVE IT TILL TOMORROW TO UNPACK MY CASE
HONEY DISCONNECT THE PHONE
I'M BACK IN THE USSR
YOU DON'T KNOW HOW LUCKY YOU ARE BOY
BACK IN THE USSR

WELL THE UKRAINE GIRLS REALLY KNOCK ME OUT
THE LEAVE THE WEST BEHIND
AND MOSCOW GIRLS MAKE ME SING AND SHOUT
THAT GEORGIA'S ALWAYS ON MY MMM MIND
SHOW ME ROUND YOUR SNOW
I'M BACK IN THE USSR
YOU DON'T KNOW HOW LUCKY YOU ARE BOY
BACK IN THE USSR.

SHOW ME ROUND YOUR SNOW PEAKED MOUNTAINS
                            WAY DOWN SOUTH
TAKE ME TO YOUR DADDYS FARM
LET ME HEAR YOUR BALALAIKA WIRING OUT
(WHILE BIG FAT FANNY KEEPS ME WARM.)
I'M BACK IN THE USSR
YOU DON'T KNOW HOW LUCKY YOU ARE BOY
BACK IN THE USSR.

Another version of 'Back In The USSR', written out possibly by Mal Evans, with four lines from the end, a rather rude line which for some reason didn't make it. (Or it could have been a complicated reference to a song John liked at the time, 'Short Fat Fannie' by Larry Williams.)

Dear Prudence

Prudence was Prudence Farrow, sister of Mia, which indicates that they were not cut off totally from the celeb world in their little commune in Rishikesh. Prudence was a true believer – overmuch so, thought John. She was so busy meditating that she could not come and play with the rest of them. In fact, he thought she was going a bit barmy. The words and music are a soft, gentle, melodic attempt to encourage her to come out, to greet the brand-new day. The music is beautiful, John's voice very sensitive, but the lyrics hardly move forward, repeating the same theme – come out and smile. 'The clouds will be a daisy chain' is a nice childlike image.

Only one copy of the manuscript exists – in John's hand, small and neat – and is easy to read, though with some lines slightly different.

'Dear Prudence', from The White Album, *November 1968, in John's neat hand.*

Dear Prudence, won't you come out to
    play?
Dear Prudence, greet the brand new
    day?
The sun is up, the sky is blue
It's beautiful and so are you
Dear Prudence won't you come out to
    play?

Dear Prudence open up your eyes
Dear Prudence see the sunny skies
The wind is low the birds will sing
That you are part of everything

Dear Prudence won't you open up your
    eyes?

Look around round round
Look around round round
Oh look around

Dear Prudence let me see you smile
Dear Prudence like a little child
The clouds will be a daisy chain
So let me see you smile again
Dear Prudence won't you let me see you
    smile?

Glass Onion

Having said that in India they shed their egos and went back to basics – it
didn't quite come off, judging by this song. John throws in references to many
of their own earlier songs – including 'Strawberry Fields', 'Walrus', 'Lady
Madonna', 'Fixing A Hole', 'Fool On The Hill' – which suggests he was getting
carried away by their own importance, or too many drugs. The random lyrics,
with no narrative, no connections, were intended to confuse the fans, to teach
them not to over-analyse, but also to amuse them, if they insisted on trying to
work it all out.

Even random stuff has to come from somewhere though. The 'bent back
tulips', so Derek Taylor explained, were spotted by John on a table at a posh
restaurant. The 'cast iron shore' referred to a shore near Liverpool, awash with
junk, which had an iron factory. 'Dove-tail joints' were what we all learned to
do, or not to, in woodwork at school.

John may have been mocking people who over-interpreted their lyrics –
and having a dig at the conspiracy theorists, such as those who later insisted
that Paul was dead. By throwing in all this apparent nonsense, he was
encouraging crackpots to find crackpot meanings.

The manuscript is on the back of an envelope, written in John's hand. There
was going to be a reference to yet another Beatles song, 'Yellow Submarine', but
this was replaced by a dove-tail joint. Having checked my 1968 address book,
I don't recognize the phone numbers at the bottom as having anything to do
with the Beatles. I think they were added later.

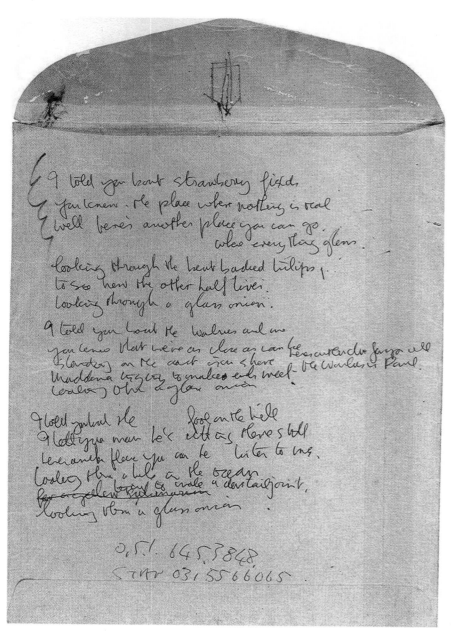

'Glass Onion', from The White Album, November 1968, written by John on the back of an envelope. Second line from the end, yellow submarine got deleted.

I told you about strawberry fields,
You know the place where nothing is
    real
Well here's another place you can go
Where everything flows.

Looking through the bent backed
    tulips
To see how the other half lives
Looking through a glass onion.

I told you about the walrus and me-man
You know that we're as close as can be-man.
Well here's another clue for you all,
The walrus was Paul.
Standing on the cast iron shore-yeah,
Lady Madonna trying to make ends meet-yeah.
Looking through a glass onion.
Oh yeah, oh yeah, oh yeah.

Looking through a glass onion.

I told you about the fool on the hill,
I tell you man he living there still.
Well here's another place you can be,
Listen to me.

Fixing a hole in the ocean
Trying to make a dove-tail joint-yeah
Looking through a glass onion

Ob La Di Ob La Da

This is Paul's take on a Jamaican ska number, about a very West Indian-sounding couple called Desmond and Molly. The title was a catchphrase used by a friend of Paul's called Jimmy Scott – a conga player whom he used to meet in the London clubs. He was in fact from Nigeria and the phrase 'Ob la di ob la da', supposedly meaning 'life goes on', was Yoruban. Paul wrote it while in India, playing and singing it one evening as they all walked out of the ashram in a little procession down to the local village.

John never liked the song, considering it twee, and there was some tension between them during the recording session, not helped by the fact that John insisted on having Yoko in the studio while they worked – which was most unusual. The other wives were normally not allowed on the actual studio floor – only upstairs, behind the glass panel in the control room.

The lyrics have a narrative, which Paul always liked, and concern two people, but don't have the power or imagery of 'Eleanor Rigby' or 'She's Leaving Home'. The manuscript, in Paul's hand, is the one he meant to sing, but in the repeat of the last four lines, he sang 'Desmond stays at home and does his pretty face' instead of Molly and her pretty face. They all liked it, so left it in. One of several transvestite lines in Beatles lyrics.

Desmond has a barrow in the market place
Molly is the singer in a band
Desmond says to Molly, 'Girl I like your face'
And Molly says this as she takes him by the hand

Ob-la-di, ob-la-da life goes on bra
La la how the life goes on
Ob-la-di, ob-la-da life goes on bra
La la how the life goes on

Desmond takes a trolley to the jeweller's store
Buys a twenty carat golden ring
Takes it back to Molly waiting at the door
And as he gives it to her she begins to sing

In a couple of years they have built a home, sweet home
With a couple of kids running in the yard
Of Desmond and Molly Jones

Happy ever after in the market place
Desmond lets the children lend a hand
Molly stays at home and does her pretty face
And in the evening she still sings it with the band

In a couple of years they have built a home, sweet home
With a couple of kids running in the yard
Of Desmond and Molly Jones, hey

Happy ever after in the market place
Molly lets the children lend a hand
Desmond stays at home and does his pretty face
And in the evening she's a singer with the band

And if you want some fun take ob-la-di-bla-da

The Continuing Story Of Bungalow Bill

This is one of John's lyrics where you think it must have come from a story he
had read in a newspaper, and then he had made up the rest, but in fact it was all
true. While they were in India, a young all-American college boy called Richard
Cooke III came out to visit his mother, who was part of the group studying
with the Maharishi. He went out on a tiger shoot, riding on an elephant, taking
his mother with him. They killed a tiger and then came back and carried on
meditating. The song is satirically but savagely mocking them in the form of a
children's story, or like Buffalo Bill, whose exploits we all followed in the fifties at
the Saturday-morning cinema. John changed it to Bungalow Bill as in Rishikesh
they all lived in bungalows.

In the studio, Yoko Ono was given a part, singing one of the little girls'
voices in the background.

The manuscript is in John's hand. The lyrics make it clear what John thought
of the young man: 'An all-American bullet-headed Saxon mother's son', which
was not very polite. When the boy later found out there was a song about him,
he didn't seem to mind much, although he later regretted killing the tiger.

Hey, bungalow bill
What did you kill
Bungalow bill?

He went out tiger hunting with his elephant and gun
In case of accidents he always took his mom
He's the all american bullet-headed saxon mother's son.
All the children sing

Deep in the jungle where the mighty tiger lies
Bill and his elephants were taken by surprise
So Captain Marvel zapped in right between the eyes
All the children sing

The children asked him if to kill was not a sin
Not when he looked so fierce, his mother butted in
If looks could kill it would have been us instead of him
All the children sing

Hey, bungalow bill
What did you kill
Bungalow bill?

Two verses of 'Bungalow Bill', from The White Album, *in John's hand.*

While My Guitar Gently Weeps

Some Beatles experts have stated that George wrote this song in India, and it does sound likely from the lyrics, but in *I Me Mine* he says the idea came to him while he was visiting his parents back in Liverpool. He had been delving into Chinese as well as Indian philosophy and was impressed by a line in the *I Ching* that everything is meant and connected, nothing is chance. When he picked up a book at random and the first words he saw were 'gently weeps', he decided to write a song based on the phrase. The notion of a guitar gently weeping is good one.

He tried hard to capture a weeping guitar sound in the studio, but didn't quite manage till he brought in his friend Eric Clapton. The other Beatles did not appear much impressed by the song, which made George try even harder to get it right. The music and arrangement is excellent – in fact, many experts think it is George's best tune. The first line is good, about 'a love there that's sleeping' but then come some clumsy lines, notably 'I look at the floor and see it needs sweeping'. Then he drags in words to rhyme with 'diverted' – 'perverted', 'inverted', 'alerted'.

The manuscript, in George's hand, has survived in several bits and pieces, which could suggest he was struggling with the words although most lyrics do get written in bits. In the first version, he writes 'whilst' instead of while, which is nicely archaic. There are also some lines he never used such as 'the problems you saw are the troubles you're reaping' and 'I'm sitting here doing nothing but ageing'. On the second page, and top of the third, you can see him listing possible rhymes.

It is interesting that he began the song with the word 'While', when the obvious way to begin would have been simply to say 'My guitar gently weeps'. A bit like Paul calling his song 'And I Love Her'. George, like John and Paul, was interested in words, their rhythm as much as their meaning, and would fall in love with them, often for no reason.

I look at you all see, the love there that's sleeping
While my guitar gently weeps
I look at the floor and I see it needs sweeping
Still my guitar gently weeps.

I don't know why nobody told you
How to unfold your love
I don't know how someone controlled you
They bought and sold you.

I look at the world and I notice it's turning
While my guitar gently weeps
With every mistake we must surely be learning
Still my guitar gently weeps.

I don't know how you were diverted
You were perverted too
I don't know how you were inverted
No one alerted you.

I look at you all, see the love there that's sleeping
While my guitar gently weeps
Look at you all …
Still my guitar gently weeps.

'While My Guitar Gently Weeps', from The White Album, three versions of it (two overleaf), all in George's hand, with various changes.

I look at the (world) and I notice it (turning)
While my guitar gently weeps
with every mistake we must surely be learning
Still (yet) my guitar gently weeps!

I don't know (how) why (burning, clinging, learning, yearning)
You were perverted (too) — You were diverted
I don't know (why) you got inverted
no one alerted you
I look at the ... know that he ...
... that was ... that is caging
(as) I'm sitting here doing nothing but aging

NEMS ENTERPRISES LTD
SUTHERLAND HOUSE, ARGYLL STREET, LONDON, W.1
TELEPHONE: 01-734 3261   CABLES: NEMPEROR, LONDON, W.1

, Tampering — tapering, Tempering, Thundering
Tittering Tottering, Towering, Toppling ✓
Wandering, Watering, Wavering, Weathering
Whimpering, Wintering, Whispering, Wondering ✓
——————— and love that sleeps
whilst my guitar gently weeps.

I look at you all see the love there that's sleeping
While my guitar gently weeps.
I look at the floor and I see it needs sweeping
Still my guitar gently weeps.
I don't know why — nobody told you, how to
unfold your love
O, don't know how, someone controlled you, how they
blindfolded you.

Happiness Is A Warm Gun

Probably John's most John song – full of meaningless meaningful things, nonsense which has you wondering whether it makes any sense, random thoughts that appear connected, all done so powerfully that you stop and think and wonder. It does have a punch, but the nearest thing to a punchline is the title, which does not appear until towards the end of the lyrics.

It began, so John said, in the recording studio when he happened to pick up a copy of an American gun magazine that had been left lying around; the headline read 'Happiness is a Warm Gun'. Steve Turner, author of the excellent *A Hard Day's Write,* has recently tracked down the exact magazine – the May 1968 issue of *American Rifleman.*

The lyrics would appear to be an amalgamation of several scraps of different songs, which is why we don't get to the warm gun reference until later. The first part, about a girl who doesn't miss much, finishes on the National Trust. The second begins on 'I need a fix' probably ends on 'going down', while the 'Mother Superior jump the gun' line, repeated four times, does not appear to be connected to anything.

Then we get to 'Happiness is a warm gun', which seems to be connected to the final suggestive lines: 'When I hold you in my arms / and I feel my finger on your trigger', but I suspect that began as yet again another separate scrap, this time about Yoko, his love heart. All in all, jolly complicated.

The May 1968 edition of American Rifleman *had a story by a man recalling the happy years shooting game with his son – which gave John an ironic title for his song.*

Derek Taylor, the Beatles PR and friend, tried to explain a few of the obscurities. The man with mirrors on his boots was apparently a Manchester City supporter who used them to look up girls' skirts. 'Lying with his eyes while his hands are busy working overtime' came from another newspaper story – about a man who had fake hands which he rested on the counter while he was stealing stuff with his real hands. The Mother Superior jumping the gun has yet to be explained, but it doesn't really matter – it was just disconnected stuff, emptied from John's brain at one particular moment. The next day, he would have dragged out another set of images. After all, why should lyrics tell a story or even make sense? They're just words that have their own sounds.

Well done anyway, getting away with it, and putting all those odd words to music. It took ninety-five takes – with Paul and George working hard with John on the complicated music – so no one can say they just knocked it off.

The manuscript, neatly written out, in Mal's hand. The numbers could refer to the timing or the tapes.

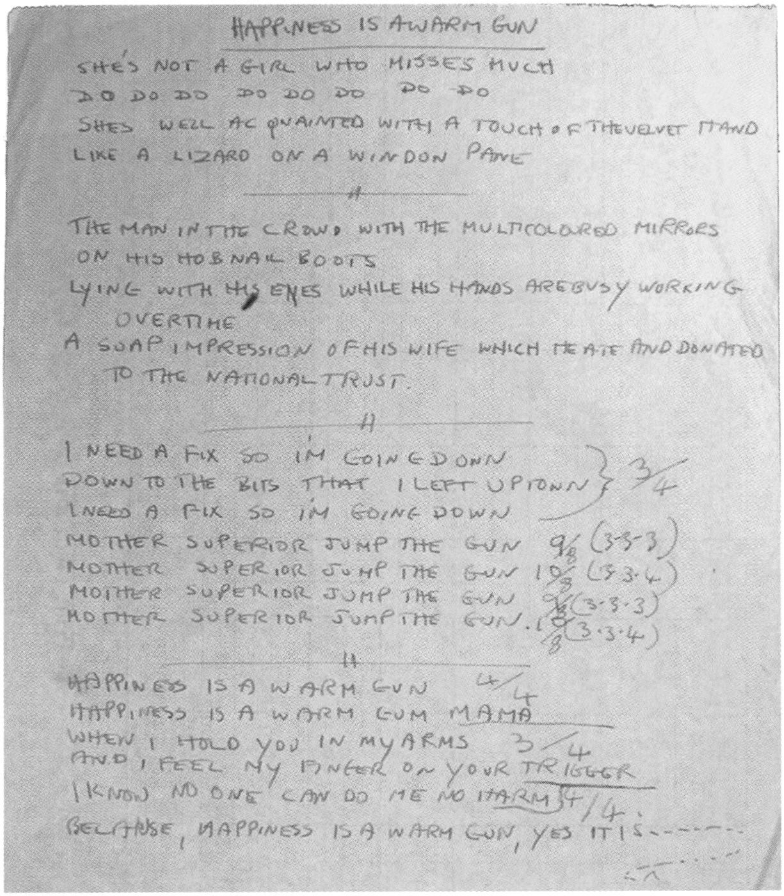

'Happiness Is a Warm Gun', from The White Album, *in Mal's hand, with timing.*

She's not a girl who
misses much
Do-do-do-do-do, oh yeah

She's well acquainted
With the touch of a velvet hand
Like a lizard on a window pane

The man in the crowd

With the multicoloured mirrors
On his hobnail boots
Lying with his eyes
While his hands are busy
Working overtime

A soap impression of his wife
Which he ate and donated
to the National Trust

I need a fix 'cos I'm going down
Down to the bits that I've left up town
I need a fix 'cos I'm going down
Mother Superior jumped the gun
Mother Superior jumped the gun
Mother Superior jumped the gun

Happiness is a warm gun
(bang bang shoot shoot)
Happiness is a warm gun, yes it is
(bang bang shoot shoot)

When I hold you in my arms (oh yes)
And I feel my finger on your trigger (oh
    yes)
I know no one can do me no harm
Because
happiness is a warm gun, momma
Happiness is a warm gun

-Yes it is.
Happiness is a warm, yes it is…
Gun!
Well don't ya know that happiness is a
    warm gun, momma? (yeah)

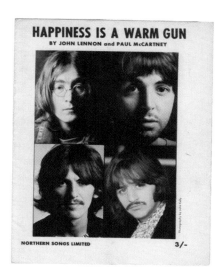

Martha My Dear

I still have fond memories of Martha. In fact her photograph is in front of me
now. There she sits, proudly beside Paul and Jane, in Cavendish Avenue. The
photo was taken by Ringo, who did special photographs of all four Beatles
in the spring of 1968, exclusively for my biography, which came out in the
September. Alas we had a flood upstairs a few years ago and all four photos –
the original prints – got damaged. Martha is now a bit blurred, and her white
fluffy fur even fluffier.

She was of course an Old English sheep dog, aged three in 1968, whom
Paul used to take for walks on Primrose Hill. Jane was Jane Asher, to whom,
after a long courtship, Paul got engaged at Christmas 1967. By July 1968 it had
all collapsed after she discovered Paul had been unfaithful.

The song began as a piano exercise. Paul was teaching himself to play
properly, trying something a bit beyond his competence, and having got a
good bit going he looked around for some words and there was Martha my
dear. He has always said it was just about his love for the dog, but others,
obviously cleverer, have said ah ha, it is about a girl, possibly Jane herself, who

has ditched him. She had been his inspiration and he hopes they will always remain friends and she won't forget him. (Jane married the cartoonist Gerald Scarfe in 1981 and has never given interviews about her long and at the time loving relationship with Paul.)

It remains one of my favourite songs – I love the bouncy, cheerful, tinkly, Scott Joplin piano playing, the gentle harmonies, the change of rhythms, and Paul's singing. This was another record on which the other Beatles did not take part. Paul did it all: vocals, bass guitar, drums, and even the hand claps, though a mini orchestra helped out.

The lyrics are not exceptional; we are told very little, possibly because he was holding back. They are nicely wistful though. I like the way he enunciates 'I spend my days in conversation' and 'you have always been my inspiration'. These lines are not there to rhyme, dragged in as George might have done, as they are so far apart, but seem natural and sincere.

It was recorded in October 1968 – by which time Linda Eastman had come into Paul's life.

The manuscript, in careful capitals (possibly by Mal), has a few crossings out. You can see that 'hold your head up' was going to be repeated, but second time round it became 'hold your hand out'. Now if he had really been thinking of a dog, he would surely have had a paw in there somewhere. So, must always have been a girl. And probably directed at Jane – not to forget him.

Martha my dear
Though I spend my days in conversation
Please remember me
Martha my love don't forget me
Martha my dear

Hold your head up you silly girl
Look what you've done
When you find yourself in the thick of it
Help yourself to a bit of what is all around
  you

Silly girl take a good look around you
Take a good look you're bound to see
That you and me were meant to be
For each other silly girl

Paul, Jane Asher and the famous Martha, photographed by Ringo, 1968.

'Martha My Dear', from The White Album, *Paul's song, but written out by Mal.*

Hold your hand out you silly girl
See what you've done
When you find yourself in the thick of it
Help yourself to a bit of what is all around you
You silly girl

Martha my dear
You have always been my inspiration
Please be good to me
Martha my love don't forget me
Martha my dear

I'm So Tired

John wrote this after three weeks in India – the period of time he mentions in the lyrics. He loved sleeping, as we know, but this time he is unable to. After too much meditating, his brain could not settle. He was also at this stage missing Yoko, whom he had met by now but had left behind. The Maharishi had banned drink and drugs, but John managed to get some alcohol and cigarettes smuggled in.

The song starts off all sleepy and drowsy, then suddenly jumps into life with explosive crescendos – and then it fades. It was following the pattern of his mood, his sudden anger and fury at being cut off from Yoko, before subsiding into resignation.

'Fix myself a drink' sounds to me an Americanism. I can't remember Brits using that phrase at the time, but John had visited the USA several times by now. The last word in the lyrics is pure Merseyside, though I have always spelled it git not get. It must have totally confused American Beatle fans.

Blaming Walter Raleigh – known for making tobacco popular in England – is funny, a silly joke dropped into the middle of his angst.

The manuscript, nicely written by John, is missing the last verse. In the final lines the words were slightly changed from the original – 'I'd give you all I've got if you gimme little peace of mind.'

I'm so tired, I haven't slept a wink
I'm so tired, my mind is on the blink
I wonder should I get up and fix myself
    a drink
No, no, no.

I'm so tired I don't know what to do
I'm so tired my mind is set on you
I wonder should I call you but I know
    what you would do

You'd say I'm putting you on
But it's no joke, it's doing me harm
You know I can't sleep, I can't stop my
    brain
You know it's three weeks, I'm going
    insane

You know I'd give you everything I've
    got
for a little peace of mind

I'm so tired, I'm feeling so upset
Although I'm so tired I'll have another
    cigarette
And curse Sir Walter Raleigh
He was such a stupid get.

'I'm So Tired', from The White Album, *in John's hand, but missing the stupid git.*

I'm So Tired.

① I'm so tired, I haven't slept a wink
I'm so tired, my mind is on the blink
I wonder should I get up and fix
myself a drink – no-no-no.

② I'm so tired, I don't know what to do.
I'm so tired
I wonder should I call you but I know
what you would do

③ You'd say I'm putting you on
but it's no joke – it's doing me harm
because I can't sleep I can't stop my
brain – you know it's 3 weeks and
I'm going insane and I'd give
you all I've got if you
gimme little piece of mind.

Blackbird

I have heard Paul, on stage at the O2, explain that in this song he was thinking of the position of the blacks in the USA, encouraging their civil rights campaign and struggle for equality. But I never heard him give this explanation at the time of the song's release in 1968.

On 30 November 1968 the *New Musical Express* quoted an interview with Paul that had been aired on Radio Luxembourg, stating that 'Blackbird' was 'just one of those pick and sing songs. It doesn't need anything else in the backing because as a song there is nothing else to it. We added a blackbird sound at the end, but that was all.' He made no comment about the words.

I suspect it was only with hindsight he decided that he was thinking about black civil rights, after an American writer had suggested it – although perhaps unconsciously he always had been. Creative people don't always know from whence inspiration comes.

Whatever the inspiration, it is one of Paul's most beautiful songs. I forced my dear wife to choose it when she went on *Desert Island Discs* – having been made to listen to me playing Beatles songs for decades, I insisted she had at least one.

Paul has said he first started the song when he was in his remote Scottish country cottage, and in his mind he was trying to compose something along the lines of Bach.

The lyrics are excellent. He is clearly not just thinking of a literal blackbird but people generally struggling to be free, to fly away from persecution or just from a bad relationship. But I do worry about 'take these broken wings and learn to fly' – how would giving broken wings help anyone to fly? Surely it should have been 'use your broken wings', i.e. because you are broken and downtrodden, and then learn to fly.

No manuscript version has turned up – which is unusual for this period. Since 1965, as we have seen, some sort of manuscript has survived for the vast majority of their songs.

Piggies

This is George in a rant, worked up about fat horrible business piggies in their starched white shirts, with their piggie wives, stuffing their faces. In the sixties, 'pigs' usually meant policemen, but it could also refer to capitalist pigs. George sings it nicely, sounding almost like Paul, with some sweet harpsichord music, but the lyrics are fairly vitriolic. He explained that it was just meant to be social comment, not a call to arms, despite the line 'they need a damn good whacking'. He said that line was contributed by his mother when he was looking for a rhyme for 'backing' and 'lacking'.

However, in 1969 in California, the Charles Manson gang took it literally, when they began slaughtering their victims, using knives to finish them off and writing the word 'pigs', using their blood. Manson himself was a fanatical Beatles fan. When he was arrested, it was found that he had been reading my biography. His followers, calling themselves the Family, believed that there was going to be an uprising and the white establishment would be overthrown in a racial war. In all, they were linked to eight murders, including the film actress Sharon Tate.

George's manuscript shows that he had an extra verse, marked no. 3, not used, which is pretty good, keeping up the invective and the images.

'It's a pity that the piggies always deal in dirt – having played their games for years – they've become experts – pressures they exert from every angle.'

'Piggies', from The White Album, *in George's hand, including a final verse which was not used.*

Have you seen the little piggies
Crawling in the dirt?
And for all the little piggies
Life is getting worse
Always having dirt to play around in.

Have you seen the bigger piggies
In their starched white shirts?
You will find the bigger piggies
Stirring up the dirt
Always have clean shirts to play around in.
In their sties with all their backing
They don't care what goes on around
In their eyes there's something lacking
What they need's a damn good whacking.

Everywhere there's lots of piggies
Living piggy lives
You can see them out for dinner
With their piggy wives
Clutching forks and knives to eat their bacon.

Everywhere there's lots of piggies playing piggy pranks
You will see them on their trotters at the piggy banks
Paying piggy thanks to the pig brother

Rocky Raccoon

Began as a joke, with Paul in India improvising a pretend Wild West song, aided and abetted by Donovan. The hero was originally called Rocky Sassoon but got changed to Rocky Raccoon. It's the sort of Cowboys and Indians saga we used to see at the Saturday-morning movies. It still is a joke piece, after all these years, with not even the most ardent analysts able to detect deeper meanings – apart from perhaps Charles Manson, who could twist anything, if he wanted to.

Don't Pass Me By

At last Ringo had done it – composed his first Beatles song. He first wrote it back in 1964, four years earlier, but it never got finished. Paul and John never found time or space or interest in including it in any of the albums. I wonder why it finally made the cut? Could it be that this time they had agreed to a double album and needed a whopping twenty-eight songs to fill the space between the grooves? Or were they keeping him sweet?

It's a country and western number with a mean fiddle, a perfect sing-along tune, but oh, the words. 'You were in a car crash / and you lost your hair.' Couldn't Paul or John have saved him from such bathos?

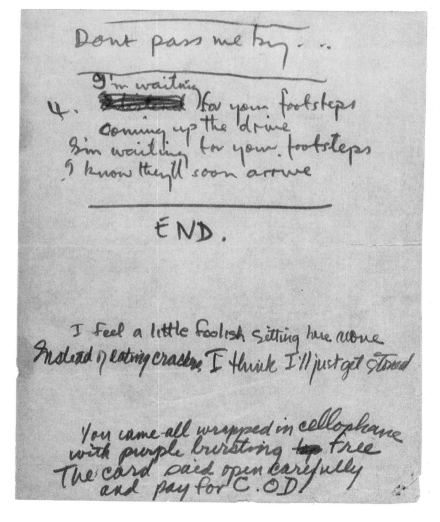

*'Don't Pass Me By',
from* The White
Album – *at last a
song from Ringo,
but the top lines
appear to be in
Paul's hand, with
other hands below.*

The manuscript has the first four lines in Paul's hand – which are not bad, though they got changed slightly on the record. The other lines, below, might or might not have been meant to be included. The first two, funny in their awfulness, appear to read:

I feel a little foolish, sitting here alone
Instead of eating crackers, I think I'll just get stoned

The final ones are a bit wittier

You came all wrapped in cellophane
with purple bursting free
The card said open carefully
And pay for C O D

Had he persevered, Ringo could well have become a modern-day William McGonagall.

I listen for your footsteps coming up the drive
I'm waiting for your footsteps I know they'll soon arrive
Waiting for your knock, dear, on my old front door
I don't hear it, does it mean you don't love me anymore?

I hear the clock a ticking on the mantel shelf
See the hands a moving but I'm by myself
I wonder where you are tonight and why I'm by myself
I don't see you, does it mean you don't love me anymore?

I'm sorry that I doubted you, I was so unfair
You were in a car crash and you lost your hair
You said that you would be late about an hour or two
I said that's all right, I'm waiting here, just waiting to hear from you

Don't pass me by, don't make me cry, don't make me blue
Cause you know darling I love only you
You'll never know it hurt me so, how I hate to see you go
Don't pass me by, don't make me cry

Why Don't We Do It In The Road?

A similar criticism could be made of this offering by Paul – how on earth did it get on the album? The only explanation is that it was a useful link track, a bit of fun. And it did come out later as a single in Nicaragua.

I think of all the Beatles songs this is the only one I disliked on first hearing – and still do. It's not because of the saucy title – for the background to that is quite interesting. He was in Rishikesh and saw two monkeys in the road, one of which jumped on the back of the other and gave her one, then hopped off again and walked away as if nothing had happened. Paul wondered why humans don't do that – well not very often. But he didn't work on any words. It consists of just two lines, the title and one other line – 'no one will be watching us' – plus a lot of raucous shouting in a phoney American accent. Fortunately, it doesn't last long.

John was upset that Paul recorded it without involving him, or asking him to work on it – but then John did the same with his 'Revolution 9' (the sound collage number, which appears on side 4 of the album).

The manuscript is in Paul's hand, written on a napkin and dated 2010, which suggests it was written out relatively recently and given to someone or some charitable cause.

Why don't we do it in the road?
No one will be watching us
Why don't we do it in the road?

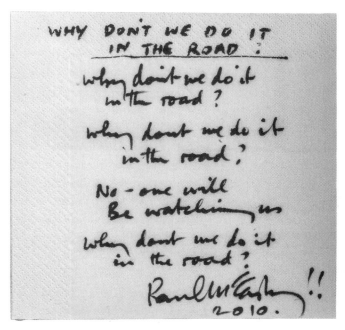

'Why Don't We Do It In The Road?', originally written for The White Album *in 1968 but the so-called lyrics copied out by Paul in 2010.*

I Will

Paul at his very best: great song, great harmonies, good words. He came up with the tune in India, and played it to various people, including Donovan, but it was only on his return that he managed to fit some suitable words to it.

The lyrics are very simple, no clever tricks, no puns or allusions, just an old-fashioned I-love-you-with-all-my-heart, the sort of thing they had not done for some time, having apparently given up all that soppy love-song stuff. It would appear to be the first song he wrote about his new love, Linda, while they were recording *The Double White Album*. She was due to visit him soon, along with her daughter Heather.

Julia

This time John at his sweetest and best – no tricks, no complications, no deliberate incomprehensibility. It is named after his mother, who died when John was only seventeen, and is the first time he had sung about her by name. It is also a love song to Yoko. 'Ocean child' refers to the fact that Yoko in Japanese means child of the ocean. She wrote to him in India, where he came up with the song, and in one letter she tells him 'I am a cloud, watch for me in the sky' which comes out in the reference to 'silent cloud'. John believed that Yoko took the place of his mother, as an influence and inspiration and love object, and later on he often addressed her as Mother.

The finger-picking guitar style was taught to him by Donovan, while they were in India.

I always thought the first line – 'half of what I say is meaningless' – was original to John, as it sounds so like him. You can take it two ways (meaningless or meaning less), but it turns out he lifted the phrase from a book of Lebanese proverbs by a mystic called Khalil Gibran: 'Half of what I say is meaningless, but I say it so the other half reaches you.'

The manuscript, in John's hand, is an early draft, and the words are a bit hard to read. The last few lines, not all of which were used, appear to read:

Beautiful Julia, silently calls me
As I sing a song of love for you, Julia
Her hair like saffron shimmering glimmering

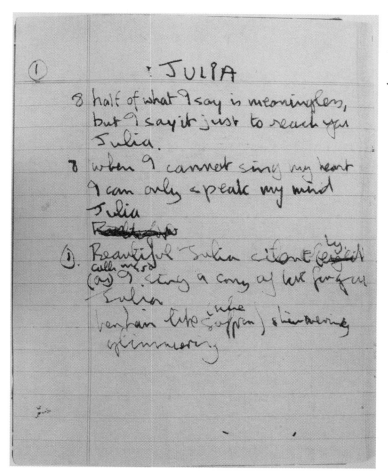

'Julia', from The White Album, *a song about John's mother, an early draft in John's hand.*

Half of what I say is meaningless
But I say it just to reach you,
Julia

Julia, Julia, oceanchild, calls me
So I sing a song of love, Julia
Julia, seashell eyes, windy smile, calls
    me
So I sing a song of love, Julia

Her hair of floating sky is shimmering,
    glimmering,
In the sun

Julia, Julia, morning moon, touch me
So I sing a song of love, Julia

When I cannot sing my heart
I can only speak my mind, Julia

Julia, sleeping sand, silent cloud, touch
    me
So I sing a song of love, Julia
Hum hum hum hum … calls me
So I sing a song of love for Julia, Julia,
    Julia

Birthday

Lyrics-wise, not a great song; in fact the words are deliberately simple and obvious and hardly worth considering, but it was done quickly, almost instantaneously, with no thought or work on the words. The point was to have fun in the studio, starting from scratch, with nothing prepared, knocking out a foot-stomping rocker. It was Paul's idea, but he can't remember if anyone he knew had a birthday coming up. The thinking behind it was that a birthday song, like a Christmas song, would always get lots of plays if it was any good. In fact on the day they were recording Linda's twenty-seventh birthday was only six days off (24 September 1968); he knew she was arriving, but may not yet have been aware of her birthday date. Or that she was one year older than him.

During the recording session, they all went round to Paul's house to watch a rock 'n' roll film, *The Girl Can't Help It*, which featured Little Richard, Eddie Cochran and Gene Vincent. (No video recording equipment in these days.) Then they returned to the studio to finish off the song.

When asked, twelve years later, what he remembered of the song, John replied, 'Garbage.'

The manuscript, mostly in Mal Evans's hand, with instructions by Paul, runs to two pages, the second one has some instructions and order of play. Not sure what 'Staggers' means. Surely they were not reading the *New Statesman* while recording? On the back of the notes (which were sold at Sotheby's in September 1996 and the proceeds donated to charity) are scribbles in Japanese script by Yoko in which she lists male names. (She was pregnant at the time – but two months later suffered a miscarriage.) She was not only present at the recording but provided backing vocals.

You say it's your birthday
It's my birthday too, yeah
They say it's your birthday
We're gonna have a good time
I'm glad it's your birthday
Happy birthday to you.

Yes we're going to a party party

Yes we're going to a party party
Yes we're going to a party party

I would like you to dance (Birthday)
Take a cha-cha-cha-chance (Birthday)
I would like you to dance (Birthday)
Dance

RIFF

THEY SAY ITS YOUR BIRTHDAY
WELL ITS MY BIRTHDAY TOO YEAH
THEY SAY ITS YOUR BIRTHDAY
WE'RE GOING TO HAVE A GOOD TIME
IM GLAD ITS YOUR BIRTHDAY
HAPPY BIRTHDAY TO YOU

DRUMS

E ⑧ _ _ _ _ _ _

I WOULD LIKE YOU TO DANCE
TAKE A CHA CHA CHA CHANCE
I WOULD LIKE YOU TO DANCE

SOLO

STAGGERS

THEY SAY ITS YOUR BIRTHDAY
WELL ITS MY BIRTHDAY TOO YEAH
THEY SAY ITS YOUR BIRTHDAY
WE'RE GOING TO HAVE A GOOD TIME
IM GLAD ITS YOUR BIRTHDAY
HAPPY BIRTHDAY TO YOU.

'Birthday', from The White Album, *mostly in Mal's hand, but Paul has written the instructions.*

Yer Blues

This is such a despairing, depressing song you have to be sorry for John writing it, feeling forced to write it, unable to help himself writing it, telling the world he was feeling suicidal. 'I'm so lonely I want to die – if I ain't dead already.'

There were millions of dedicated fans, such as my younger self, who on first hearing this wailing immediately thought, Oh my god, John, give us a break, John, keep it to yourself, John, we want fun and cheerfulness, yes, a bit of sadness and misery is fine, but within reason. Couldn't you have got Paul to cross out a bit of the agony and give us some hope?

But this was all John's work, written in India. So much for prayer and meditation, peace and tranquillity, getting away from the nasty world – it obviously wasn't much help to a troubled soul like John. He had already told us he was so tired, yet couldn't sleep. Now he wanted to top himself.

The problem was Yoko – or at least, he had decided that his salvation and hope for the future was Yoko. But how and when was he going to tell Cynthia? And if he didn't tell her, how could he go on? That was his dilemma. (He did, in fact, confess his infidelities to Cynthia on the plane home from India, to her surprise and distress; it marked the beginning of the end of their marriage.)

With its heavy, moany, shouty, deep blues parody style, it's nothing like a Beatles tune, having more in common with the sort of songs he was to write later with Yoko in their Plastic Ono life.

The lyrics, it must be said, are powerful: black clouds across his mind, blue mist around his soul. I suppose the vaguely jocular reference to Dylan's Mr Jones (from Bob Dylan's 'Ballad of a Thin Man') and his despair being so great he even hates his rock'n'roll, do slightly leaven the overall anguish, but even so, it is an uncomfortable listen. God knows what Manson made of it.

The manuscript is typed, which is unusual, with corrections in John's hand. He has altered 'If I'm dead already' and made it 'If I ain't dead already'. And he has substituted the word 'suicidal' for what in the original appears to be 'so' – then something illegible.

Yes I'm lonely wanna die
Yes I'm lonely wanna die
If I ain't dead already
Ooh girl you know the reason why.

In the morning wanna die
In the evening wanna die

If I ain't dead already
Ooh girl you know the reason why.

My mother was of the earth
My father was of the sky
But I am of the universe
And that's the reason why

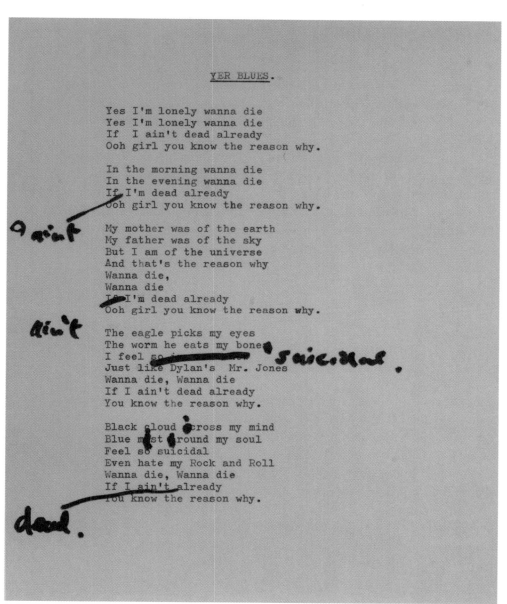

'Yer Blues', from The White Album, *typed out, with hand corrections by John. What was the word which 'suicidal' replaced?*

The eagle picks my eye
The worm he licks my bones
I feel so suicidal
Just like Dylan's Mr. Jones
Lonely wanna die
If I ain't dead already
Ooh girl you know the reason why.

Black cloud crossed my mind
Blue mist round my soul
Feel so suicidal
Even hate my rock and roll
Wanna die yeah wanna die
If I ain't dead already
Ooh girl you know the reason why.

Mother Nature's Son

So is this what we all wanted instead? Paul had supposedly been inspired by a lecture from the Maharishi on the unity between man and nature, but he actually composed this in Liverpool, after a visit to his dad. The first line begins 'born a poor young country boy'. Don't most people get born young? He presumably needed the right number of words to fill out the line and didn't give much thought to their meaning. The boy is singing amongst the daisies and mountain streams, and it's all very nice, pretty and sweet and melodic – but it does seem as if Paul himself had second thoughts, unable to manage more than six lines. Instead of thinking up any more verses he contented himself with doooo doooing and hummm humming. Very nicely, mind you.

Everybody's Got Something to Hide Except Me and My Monkey

Another shouty one from John with the longest title in the Beatles canon, but with more melody and some nice lines. In his mind, he and Yoko – whom I take to be his monkey, though others have suggested it refers to heroin – were on their own, the world against them, only they knew what was true and good and joyous. He had by now confessed about Yoko to Cynthia, and was leaving her; in the meantime he was having arguments with Paul and the others, who did not care for Yoko coming to the studio and taking part in musical discussions. Then there was trouble with their company, Apple, leading them to close their Baker Street boutique in August. So, the anguish went on, and John felt everyone had something to hide, except him.

Sexy Sadie

Appeared at the time to be a song about a girl who teased and turned everyone on, then made a fool of them all. Then we discovered that it was not about a girl but the Maharishi. In the original recordings, John sang his name; but when he realized he could end up in court, it was changed to a girl's name.

Bootlegs which were somehow spirited out of the recording sessions revealed John shouting obscenities about Maharishi. That evidence, plus gossip and rumour, eventually led to most fans learning about the true background to the song.

It was begun by John while still in India, but thinking of coming home, after he had become disillusioned. There were stories circulating in the camp about the Maharishi making approaches to a girl (never proved), and that he was really after their fame and money. This was supposedly what made John suddenly decide to leave.

No manuscript has so far turned up, but a piece of wood was auctioned in 2007, said to have been carved by John on his return to Kenwood, on which the lyrics are written – with the name Maharishi all the way through and no mention of Sexy Sadie. It is of course, as you already know, the only Beatles song in which the word sex or sexy appears.

Helter Skelter

Paul then decided to do his shouty bit, showing he could keep up with John and also with the fashion at the time for loud heavy music, as exemplified by Pete Townshend and The Who. While up at his Scottish cottage, he read a review in a music newspaper about The Who's latest record being the loudest, rawest and dirtiest they had done. This inspired Paul to have a go at something that would freak everyone out and prove that he wasn't just a ballad writer. Even the late Ian MacDonald, normally the most cerebral and technical and wordy of music critics, called it a 'drunken mess'.

The subject matter is clear enough to most Brits – because we all know that a helter skelter is a fairground ride, a fast, furious, scary spiral ride, where you ride on a mat at breakneck speed from the top of a winding slide all the way down the bottom, so the analogy of taking a ride on a girl who is coming down fast, whom he might break, is readily understood sexual innuendo. The term 'helter skelter', meaning a headlong, disorderly haste or scramble, had actually been in popular use long before the fairground ride came along.

All this was lost on American Charles Manson, alas. He took it be a literal incitement to kill. The crazy, wild, dirty, incredibly loud music encouraged his dangerous fantasies. He managed to see hidden meanings in almost all of the songs on the album, finding references to the black races in 'Rocky Raccoon' – 'coon' being a derogatory term for a black person – and in 'Blackbird'. But it was 'Helter Skelter' that became the soundtrack to his killing spree. When he was arrested, Manson talked specifically about the record and how it was about confusion which you can't see, coming down fast, so you have to kill or be killed.

The lyrics, and the music, sound highly sexual, and pretty frantic at that, but when interviewed by Barry Miles in 1996, Paul said the helter skelter was merely a symbol of descent from top to bottom 'like the rise and fall of the Roman Empire'. You what?

On the record, which took fifty-two takes to get right, you can hear Lennon at the end saying 'How's that?' and Ringo replying 'I got blisters on me fingers.'

The part manuscript is in Mal Evans's careful handwriting, but the instructions for the recording of the song are written by Paul.

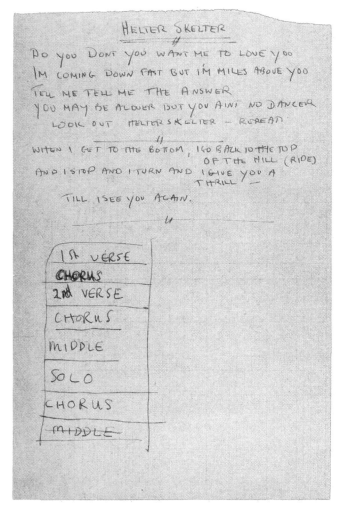

'Helter Skelter', from The White Album, *lyrics in Mal's hand, instructions by Paul.*

When I get to the bottom I go back to the top of the slide
Where I stop and I turn and I go for a ride
Till I get to the bottom and I see you again.

Do you don't you want me to love you
I'm coming down fast but I'm miles above you
Tell me, tell me, tell me, come on tell me the answer
You may be a lover but you ain't no dancer.

Helter skelter, helter skelter
Helter skelter.

When I get to the bottom I go back to the top of the slide
Where I stop and I turn and I give you a thrill
Till I get to the bottom and I see you again.

Will you, won't you want me to make you
I'm coming down fast but don't let me break you
Tell me, tell me, tell me the answer
You may be a lover but you ain't no dancer.

Well do you, don't you want me to love you
I'm coming down fast but don't let me break you
Tell me, tell me, tell me the answer
You may be a lover but you ain't no dancer.

Look out
Helter skelter, helter skelter
Helter skelter.

Look out helter skelter
She's coming down fast.
Yes she is.
Yes she is

(I got blisters on me fingers)

Long Long Long

George's soppy love song – at least, that is how it appears, with stuff like oh how I love you, and want you, and need you, so happy I found you, etc. You come away convinced it must be about his wife Pattie or some girlfriend. But in *I Me Mine* George says it was not about a girl, but God. Hmm.

The sound is interesting, with George almost whispering the words, and with a distant drumbeat, but the words are clumsy: 'How can I ever misplace you' makes God, or the girl, sound like a parcel.

The manuscript, in George's hand, was written on a sheet torn out of a diary for the week of 11 August 1968. Not often we can date the composition of a song. It was then recorded 7–9 October.

At the bottom, George has listed some of his other songs – 'Savoy Truffle' and 'Piggies', plus 'Not Guilty' which was not recorded by the Beatles but by George himself in 1979.

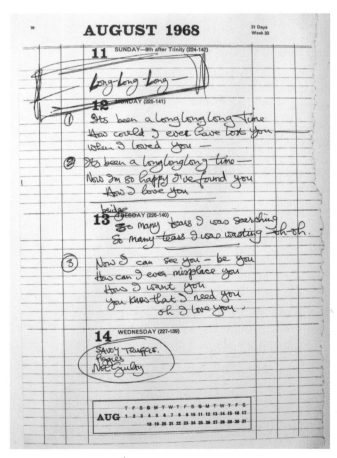

It's been a long long long time,
How could I ever have lost you
When I loved you.

It's been a long long long time
Now I'm so happy I found you
How I love you

So many tears I was searching,
So many tears I was wasting, oh.
Oh—

Now I can see you, be you
How can I ever misplace you
How I want you
Oh I love you
You know that I need you.
Ooh I love you.

'Long Long Long,' from The White Album, *in George's hand, on the very day he wrote it?*

Revolution 1

The same lyrics as on the B side of 'Hey Jude', except for that one vital addition – 'in' added to 'out', sounding like a quick afterthought, and easy to miss. The tempo is much slower and relaxed and amused, and at the end he adds a bit of a chorus where they go shooo bee doo.

Honey Pie

Oh, didn't Paul write some fun songs, brilliant pastiches which sound better, more polished, more realistic, more genuine than the songs being parodied. In this case a 1920s ragtime song about a North of England girl who makes it big in Hollywood – a little present to his father, who played these sort of old music-hall songs in his jazz band days. It begins as they all did – with a very slow, almost spoken introduction – before we are into the action of the music, with everyone wanting to get up and dance or sing, or both, like in ye good old days. Oh, we were happy them.

On the first side of the album, there is another song called 'Wild Honey Pie', but it is a mere scrap, under a minute long, with no real lyrics apart from the repetition of the words 'Honey pie'. Another piece of self-reflection.

The 'Honey Pie' manuscript shows some minor changes in the intro. The contract for the song has also somehow emerged – which is interesting as it shows that in 1968 the publisher, Northern Songs (Dick James Company), was still taking 50 per cent of the fees.

How the performing rights fees were divided for 'Honey Pie', 1968 – half to Northern Songs, half to John and Paul.

C/197

Publisher's Name   NORTHERN SONGS LIMITED,

Address   James House, 71/75, New Oxford Street, LONDON, W.C.1.

Date 15th October 1968.

To the Secretary,
THE PERFORMING RIGHT SOCIETY, LTD.,
29/33 BERNERS STREET,
LONDON, W.1.

Notice of agreement to vary the division of fees, pursuant to Rule 5 (f) of P.R.S. Rules.

We, the undersigned, desire to notify you that we have agreed that all fees payable by the Society in respect of performances on and after 15th October 1968. of the work(s) entitled:—

" HONEY PIE "

shall be divided between us in the following proportions instead of in the normal proportions specified in the Society's authorised plan of division of fees for British works, namely, for original works, two-thirds to the writer or writers and one-third to the publisher, or, for arrangements of non-copyright music, as provided in the plan of division for graded works.

	General fees	Broadcasting fees	Film fees
Composer share, or (if an arrangement of non-copyright music) arranger share	6/12ths to Maclen (Music)Ltd.,		
Author share			
Publisher share	6/12ths to Northern Songs Ltd.,		

and we hereby authorise and request the Society to act accordingly.

It is understood that the share of any signatory hereto who is not a member of the Society or of any of its affiliated societies shall in respect of all performances prior to the distribution period during which he is elected to membership of any such society, be paid to the publisher where the latter is the assignee of the performing right.

Signature(s) of Composer(s) or (if an arrangement of non-copyright music) of Arranger   JOHN LENNON

Signature of Author(s)   PAUL MCCARTNEY

HONEY PIE.

INTRO.
~~FIRST~~ SHE WAS A WORKING GIRL
NORTH, OF ENGLAND WAY
NOW SHE'S HIT THE BIG TIME
IN THE U.S.A. ~~COULD ONLY~~.
~~NO~~ AND, IF SHE ~~CAN~~ HEAR ME,
THIS IS WHAT ID ~~LIKE TO~~ SAY

(1) HONEY PIE YOU ARE MAKING ME CRAZY
IM IN LOVE BUT IM LAZY
SO WON'T YOU PLEASE COME HOME.

(2) HONEY PIE MY POSITION IS TRAGIC
COME AND SHOW ME THE MAGIC
OF YOUR HOLLYWOOD SONG.

MIDDLE
YOU BECAME A LEGEND OF THE SILVER SCREEN
AND NOW THE THOUGHT OF MEETING YOU
MAKES ME WEAK AT THE KNEE

(3) HONEY PIE YOU ARE DRIVING ME FRANTIC
SAIL ACROSS THE ATLANTIC / TO BE WHERE YOU BELONG.

MIDDLE
WILL THE WIND THAT BLEW HER BOAT
ACROSS THE SEA
KINDLY SEND HER
SAILING BACK TO ME. — — TSK TSK TILL

REPEAT IST. VERSE

OR OUT ON SOLO.
COME ~~COME BACK FOR LITTLE DOVE~~

'Honey Pie', from The White Album, *1968, in Paul's neat capitals, but with some changes.*

She was a working girl
North of England way
Now she's hit the big time
In the U. S. A.
And if she could only hear me
This is what I'd say.

Honey pie you are making me crazy
I'm in love but I'm lazy
So won't you please come home.
Oh honey pie my position is tragic
Come and show me the magic
of your Hollywood song.

You became a legend of the silver
　　screen
And now the thought of meeting you
Makes me weak in the knee.
Oh honey pie you are driving me
　　frantic
Sail across the Atlantic

To be where you belong.
Will the wind that blew her boat
Across the sea
Kindly send her sailing back to me.
Honey pie you are making me crazy
I'm in love but I'm lazy
So won't you please come home.

Savoy Truffle

The first words 'crème tangerine' and 'pineapple heart' might make you think
this was John, going back to Lucy and marmalade skies – but it is George,
emptying a box of chocolates, naming each one as he goes. Almost all the
words are real names of choccies in a box of Mackintosh's Good News. It
started because of Eric Clapton and his love for chocolates, which George told
him would lead to all his teeth falling out – and they did. When he got stuck
for some bridging words, Derek Taylor suggested the phrase from of a film
he had just seen, *You Are What You Eat*, which George turned into 'you know
that what you eat you are'. The origin of the phrase goes back to the French
epicure Brillat-Savarin in 1826 when he wrote 'Tell me what you eat and I will
tell you what you are'. There is a brief pause to try and make the words more
meaningful, as if he might also be thinking of a girl with the line 'I feel your
taste all the time I am apart'. But so far as the lyrics go it's a bit of a cheat and
pretty pointless. It's almost as if the Beatles at this stage, with a double album
to complete and vast sales assured, are saying to themselves, We can write any
old song on any old thing, just watch us – and listen. And they did.

George's manuscript has a few changes, but all heavily scored out.

Crème tangerine and Montélimar
A ginger sling with a pineapple heart
A coffee dessert – yes you know it's good news
But you're going to have to have them all pulled out
After the Savoy truffle.

Cool cherry cream, nice apple tart
I feel your taste all the time we're apart
Coconut fudge – really blows down those blues

But you'll have to have them all pulled out
After the Savoy truffle.

You might not feel it now
But when the pain cuts through
You're gonna know and how
The sweat is going to fill your head
When it becomes too much
You'll shout aloud

But you'll have to have them all pulled out
After the Savoy truffle.

You know that what you eat you are,
But what is sweet now, turns so sour—
We all know Obla-Di-Bla-Da
But can you show me, where you are?

'Savoy Truffle', from The White
Album – *George's lyrics, all about
real chocolates, but some he had
second thoughts about.*

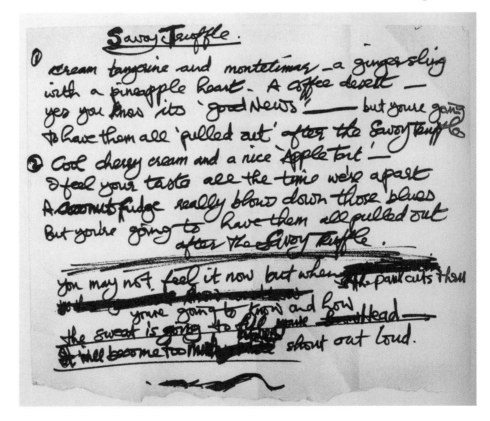

Creme tangerine and Montélimar
A ginger sling with a pineapple heart
A coffee dessert – yes you know it's good news
But you'll have to have them all pulled out
After the Savoy truffle.
Yes, you'll have to have them all pulled out
After the Savoy truffle.

Cry Baby Cry

This was one of the scraps of songs John told me about in 1967 while doing the biography. 'I've got another song here, a few words, I think I got from an advert: "Cry baby cry, make your mother buy." I've been playing it over on the piano. I've let it go now. It'll come back if I really want it. I do get up from the piano as if I have been in a trance. Sometimes I know I've let a few things slip away.'

The title lines were taken from a TV advertisement, as John never turned the TV off, regardless of what was on. He eventually fitted lyrics to the tune while in India, relying on half-remembered childhood nursery rhymes, the kind you might sing to a baby, such as 'Sing a Song of Sixpence': 'The Queen was in the parlour, eating bread and honey …' The Duchess of Kirkcaldy appealed to him because he liked Scottish names and places. (And the Beatles did actually play in Kirkcaldy, back on 6 October 1963.) The music is rather haunting, even if the words are mainly random. John later described the song as rubbish.

Revolution 9

No lyrics, as such, so does not concern us here. In fact, I doubt if many Beatles fans have ever played it since 1968 when they first heard it – though musicologists and techies and avant-gardists have had good fun trying to work out how it was done. Putting a load of old sounds together, backwards tapes, overheard conversations, scraps from the archives – that's how it was done. The *New Musical Express*, in its review on 9 November 1968, described it as 'a pretentious piece of old codswallop'.

Before it begins, after the end of 'Cry Baby Cry', we hear a few seconds of Paul singing, 'Can you take me back'. It sounds as if it could have been turned into a nice song, like 'I Will', but we only get a few bars. The rest was not released. Then it's into the dreaded 'Revolution 9' – all eight minutes of it.

The repetition of 'Number nine, number nine' constitutes the only words you can hear clearly, and they came from some old Abbey Road archives of a taped music examination for Royal College of Music students.

John, George and Yoko did this together while Paul was away, and he wasn't exactly thrilled by the result, though he too was keen on avant-garde music. 'Revolution 9' was the extended ending to 'Revolution'. Presumably it was all meant to be a revolution in music, that you should change your normal acceptance of how music should sound, rise up, open your ears. To Manson of course it all made perfect sense – and perhaps it was this track that drove him truly mad.

Good Night

I can't say I like 'Good Night' any better – though I can see why it was stuck in after 'Revolution 9' right at the end of the album, bringing it all to a close. It is a pastiche of lush Hollywood movie music, all lush strings and over-the-top harmonies and treacly choruses, sung by the Mike Sammes Singers.

It's a John song, surprisingly – well, I was surprised, always having assumed from its schmaltziness that it must be by Paul. John's defence was that he wrote it as a bedtime song for Julian, his son. All it says is good night, sweet dreams, with no wit or irony or half-decent similes, and even 'The sun turns out his light' is corny. John gave it to Ringo to sing – not wanting his own image to be tarnished.

Ah well, it was a long album. An amazing achievement, to record in so short a time so many new songs, some of which are dreamy and beautiful and lyrical and others loud and exciting and shattering and yes, revolutionary. Especially when you know all the other things which were happening in their young lives …

12

YELLOW SUBMARINE

1969

The Beatles were under contract to United Artists to do another film, but they were not keen. They had not really enjoyed making *Help!* and *Magical Mystery Tour* had been hammered by the critics, so why bother, when they had so many other new things, and new people and plans, going on in their lives?

Were they getting spoiled, too big for their boots, too bored? Probably a bit of each. On the other hand, they felt trapped by various managements and companies who had made a fortune out of them, such as United Artists and Northern Songs, who had them under contracts that they had signed ages ago when they didn't quite know where they were going and what they might want to do.

So when the idea of an animated film came up, a cartoon based on a story spun out of their earlier children's song 'Yellow Submarine' (released in 1966 on their *Revolver* album), in which they would not have to act, but would get away with doing only one cameo appearance in the final sequence, they agreed. Initially the fans assumed and hoped their real voices would be used, but in the end their words were spoken by actors.

The film opened in July 1968 but the LP did not come out till January 1969. Only four new songs were provided by them for the film, and for the LP. And even then, there was a feeling these were left-over songs, not considered good enough for earlier albums or singles. The other songs in the film were old songs, recorded some time ago, such as 'When I'm Sixty-Four'. On the LP a lot of the space was filled up with instrumental numbers, composed and orchestrated by George Martin for the film score.

The film turned out to be enjoyed by fans and critics alike, and is seen now as a pioneer in the field of animation; even the Beatles later said they thought it was really good. The album, however, compared with all the treasures on *The Double White Album*, was disappointing; it seemed a bit of a cheat, putting it out as if it were filled with new Beatles songs.

Derek Taylor did the sleeve notes for the album – and it seemed even he could not be roused to do any work. He told us his name was Derek, a name given by his mother, and he had been asked to write the notes for this album, but really he had nothing new to say about the Beatles. Instead he reprinted a review of *The Double White Album*, written by Tony Palmer. Which wasn't even new either, having appeared in the *Observer*.

Only A Northern Song

I am amazed George got away with this – and it did appear as if he did not want to write the song at all. George was a very small minority shareholder in Northern Songs – just 1.6 per cent shared with Ringo, compared with Paul and John who had 15 per cent each. He still got a performing royalty, but he felt he was only working for others' gain. (It was later in 1969, after the *Yellow Submarine* album was released, that Dick James, without telling them, sold his share to ATV and Lew Grade, followed a few months later by Paul, John and George.)

The title gives it away – disparaging itself, suggesting it was only a bit of inferior, provincial material. He tells us that if we think the chords are going wrong, they are, that's how he wrote it; and if you think the harmony is out of key, you are right, because there is nobody there, nobody bothering to do it properly, so up yours, Northern Songs Ltd.

In *I Me Mine* he describes it as 'a joke, relating to Liverpool, the Holy City in the North of England. In addition the song was copyrighted Northern Songs, which I don't own, so: it doesn't really matter what chords I play, as it's only a Northern Song …'

The basic recording was made in February 1967, during *Sgt. Pepper*, but wasn't used at the time, an indication perhaps that they all felt it was a pretty feeble effort.

In the manuscript, George writes in the first verse that 'he wrote it like that' but in the recorded version he sings 'we wrote it like that', thus spreading the blame. There was also another verse, the fourth one, about his clothes, not in the manuscript.

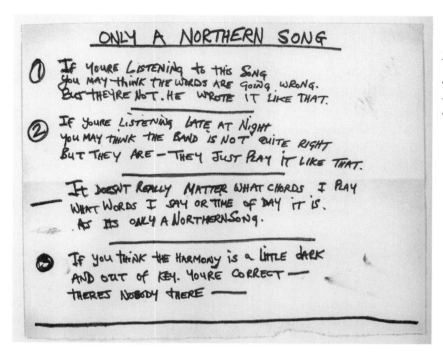

'Only A Northern Song', from the Yellow Submarine *album, January 1969, in George's hand.*

If you're listening to this song
You may think the chords are going wrong
But they're not
I just wrote it like that

When you listen late at night
You may feel the words are not quite right
But they are, I just wrote them myself

It doesn't really matter what chords I play
What words I say or time of day it is
As it's only a Northern song.

It doesn't really matter what clothes I wear
Or how I fare or if my hair is brown
When it's only a Northern song

If you think the harmony
Is a little dark and out of key
Then you're right
'Cos I sing it myself

All Together Now

This time it's Paul getting away with murder – doing a sing-along song, reciting the letters of the alphabet with some childlike activities thrown in, such as skip the rope, sail the ship. So, no lyrics worth commenting on. The 'All Together Now' chorus sounds as if it might by now have been appropriated as a political party anthem or as a football chant – but I have not heard it sung anywhere. Football fans around the world prefer to sing along to 'Yellow Submarine' or 'Hey Jude'.

Hey Bulldog

Considering that John said this was meaningless, and therefore we can presume there was no bulldog nor bullfrog, which was the original idea, the words are not bad – very like some of his earlier poetry: 'What makes you think you're something special when you smile.'

The third line 'Some kind of happiness is measured out in miles' was originally 'some kind of happiness is measured out in news' but got misheard, and it was decided to use the misheard version. Either way it sounds familiar – with echoes of 'I have measured out my life in coffee spoons' from T.S. Eliot's 'Prufrock'. On the record, a lot of John's words are indistinct, as he messes around, amusing himself, but, as he said, it was all fairly meaningless.

It's All Too Much

George's version of a childish nonsense verse – 'sail me on a silver sun', 'all the world is birthday cake' – but there are some fairly good lines – 'the more I learn the less I know' – and just when he's getting too pretentious he concludes 'and get me home for tea'. Some of the other lines sound a bit derivative and corny, such as long blonde hair and eyes of blue – which were used by the McCoys in their 1965 song 'Sorrow'.

George said that he wrote it 'after some LSD experiences which were later confirmed in meditation'. So any plagiarism was not his fault. But it's a good song, worth digging out. The recorded song has some more verses – and a lot of repetition.

When I look into your eyes
Your love is there for me
And the more I go inside
The more there is to see

It's all too much for me to take
The love that's shining all around you
Everywhere it's what you make for us
    to take
It's all too much

Floating down the stream of time
From life to life with me
Makes no difference
    where you are
Or where you'd like
    to be

It's all too much for
    me to take
The love that's
    shining all around
All the world is
    birthday cake
So take a piece, but
    not too much

Sail me on a silver
    sun
Where I know that
    I'm free

Show me that I'm everywhere
And get me home for tea
It's all too much for me to see
The love that's shining all around here
The more I learn, the less I know
And what I do is all too much

With your long blonde hair and eyes of
    blue
You're too much – aah
We are dead
Too much, too much, too much . . .

Get Back

'Get Back' was released as a single in April 1969, two months after the *Yellow Submarine* album. The song had been Paul's idea, and John helped out with the lyrics. In an improvised early version, mucking around in a jamming session – which was a feature of most of their creative sessions – 'Get Back' acquired for a while a deeper meaning, possibly in reaction to a news story on that day. Newly arrived Pakistanis in the UK were being told to go home by right-wing fascist groups and Enoch Powell was forecasting rivers of blood. So the title they were already working on picked up that mood.

But as they worked on it they gradually realized that it was open to misinterpretation and people might use it the wrong way. In one of the bootlegged tapes, there was a line that referred to Pakistanis, but they later redid the lyrics and dropped all references to Asian immigrants and the like, substituting neutral locations such as Tucson, Arizona, and introducing a frivolous element: a man who thought he was a woman. Thus the notion 'get back' – as in go back – could be interpreted almost any way you liked. 'I often left things ambiguous,' Paul said about the song. 'I like doing that in my songs.'

Most people probably never worried or even took in all the words, as the beat was so infectious, an exciting trainride of a rocker that got to number 1 all over the world.

The part manuscript is typed with the second verse corrected in John's hand – turning 'in the Californian grass' into 'for the Californian grass' which suggests a rather different meaning. You can also read the reference to Pakistanis in the third verse.

Jojo was a man who thought he was a loner
But he knew it wouldn't last
Jojo left his home in Tucson, Arizona
For the California grass

Get back, get back
Get back to where you once belonged
Get back, get back
Get back to where you once belonged
Get back Jojo. Go Home.
Get back, get back.

'Get Back' single, April 1969, part typed, with Paul's corrections.

Sweet Loretta Martin thought she was a woman
But she was another man
All the girls around her say she's got it coming
But she gets it while she can

Get back, get back
Get back to where you once belonged
Get back, get back
Get back to where you once belonged
Get back, Loretta. Go home.

Your mother's waiting for you
Wearing her high-heel shoes
And her low-neck sweater
Get on home Loretta
Get back, get back.
Get back to where you once belonged

Don't Let Me Down

John is supposed to have commented, when they were working on 'Get Back', that Paul really meant it to refer to Yoko, whom he wanted to go back, as she was now constantly in the studio. That was how John felt – that everyone was against Yoko.

Now in this song he is wondering that one day she might let him down and leave him. The song – the B side of 'Get Back' – is for Yoko, one of the most heartfelt, moving love songs John ever wrote, a late flowering in a way, getting back to a simple message and a simple rhythm, with no cluttered-up psychedelic sounds or nonsense lyrics.

He says he is in love for the first time, which must have saddened the now deserted Cynthia, and he is sure it is going to last for ever: 'A love that has no past.' He has fun with the past tense of 'do', deliberately using bad grammar, 'she done me good' instead of she did me good. It is a common colloquial usage, as is its sexual connotation: 'I guess nobody really done me – she done me, she done me good.' And yet the lyrics don't hark on the sexual element – it is all about true love, and whether it will last. John comes across as incredibly needy and fragile, which of course he often was, scared that people would let him down. That's what he believed had happened to him in the past, when his parents let him be brought up by Mimi.

I got a letter from John in 1968, about a year before this record was released, in which he adds a PS: 'Don't let me down.' It was about a small matter in my biography, which he wanted me to see Mimi about, but it shows that this was a phrase he used often.

In the manuscript, mostly in Mal's hand with corrections by John, you can see John is undecided whether to opt for correct grammar with 'does', or go with 'do' instead.

Don't let me down
Don't let me down
Don't let me down
Don't let me down

Nobody ever loved me like she do me
Ooo she does, yes she does
And if somebody loved me like she do me
Ooo she do me, yes she does
I'm in love for the first time

Don't you know it's gonna last?
It's a love that lasts forever
It's a love that had no past

And from the first time that she really
    done me
Ooo she done me, she done me good

I guess nobody ever really done me
Ooo she done me, she done me good

Hey, don't let me down
Can you dig it?
Don't let me down

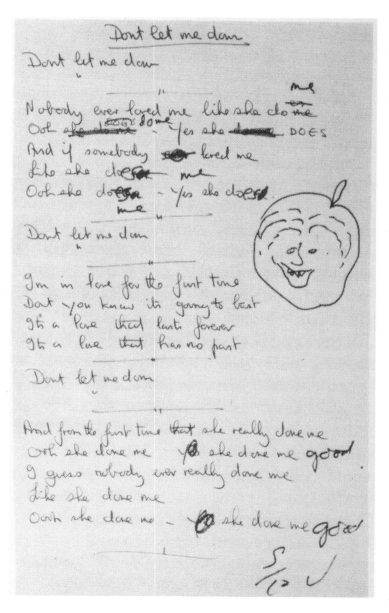

'Don't Let Me Down', the B side of the 'Get Back' single, in John's hand, with some interesting grammatical changes.

The Ballad Of John And Yoko

Not a ballad in one sense; instead of slow, strumming music, this was a fast rocker, so you could just go along for the ride. But it is lyrically a ballad in that it has a straight narrative, telling a rather sad story. And the story is …? John's.

It's a recitation of true stuff, what had been happening to him in real life – and in his head. In real life they did try to set off to sail from Southampton, hoping to get to Holland or France, but never made it. Peter Brown was the management figure at Apple who did tell them they could get married at Gibraltar (which they did in March 1969). They went to Amsterdam for a bed in, and yes, the references to fifty acorns is true. They sent them to world leaders, asking them to plant them for peace. So the narrative is straight and factual.

But what about the narrative in his head? John finishes by singing 'they're gonna crucify me'. It is true that he and Yoko were being mocked by the media in most parts of the world, scoffed at for thinking that staying in bed for two weeks would somehow lead to peace. But the idea of being crucified was ridiculous, wasn't it? Total paranoia, surely? Well, he'd harboured such delusions before. Even while only twenty, writing to his friend Stu from Hamburg, he was going on about being crucified, feeling the world was against him – and yet he had done nothing or said nothing to offend the world at large.

Now, he felt he really was being got at by everyone. And it did feel like being crucified. And in a sense, that is what happened to him in the end …

Old Brown Shoe

Written by George, the B side of 'The Ballad of John and Yoko' single, which came out in June 1969. It has a couple of very good lines at the beginning: 'I want a love that's right / But right is only half of what's wrong' – which makes sense, if you think about it long enough. The second line though, developing the theme, descends into bathos, wanting a short-haired girl who sometimes wears it twice as long.

On the surface, it is a simple, fairly corny love song – 'for your sweet top lip I am in the queue' – but George is agonizing away behind the scenes, trying to tell us that opposites, right and wrong, left and right, love and hate, are all part of each other. And in heaven we are all one anyway. The material world is an illusion. In *I Me Mine*, he tells us the song is about the 'duality of things'.

The title, 'Old Brown Shoe', comes from a passing remark in the first verse – 'stepping out of this old brown shoe' – which I take to mean stepping out of this old worn-out materialistic life down here.

The manuscript is interesting as you can see clearly some of his thought processes, with crossings-out and changes. The last verse has lines that never made it, about him being wakened by people knocking at his door.

'Old Brown Shoes', the B side of 'The Ballad Of John And Yoko', an early version in George's hand, with an unused last verse.

I want a love that's right but right is only half of what's wrong.
I want a short haired girl who sometimes wears it twice as long.
Now I'm stepping out this old brown shoe, baby, I'm in love with you.
We're so glad you came here, it won't be the same now, I'm telling you.

Though you pick me up from where some try to drag me down
When I see your smile replacing every thoughtless frown
Got me escaping from this zoo
Baby I'm in love with you
So glad you came here
It won't be the same now, now that I'm with you

If I grow up I'll be a singer wearing rings on every finger.
Not worrying what they or you say I'll live and love and maybe someday
Who knows, baby, you may comfort me.

I may appear to be imperfect but my love is something you can't reject
I'm changing faster than the weather
If you and me should get together
Who knows baby? You may comfort me

I want that love of yours
To miss that love is something I'd hate
Make an early start, making sure that I'm not late

For your sweet top lip I'm in the queue
Baby I'm in love with you
So glad you came here
Won't be the same now, when I'm with you

I'm so glad you came here
It won't be the same now, now that I'm with you

13

LET IT BE

1969–1970

I nearly made it on to the *Let It Be* album – not as myself, but as the inspiration for a song. Or at least, so I have imagined, so I tell myself. Complete fantasy, I am sure, but we can all dream.

Late one night in December 1968, when my wife and family and I were living in a converted sardine factory right on the beach at Praia da Luz in the Algarve, there was loud banging and shouting from outside, which we thought at first must be drunken fishermen. I opened the door to find a rather cross taxi driver, who was demanding to be paid, having driven his fares all the way from Faro Airport, only to find they now said they had no money. Out of the taxi spilled Paul and a blonde American woman called Linda whom I had never seen before. When we had left London nine months earlier, Paul was still engaged to Jane Asher.

It gradually emerged that he had got together with Linda, a photographer. And she had a six-year-old daughter called Heather, who was also with them. That evening, in London, Paul had suddenly decided to come out and visit us, knowing we had two young children, just a bit younger than Heather. They didn't ring, as we didn't have a phone, but they knew our address as I had written to him. They simply asked Neil Aspinall, their road manager, to book them a private jet, and off they went.

They stayed for about two weeks, and we all had a jolly time, going on local expeditions, up in the hills, mucking around on the beach. Paul had brought his guitar with him, as always, and even used to take it with him to the lavatory. One evening I happened to reveal that my real first name is Edward, but I had never ever been called that, only by my second name, Hunter. For some reason, Paul thought this was awfully funny – though I can't think why, as Paul is not his real first name either; he was christened James Paul.

So he went off to the lavatory and when he came back he played us four bars of a song he had apparently just written called 'There You Go Eddie'. He only had four lines – which consisted of the title repeated three times, then the line 'Eddie you've gone'. I thought it was pretty good, and naturally encouraged him to finish it. He said he might, one day.

When we got back to London in 1969, I rushed to buy their next two albums – which alas, turned out to be their final two albums – hoping that Eddie would have been worked on, polished up, or even subsumed into another song, but nope, no sign of Eddie, in any form.

Quite recently, I heard a copy of a song about Eddie that had been found on a bootleg tape of the *Let It Be* recording sessions. (Apparently one hundred hours' worth of bootlegs have crept out over the years.) You can hear Paul singing and playing the Eddie song to John. He had obviously worked on it a bit, as it had acquired a second verse and quite a decent middle section. In it, Eddie is referred to as 'Eddie you dog' who thinks he is one of the 'In Crowd'. Surely I never thought that about myself? It had become a fairly decent song, as whole and complete as some of the songs they used to fill up their final album. But, curses, it never made the cut. On the bootleg tape, John can be heard muttering in the background. Paul does several versions, changing Eddie to Tiger, Bernard, Nigel and then to Mimi, which makes John laugh. When Paul has finally finished singing it, there is silence from John.

The *Let It Be* album was a fairly chaotic, unhappy, unsatisfactory experience for them all – and it ended up being delayed well over a year, for various reasons. Technically, it was their last album, being the final to appear, but it was in fact the penultimate album that they worked on and recorded.

The original idea was to make a film of them recording, which was a good idea, observing them at work, watching them create their music – something all Beatles fans would have loved to see. In the event, they spent most of the recording sessions arguing amongst themselves. George fell out with Paul and John in January 1969, while they were recording, and left the group for a week, but was persuaded back. He was fed up with being bossed around by Paul and thought John was just messing about, not working hard enough. They were arguing about Apple, particularly about Allen Klein, who had been brought in to manage their affairs by John, George and Ringo – but not by Paul, who wanted someone else. By this time they were also each going their separate ways, with their own individual projects – and partners. John and Paul had rows. Then the lawyers were brought in. The whole thing became a sorry, sad mess, something I had never ever expected. I had often morbidly, gruesomely imagined the Beatles all dying suddenly in a plane crash – just because there had been periods in their lives when so many people around them, friends and relations, had suddenly died. I hadn't expected them to splutter and splinter apart over what seemed to the outside world to be petty, piddling, personal and business differences. Dear God, surely they could have worked it out.

The *Let It Be* film, when it eventually emerged, allowed us to see the effects of some of these differences, capturing their strained relationships and petty bickering. The film was only 81 minutes long, cut down from miles of material, and its release was endlessly delayed.

The album was also delayed. Allen Klein was not happy with it and ordered several remixes. Then Phil Spector was brought in to add some polish to it, which made Paul furious as he hadn't been consulted and was upset by what Spector was doing to some of his songs. Paul then announced his departure from the Beatles, though John had already decided he was off, having had enough, but was persuaded not to announce it before a new EMI contract was signed.

So by the time the *Let It Be* album was eventually released in May 1970, along with the film, the Beatles were no more. The album 'as reproduced for disc by Phil Spector' – came in a fancy black box set, complete with a 160-page glossy book, mostly colour photos, plus some overheard, rather pretentious chat that took place during the making of the film. The book is entitled *The Beatles Get Back*, as that was originally going to be the title of the album, and it has the publication date 1969, indicating how long it had been delayed. The original creation and recording of most of the songs on the album had taken place almost eighteen months earlier, in January 1969. In relatively happier times

One of those happy times, as captured in some historic photos in the book, shows them on the roof of the Apple office in Savile Row on 30 January 1969, when they played their last ever live session. Not to a paying public, but to thousands of gapers in the streets below, listening to their live performance – until the police came along and put a stop to it. In the film, and in the photographs, you can see how much they were enjoying themselves, playing together, larking around, amused by such a funny stunt, such a funny location, and also by themselves, having fun together.

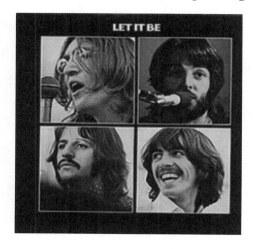

Two Of Us

The two were not Paul and John, despite the fact that in the film you see them head to head in the studio, sharing the same microphone, singing away. The two of them were now Paul and Linda, his new loveheart, soul mate, companion. The song was recorded in January 1969, just after they had got back from their Portuguese holiday.

Linda used to encourage Paul to jump in the car, drive off and get lost, as they did in Portugal – and naturally Paul wrote a song about it, writing it as it happened, standing solo, wearing raincoats, then driving home again, singing that we're going home. There's a reference to chasing paper, which could be a reference to the Apple mess and all the documents and court cases – but he doesn't dwell on this. It's a happy, cheerful, totally straightforward road song – no memorable lyrics, but a proper song, with a chorus and verses.

It's the first song on *Let It Be*, but before Paul starts singing 'Two of Us', you can hear John announcing 'I dig a pygmy by Charles Hawtrey and the Deaf Aids (Ha ha ha). Phase one, in which Doris gets her oats …'

Charles Hawtrey was an English actor who appeared in many *Carry On* films. 'Getting your oats' meant sexual intercourse, a phrase you hardly hear these days, modern usage being much more blunt.

Professor Campbell, in his compendium, transcribes these two lines as being part of the lyrics of 'Two of Us', but I have ignored them. It is just John playing silly buggers.

The manuscript, possibly in Mal Evan's hand, is neatly done on Apple notepaper. At the end it says 'A Quarrymen Original' – a joke, harking back to the days when they wrote 'Another Lennon–McCartney original' on every song scrap.

Holiday snap, Portugal, 1968: (left to right) Hunter Davies, Linda McCartney, Paul, Hunter's wife Margaret, and children.

Two of us riding nowhere
Spending someone's hard
    earned pay
You and me Sunday driving
Not arriving on our way back
    home

We're on our way home
We're on our way home
We're going home

Two of us sending postcards
Writing letters
On my wall
You and me burning matches
Lifting latches on our way back home

You and I have memories
Longer than the road
That stretches out ahead

Two of us wearing raincoats
Standing solo in the sun
You and me chasing paper getting
   nowhere
On our way back home

'Two Of Us', the first track on the Let It Be *album, released May 1970, in Paul's hand on notepaper from Apple's Savile Row office, from the roof of which they did their last performance. Most of* Let It Be *was recorded at Savile Row.*

Dig A Pony

Pure self-indulgence; John was trying to see how far they could make things up as they went along, without preparation. Somewhere inside all the pony, road hog, moon dog nonsense (which John admitted was garbage), and forced rhymes like penetrate, radiate, imitate, indicate, syndicate, there is a half-decent song trying to get out. It surfaces briefly in the two-line chorus where John movingly sings about Yoko: 'All I want is you / Everything has just got to be like you want it to.' This suggests that he saw Yoko forever organizing him and their life together – which was roughly true. Paul's Linda, by comparison, was laidback, let it all hang out, play it by ear, let's go off and get lost, see what happens – which was also roughly true. This aspect of the character of each of their respective new loves greatly appealed to each of them. John had felt lost and wanted to be led. Paul was fed up with the constraints of being engaged to Jane, and caught up in Apple and the legal problems, being forced to be the leader and boss, as he saw it, in order to get anything done.

The original working title of 'Dig A Pony' – which doesn't mean anything – was 'Con a Lowry', thought to have been a reference to a make of organ lying around in the studio. I have always wondered if instead it could have anything to do with Brian Epstein's collection of Lowry paintings (which Brian had bought with the money the Beatles had made for him).

Across The Universe

John's most poetic lyrics for some time. They appear slightly stream-of-consciousness but are all worked out and make sense, with excellent imagery. Certainly not garbage. 'Words are flying out like endless rain into a paper cup … pools of sorrow, waves of joy are drifting through my open mind.'

This was a song I heard him struggling with some time early in 1968, perhaps even late 1967, when he was still living at Kenwood with Cynthia, but at the time he only had a few bars and a few lines. In the *Playboy* interview he said he had been lying in bed next to Cynthia and she had been reproaching him for something. 'I went downstairs and turned it into a sort of cosmic song rather than an irritated song.' He had certainly worked hard on it by the time he came to record it in February 1968, then it was later remixed by Phil Spector for the *Let It Be* album

It was being recorded on a Sunday, when it was difficult to suddenly order up any backing singers, so two of the so-called Apple Scruffs – girl fans who hung around every day outside Paul's house or the Abbey Road Studios – were called into the studio to help out, a fantasy come true. All they had to do was sing 'Nothing's gonna change my world' over and over again for two hours. One of them was Lizzie Bravo, a sixteen-year-old Brazilian who had been given a trip to London by her parents as a birthday present, then had stayed on, getting a job as an au pair. (She went on to work in Brazil as a singer and publisher, and is now a grandmother, living in Rio – and about to release her memoirs of her time in London.)

I Me Mine

George in his book of the same name tried to tell us what he was saying in this song, but alas I was little wiser. 'There are two "I's": the little "i" and the big "I" i.e. OM, the complete whole, universal consciousness that is void of duality and ego.' Hmm.

So I went back to the song itself and decided that what he is saying is that there is too much ego in the world – everyone is saying something is mine, it's I and me all the time. Which is all perfectly true. But how does he know that out there in the void things aren't much the same – or worse?

If you didn't have the words written down, it would be hard to work out what George is actually singing. He rolls the three words together, so it comes out as someone's name – Hymie Mine.

The manuscript in George's hand is much neater than his normal writing, as if determined to make things really clear to use in his book.

All through the day I me mine,
  I me mine, I me mine,
All through the night I me mine,
  I me mine, I me mine,
Now they're frightened of leaving it,
Everyone's weaving it,
Coming on strong all the time,
All through the day I me mine.
(Chorus)

All I can hear I me mine, I me mine,
  I me mine,
Even those tears I me mine, I me mine,
  I me mine,
No-one's frightened of playing it,
Everyone's saying it,
Flowing more freely than wine,
All through your life I me mine.
(Chorus)

I ME MINE

All thru' the day, I·Me·MINE
All thru' the night, I. Me, Mine
Now they're frightened of leaving it,
Everyones weaving it, coming on strong
all the time --
All through the day I·ME - MINE.
          BOP.
All I can hear, I · Me · Mine,
Even your tear , I·ME·MINE.
No one's frightened of playing it
Everyone's saying it, flowing more
freely than wine,
All through your Life - I·Me·Mine.

'I Me Mine', from Let It Be, *in George's ever so nice handwriting.*

Dig It

Really silly and pointless lyrics, with made-up words and lists of names out of their heads or out of the newspapers – such as FBI, BBC, Doris Day. All the names and initials are understandable by most people today, except perhaps for Matt Busby, unless you happen to be a British football fan. He was the manager of Manchester United Football Club.

The song, mercifully, is very short, just fifty seconds, and with only six lines, carved out of a much longer jam session. On the album, you can hear them mucking around, as they did in the film, playing up to the cameras, knowing they were being filmed. At the end of this track, John is heard doing stupid voices at Paul's expense. 'Now we'd like to do "'Ark the Angels Come",' he says in a high-pitched Lancashire Wee Georgie Wood voice – introducing the next song, Paul's serious and heartfelt song about his mother. Not very kind.

Let It Be

In the midst of all the angst and anger, rows and recriminations during this awful year, while Paul was trying to organize them, sort out the problems and frictions – and getting no thanks for it – he was lying awake one night, feeling paranoid, when he imagined that his mother Mary, who died when he was fourteen, was saying to him, Don't worry, it will turn out OK. 'I'm not sure if she actually said "Let it be", but that was the gist. I felt blessed to have that dream.'

Released as a single in March 1970, before the album itself came out, it is far and away the most commercial number on the album.

While it is almost a pastiche of a choral hymn, with lots of biblical overtones and allusions such as 'hour of darkness', 'a light that shines on me' and of course the image of Mother Mary, it is nonetheless sincere and moving. When Paul has played it over recent years, the hall lights go down and the audience often light candles, cigarette lighters or hold up their mobile phones to shed light. It does then begin to feel almost like a prayer meeting.

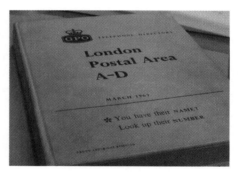

The London 1967 phone book with the slogan 'You have their name? Look up their number', which inspired John.

You Know My Name (Look Up The Number)

This was the B side of the 'Let It Be' single (though not used on the LP), first recorded in 1967 after completing *Sgt. Pepper*. Again, they were just larking around, stoned a lot of the time, hence its delayed release. It's a joke song, a comedy number, a *Goon Show* pop song. The general public will be hard pressed to remember it now, but its origins are interesting, and amusing. The inspiration was typical of many of John's songs, some of which turned out to be excellent, whose words were taken from other sources, in this case a telephone directory.

John was in Paul's house, waiting for him to arrive, when he noticed a copy of the London phone book for 1967 lying on the piano. On the front cover was the slogan: 'You have their name? Look up the number'.

John started playing with the words, and soon came up with a rhythm. Later, in Abbey Road Studios, he told Paul he had a new song, the title of which was 'You Know My Name, Look Up the Number'. When Paul asked to hear the lyrics – John told him that was it, there were no other words.

In recording it, repeating it over and over like a mad mantra, they ad-libbed some jokey remarks, introducing Paul by saying 'Welcome to staggers' and 'Let's hear it for Denis O'Bell'. The initial recordings were abandoned, and it was not worked on again until *Let It Be* – but nobody bothered to tell Denis O'Dell, a producer friend of theirs who had worked at Apple and on *A Hard Day's Night*.

When the single came out, O'Dell suddenly received a torrent of late-night phone calls from drugged-up hippies in California. Then groups of people, sometimes as many as ten, started arriving at his door, having tracked down his address, saying they were coming to live with him. He was forced to go ex-directory.

I've Got A Feeling

The first side of *Let It Be* finishes on a burst of 'Maggie May', a traditional Liverpool song which they used to perform in their early years. John's heavy Scouse accent is supposed to be funny but is a bit embarrassing.

Side two begins on 'I've Got A Feeling', which was originally two songs, one by Paul the other by John, knocked into one – just like in the good old days. They are both in fact good songs.

Paul begins it with the feeling he's got deep inside; obviously about Linda. John eventually comes in, telling us that everybody had a hard year. Which was true. Apart from all the long-running Apple rows, he had got himself arrested for drug possession and Yoko had a miscarriage. But he tries to keep his chin up, mocking himself in clichés like 'pull your socks up', 'let your hair down'.

After their individual bits, Paul returns with his song while John counterpoints in the background. It ends on a sort of 'Day In The Life' crescendo, although not as intense. The lyrics do have some sexual references – such as 'wet dreams', and at the end you can hear John saying 'it's so hard' – which were not in their early love songs.

One surviving manuscript, in Paul's hand, is only a scrap, but it gives a snippet of each song. The other is longer, but does not have John's contribution about their hard year.

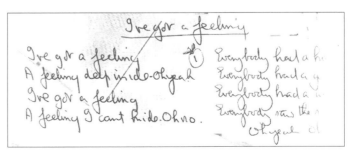

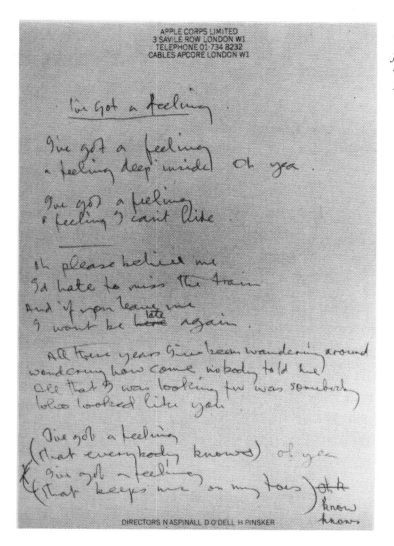

*'I've Got A Feeling',
from* Let It Be, *the
verses Paul wrote, in
Paul's handwriting.*

I've got a feeling, a feeling deep inside
Oh yeah, Oh yeah. (that's right.)
I've got a feeling, a feeling I can't hide
Oh no. no. Oh no! Oh no.
Yeah! Yeah! I've got a feeling. Yeah!

Oh please believe me, I'd hate to miss the train
Oh yeah, yeah, oh yeah.
And if you leave me I won't be late again
Oh no, oh no, oh no.
Yeah Yeah I've got a feeling, yeah.
I got a feeling.

All these years I've been wandering around,
Wondering how come nobody told me
All that I was looking for was somebody
Who looked like you.

I've got a feeling that keeps me on my toes
I've got a feeling, I think that everybody knows.
Oh yeah, Oh yeah.
Oh yeah, Oh yeah, Oh yeah.
Yeah! Yeah! I've got a feeling. Yeah!

Ev'rybody had a hard year.
Ev'rybody had a good time.
Ev'rybody had a wet dream.
Ev'rybody saw the sunshine.
Oh yeah, Oh yeah. Oh Yeah.
Ev'rybody had a good year.
Ev'rybody let their hair down.
Ev'rybody pulled their socks up. (yeah.)
Ev'rybody put their foot down.
Oh yeah. Yeah!
Oh my soul
Oh it's so hard

One After 909

Probably the oldest known Lennon–McCartney number, written by John not long after they first met back in 1957, in their Quarrymen days when they would bunk off school and go to Paul's house. They were trying to do a skiffle railway song, like the ones that were very popular at the time, such as 'Rock Island Line' and 'Cumberland Gap'. They had recorded it in 1963, but George Martin – who in those days was still in charge of such decisions – thought it wasn't good enough. Which it wasn't. Lines like 'Come on baby, don't be cold as ice' were not exactly poetic. Now, looking to fill up the *Let It Be* album, they decided they could get away with it. But even Paul admitted 'we hated the words'.

The Long And Winding Road

The road itself has been named by Beatles analysts as the B842, a long and winding road from Paul's cottage in Scotland with sixteen miles of twists and turns before it reaches anywhere – though Paul himself has never confirmed this was the road he had in mind. In his authorized biography, *Many Years from Now*, he says simply that he wrote it as a sad song, during some stormy recording sessions.

The lyrics are in fact very good, verging only marginally on the maudlin ('pools of tears'); rhyming 'cried' with 'tried' is a bit feeble, but as a love song, about the long and winding road that leads to your front door, i.e. to love, it is moving and poignant.

Its worth has rather been obscured by the fact that it was this song that led to so many rows and scenes. In the Beatles history books, the experts tend to concentrate on the dramas of the recording sessions, rather than on the content.

The song had been recorded quickly, and not very well. John, who had done a poor job himself, therefore decided to call in Phil Spector to knock it into shape – without telling Paul, who was busy with his own solo album. Paul was naturally furious.

Spector turned it into a lush, mushy, orchestral smoochy number, like a corny Hollywood film score, with an over-the-top female choir in the background.

John's defence was that if Paul had been allowed to work on it again, they would never have got *Let It Be* finished.

For You Blue

A George number, but unusually for him it's a happy-go-lucky, catchy blues song, with no Indian influences or mystical, magical, mysterious lyrics. He also manages a very convincing falsetto, the sort of stuff usually left to Paul. John can be heard chattering in the background, but it doesn't distract, nor mock the song. It's a love song, presumably for Pattie; he loves her because she's sweet and lovely. What could be nicer?

'For You Blue', from Let It Be, *in George's hand, with the title given a plural.*

Because you're sweet and lovely girl I love you,
Because you're sweet and lovely girl it's true,
I love you more than ever girl I do.
I want you in the morning girl I love you,
I want you at the moment I feel blue,
I'm living every moment girl for you.

I loved you from the moment I saw you,
You looked at me; that's all you had to do,
I feel it now I hope you feel it too.

The *Let It Be* album finishes with 'Get Back', which had already been released as a single.

When the delayed album finally came out in May 1970, there was alas no chance of them getting back.

14

ABBEY ROAD

September 1969

This was the last album they made, though not the last to be released. It came out seven years after their first one. And surprisingly, despite all the chaos and confusion, the splits and splinters in their personal and professional lives, they went out on a high. George Martin has said he thought it was their best album.

It was as if with *Abbey Road* they had decided to forget their differences for a moment, forget the mess they had made and were making of the *Let It Be* project, and try to go back to how they had been almost a decade earlier. They even included some soppy love songs. Plus several songs revealing how they really felt exploited and as if they were carrying the weight of the world upon their shoulders.

In Beatles' time, seven years counts as seventy years in normal human time. So much had happened to them, so much had been done by them, in such a short span, that it's hard to remember that they were playing and creating as Beatles for such a very short spell.

John, Paul, George and Ringo were still in their twenties when it all unravelled, and yet they seemed to have been around for so long that we looked upon them as elder statesmen, established figures with power and prestige. For Paul and Ringo at least, and even George, those seven years as Beatles turned out to be but a minor fraction of their adult lives. You wouldn't think so, of course, if you chanced upon a library of Beatles books, shelf after shelf of them, two thousand volumes at least, giving anyone arriving from Mars the impression they must have been on Earth for centuries, to have attracted all that attention.

Back in 1962, when they started recording, they were so young and fresh-faced, wide-eyed about being in a proper studio, walking around London, getting invited to parties. Being simple souls, they wrote songs to a simple formula, with a simple beat. Or so we thought. We lumped them together at first, as if they were interchangeable, writing and playing and together, eyeball to eyeball.

As they gathered success, homes, families, more time, more interests, more stimulants – of every sort – they began to create more on their own, bringing in songs half or nearly finished. And we began to see that they were writing different songs in different ways – being different people.

The lyrics were never as polished and crafted and slick as Gershwin, Cole Porter or Noël Coward. They were often self-indulgent, confused. But at their best, they rang true, delivering meanings and messages and emotions. And yes, they were literary, popular poetry, giving us words and phrases that have passed into the language.

They left us with a range of songs and lyrics, with narrative stories, images, emotions and dreams. And it turned out we had three composers, not one joint composer. John, Paul and George created songs that eventually would be recognized as distinctly theirs.

But these were not poems set to music. You can see from most of the scraps of the manuscripts which have survived that they were rarely whole poems completed before the band went into the studio – unless of course they were versions that got written out, when finished, for the others to see. The songs were made by fitting words and music together, not from parts completed separately.

The early songs were meant to be danced to, with not much thought given to the words, apart from appealing to a female teenage audience, which of course is not as easy as it might appear. The lyrics then moved on from boy–girl love to more complex relationships. In the third stage, they were generally more concerned with the world within.

Once they had moved on from basic love songs, and got control of their own records, there were no barriers: any subject, however apparently trivial or silly, might surface in their lyrics. While they progressed from romantic love to abstract love and concepts such as Peace and Love and Understanding, they were not politically revolutionary or iconoclastic in their lyrics. John drew back from encouraging physical violence. There was never any overtly raw sexual content. Unlike today.

On the whole, the lyrics meant what they said. Unlike Dylan, they did not often go in for metaphor or symbolism. Of course some meanings were less obvious, but that was usually intended – employing word play, word association, stream-of-consciousness, or just plain nonsense.

Looking back, at the time of *Anthology* in 1995, Paul was quite pleased with what they had achieved with their lyrics. 'There's hardly any of them that says "Go on, kids, tell them all to sod off, leave your parents." It's all very "All You Need Is Love" or "Give Peace a Chance". There was a good spirit behind it all.'

The range of their lyrics, and their songs, was helped by the fact that the band's three creative forces were in many ways polar opposites – something we had never realized, and probably they didn't either, not at first. Paul is on the whole cheerful, optimistic, thumbs up, conservative with a small c, and also wanting to be liked, craving an audience. John appeared to scowl behind his granny specs, which we thought were purely to assist with an eyesight problem, but he was often scowling inside as well. He hardly cared about being popular, being liked. He could be contrary, selfish, cruel – and yet loving. These differences created sparks which created songs.

Words were John's first concern whereas with Paul the melody came first. In the early years, it was thought by some that John was the lyric writer while Paul did the music. But each could do either, and do it as well as the other one could, thus spurring each other on. With success, they were able to reflect their true selves much more. But with success, the sparks flared into flames, igniting blazing rows. The rivalry that had once been cooperative, then competitive, became incendiary. Yet they still loved each other.

George was the biggest surprise of all. He seemed like a typical George at first, his name suggesting an ordinary, simple lad, no great depths. John, aided by Paul, kept him in his place for many years, which was on the guitar, hardly letting him sing on stage. When George first started writing songs, they were not encouraging. 'There was an embarrassing period,' John once said, 'where his songs were not that good and nobody wanted to say anything. He wasn't just in the same league for a long time. That's not putting him down – he just hadn't had the practice as a writer as we had.' Which of course is putting him down.

George himself, back in 1967, told me that he thought that all three of them had been discouraged from progressing in the early years. 'We had to go on stage all the time and do it, with the same old guitars, drums and bass. We just had to stick to basic instruments. We were held back in our development.'

In an interview with an American magazine, *Crawdaddy,* in 1977, George complained that the Beatles had helped to hold him back. 'The problem was that John and Paul had written songs for so long it was difficult. They had such a lot of tunes and they automatically thought theirs should have priority, so I'd always have to wait through ten of their songs before they would even listen to one of mine. I had a little encouragement from time to time, but it was very little. It was like they were doing me a favour. I didn't have much confidence in writing songs because of that. They never said "Yeah that's a good song." When we got into things like 'Guitar Gently Weeps', we recorded it one night and there was such a lack of enthusiasm. So I went home really disappointed because I knew the song was good.'

One of George's problems as a composer was that he didn't have a composing partner. John and Paul had each other, to criticize and encourage. He was essentially a loner, who didn't really want help or togetherness, but wanted to go his own way, do his own thing.

Yet George in many ways turned out to be the most complicated of them all. He was the first to realize it was all a nonsense, being a Beatle, being famous. He was the first to realize that exploring what was inside – and outside – was much more important. Again, this was reflected in his music.

Ringo had the only exotic name – OK, it was an assumed one, but a fancy-sounding one – yet he turned out to be the common man, the only one who didn't really change and kept his feet planted firmly on the ground. He only contributed two Beatles lyrics, so has not featured much, but he was an essential part of their success.

Over the decades, people have tried to sum up the different characters of the four Beatles. Likening them to the four seasons has been popular, and also the four apostles, the four phases of the Moon, the four corners of the Earth, the Four Stooges – or were there only three? I remember them being compared, in terms of their roles and what they contributed, with the four members of *Beyond the Fringe*, because, like them, one was Jewish. (This theory fell apart when it was pointed out that Ringo was not in fact Jewish.)

In 1973, Wilfrid Mellers, in his book about their music, had compared them to the four elements: Paul was Air and so needed John's Fire while Ringo's Earth needed George's Water. I'm not sure about George being Water, but then in 1973 George was still developing.

George did, however, reach a peak as a Beatle with *Abbey Road*, producing two of his best ever songs, 'Something' and 'Here Comes The Sun'. They knew *Abbey Road* was their swansong when they were making it, the end of that particular road, and they did try to get along, to make it work, producing some well-rounded songs – except for some on the second side which sound a bit hurried.

Abbey Road, obviously, was named after Abbey Road, where they had been recording since they began. The cover photograph was taken by the late Iain Macmillan and shows them on the pedestrian crossing on Abbey Road itself, near the EMI studios. Long-haired John, the leader, leads them over in a white suit. Ringo is next, in a black suit. Paul has bare feet. A bearded George is in jeans. Pick the bones out of that – and millions did, even analysing the significance of the registration numbers of the vehicles that can be glimpsed in the background. The crossing – which today has been moved a few yards further on, for safety reasons – is one of the most photographed locations in London, despite being utterly boring and, er, pedestrian.

No sleeves notes at all on the album alas, no printed copy of the lyrics. I did miss that.

Come Together

John wrote this during his and Yoko's 1969 Toronto bed-in – which also produced 'Give Peace a Chance' (not included here as it was not a Beatles song but a Plastic Ono Band number). Timothy Leary, while visiting John and Yoko in the bedroom, had asked John for a campaign song as he was running against Ronald Reagan for Governor of California. Leary's slogan was 'Come together – join the Party'. John made up a new tune and some words to go with the slogan and taped it. Leary got arrested for drug possession and ended up in prison.

Later, back in London, John brought it into the studio and, with Paul's help, knocked it into shape. It was chosen as the first song on the *Abbey Road* album.

Leary, thinking he had been given the song, complained to John. John explained that he was like a tailor – if he does a suit for a customer who then doesn't return, he sells it to someone else. John also had trouble when it was proved that he had lifted one of the phrases about 'old flat top' from a Chuck Berry record.

Those niggles aside, the song proved very popular, especially amongst the left-wing hippie, druggie brigade, who latched on to the line 'One thing I can tell you is you got to be free'. It seems unlikely that they understood all the other lines, but then, who does? It was just John throwing in random thoughts and phrases. Some are fairly easy to trace. The first two lines – 'He got O-no sideboard / He one spinal cracker' – refer to Yoko and her habit of giving asides during their interviews and also standing on his naked back to ease his spine.

Some clever clogs have suggested that each verse refers to a different Beatle. 'Holy roller' was the spiritual George. 'He got monkey finger, he shoot Coca-Cola' was Ringo. 'Got to be good looking cause he's so hard to see' was Paul. And the Ono sideboard remark referred to John and Yoko.

The BBC banned the record for a while. No, not because of sexual connotations in the title; it was that reference to Coca-Cola that upset them. Commercial endorsements were not allowed.

John was always proud of the record, and his voice singing it, but admitted the lyrics were gobbledygook.

Something

George, despite being fed up being a Beatle, managed to produce one of the Beatles' classics. 'Something' was quickly issued as a single – George's first A side in the UK – and has since been covered by scores of artists. After 'Yesterday', it is reckoned to be the most recorded Beatles song. And yet, poor old George, when Frank Sinatra performed it, he used to introduce it as a Lennon–McCartney number.

According to George, there was no story behind it. He just wrote it on the piano in an empty studio while the others were busy on *The Double White Album*, being bossed around by Paul. (He didn't use those words, but that's the implication.) It was too late to be included in that album, but was ready in time for *Abbey Road*, after the others had helped with the middle eight.

There is some suggestion that he pinched the first line from another singer, James Taylor, who was working at the same time at Abbey Road, though his song did not come out till later. Taylor never protested, and was flattered to think it might be true. As we know, lines have to come from somewhere – and that somewhere is not always clear or traceable.

The lyrics are probably George's best – a simple love song, clearly with Pattie in mind – who else could it have been at that stage of his life? Alas, his wondering and worrying about whether their love would grow proved correct.

In George's manuscript, there is a final verse he didn't use – just as well, as it's a bit lame, especially 'that woman don't make me blue'.

One hates to be pedantic, but there is also a spelling mistake in the third line – the sort of slip Paul rarely made.

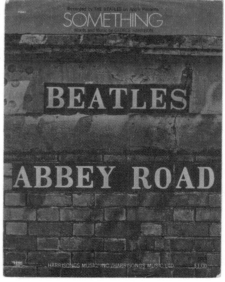

'Something', the second track on the Abbey Road *album, the last one they worked on, released October 1969. In George's hand, with a final verse he never used.*

There's something in the way she moves
Attracts me like no other lover
Something in the way she woos me
I don't want to leave her now
You know I believe and how

Somewhere in her smile she knows
That I don't need no other lover
Something in her style that shows me
I don't want to leave her now
You know I believe and how

You're asking me, will my love grow?
I don't know, I don't know
You stick around now it may show
I don't know, I don't know

Something in the way she knows
And all I have to do is think of her
Something in the things she shows me
I don't want to leave her now
You know I believe and how

Maxwell's Silver Hammer

Oh what fun Paul had writing this. Even after all these years, you can picture him smiling as he enunciates some of the tongue-twisting phrases which would have been so easy to mangle: 'Joan was quizzical studied pataphysical', 'wishing to avoid an unpleasant scene', 'painting testimonial pictures'. He is clearly laughing when he sings 'writing fifty times I must not be so'.

APPLE CORPS LIMITED
3 SAVILE ROW LONDON W1
TELEPHONE 01-734 8232
CABLES APCORE LONDON W1

MAXWELL'S SILVER HAMMER.

① Joan was quizzical
Studied pataphysical science in the home.
Late nights all alone with a test tube
oh oh oh oh.
Maxwell Edison majoring in medicine
Called her on the phone
Can I take you out to the pictures? Joan
oh. oh. oan . . . .

But as she's getting ready to go.
A knock comes on the door.
CHORUS:
Bang bang Maxwell's silver Hammer
Came down upon her head.
Clang clang Maxwell's silver hammer.
Made sure that Joan was dead,

② Back in school again (a fool)
Maxwell is on ass again
Teaching gets annoyed
Wishing to avoid an unpleasant scene —
She tells him to stay when the class has gone away.
you will wait behind.

DIRECTORS N ASPINALL D O'DELL H PINSKER

'Maxwell's Silver Hammer', from Abbey Road, in Paul's hand. Five lines from the bottom, it was originally 'ass', which got changed to 'fool'.

So what is it about? Sounds a very cruel narrative. Someone called Maxwell goes around killing people with his silver hammer, first his girlfriend, then a teacher, then a judge, all a bit scary for the children, even though children do face horrors in some of our best-loved nursery rhymes and fairy tales.

It is, of course, metaphorical. Just when things seem to be going well, bang bang, down comes disaster in the form of the hammer, and ruins everything. Things going wrong at the time with the Beatles were pretty easy to see – most of them surrounding Apple.

During the recording itself, Paul only recalled one argument – about the time taken on 'Maxwell's Silver Hammer': 'I remember George saying to me, "You've taken three days, it's only a song." "Yeah, but I want to get it right."'

John hated the song, and lots of Beatles experts have dismissed it as twee and cute, but the music is music-hall jaunty, one of Paul's many pastiche arrangements.

In the manuscript, it was originally 'Back in class again, Maxwell plays the ass again'. Playing the ass was a period phrase from the fifties when we read comics where characters called each other 'silly ass'. It had fallen from use by 1969, leading to sniggers, especially in the USA. The word class got changed to school and ass became fool, thus creating a neat internal rhyme of school/fool instead of class/ass, though either would have worked and been pretty clever. Paul always attended to detail, even at this late stage in the Beatles game.

Joan was quizzical, studied pataphysical
Science in the home.
Late nights all alone with a test tube.
Oh, oh, oh, oh.
Maxwell Edison, majoring in medicine,
Calls her on the phone.
Can I take you out to the pictures,
Joa, oa, oa, oan?

But as she's getting ready to go,
A knock comes on the door.

Bang! Bang! Maxwell's silver hammer
Came down upon her head.
Clang! Clang! Maxwell's silver hammer
Made sure that she was dead.

Back in school again Maxwell plays the fool again.
Teacher gets annoyed.
Wishing to avoid an unpleasant scene

She tells Max to stay when the class has gone away,
You will wait behind
Writing fifty times I must not be so

But when she turns her back on the boy,
He creeps up from behind.

Bang! Bang! Maxwell's silver hammer
Came down upon her head.
Clang! Clang! Maxwell's silver hammer
Made sure that She was dead.

P. C. Thirty-one said, 'We've caught a dirty one.'
Maxwell stands alone
Painting testimonial pictures oh, oh, oh.

Rose and Valerie, screaming from the gallery
Say he must go free
(Maxwell must go free)
The judge does not agree and he tells them so, oh, oh

But as the words are leaving his lips,
A noise comes from behind.

Bang! Bang! Maxwell's silver hammer
Came down upon his head.
Clang! Clang! Maxwell's silver hammer
Made sure that he was dead.

Silver Hammer Ma, a, an.

Oh Darling

Paul got it into his head he wanted to sound raw and bluesy, tough and tired, so he sang it over and over again for a week to really knacker his voice – but he sounds more like John trying too hard, instead of Little Richard, whom he used to imitate so well back in their early years. It all sounds a strain, the music and the lyrics. So let's move on quickly.

Octopus's Garden

Paul and John didn't need to write the traditional Ringo song for Ringo to sing and amuse the boys and girls – this time Ringo wrote it himself, his second and last Beatles song. The idea came to him on hols in Sardinia in August 1968 on Peter Sellers' yacht when he had temporarily left the Beatles. He had turned down the offer of an octopus lunch – not surprising, Ringo did not go for fancy, foreign foods – but the captain of the boat told him about octopuses and their habits on the seabed, such as making a garden with stones, all of which Ringo found fascinating.

It's a jolly, popular song, with a country and western beat, though perhaps not quite as popular as 'Yellow Submarine', another aquamarine ditty. Ringo's voice, with his Liverpool accent, easily manages to rhyme 'in' and 'been' in the third line, pronouncing 'been' as 'bin'.

George helped Ringo out with the words and thought it was a lovely song. 'It gets deep into your consciousness … it is very peaceful. I suppose Ringo is writing a cosmic song without even realizing it.' Which just shows you that the Beatles themselves could over-analyse Beatles lyrics as well as any fan.

The manuscript – in Ringo's hand – has some interesting spelling and grammar ('knowes were weeve been'). Ringo, unlike the others, did not attend a grammar school. It is written on a sheet of promotional paper for Ringo's 1969 film, *The Magic Christian*, in which he co-starred with Peter Sellers.

I'd like to be under the sea
In an octopus's garden in the shade
He'd let us in, knows where we've been
In his octopus's garden in the shade

I'd ask my friends to come and see
An octopus's garden with me
I'd like to be under the sea
In an octopus's garden in the shade

We would be warm below the storm
In our little hideaway beneath the waves
Resting our head on the sea bed
In an octopus's garden near a cave

We would sing and dance around

In an octopus's garden in the shade

We would shout and swim about
The coral that lies beneath the waves
Lies beneath the ocean waves
Oh what joy for every girl and boy
Knowing they're happy and they're safe
Happy and they're safe

We would be so happy you and me
No one there to tell us what to do
I'd like to be under the sea
In an octopus's garden with you

'Octopus's Garden', from Abbey Road, *in Ringo's hand, with some excellent spelling. It is written on* Magic Christian *notepaper, the film Ringo starred in with Peter Sellers.*

I Want You (She's So Heavy)

There is not a lot to say about the lyrics as John himself has little to say, using a vocabulary of just twelve words – 'I want you / I want you so bad / it's driving me mad' and 'she's so heavy'.

When I asked John why there were so few words, he told me, 'This is about Yoko. She's very heavy. There was nothing else I could say about her other than "I want you". Someone said the lyrics weren't very good, but there was nothing more I wanted to say.'

And yet the song lasts for seven minutes and forty-four seconds, making it the second longest Beatles number. (The longest is 'Revolution 9' at eight minutes and twelve seconds, third is 'Hey Jude' at seven minutes four seconds.) The reason for the length is that it is mainly an instrumental number, almost an orchestral exercise on a theme, coming back to the same notes, the same words, but in a slightly different way, worrying about it, unable to leave it alone, like a sore, returning to it all the time. The wailing, nagging, trancelike music fits with the words, even if neither of them goes anywhere.

Here Comes The Sun

Another minimalistic lyric, as if they were running out of words, had used them all up, or were getting tired, or perhaps not helping each other to correct and improve as they had done in the past. Most of the songs on *Abbey Road* were completed and arranged by the original begetter, which was not the way they'd worked in the past.

In this instance, George's inspiration only ran to ten or so lines, with a lot of repeating – but it is still a very cheerful, hopeful, excellent song. George had decided to sag off (i.e. play truant) from yet another Apple round-table board meeting about their finances and organization. He was fed up with signing endless forms, which they didn't really understand, and went off to Eric Clapton's garden. While walking round, communing with nature, he realized spring was coming, the awful winter of discontent at Apple could not possibly go on for ever – so on an acoustic guitar borrowed from Clapton, he wrote this song. One of George's best – which just seems to have come to him, out of *plein air*.

John was not involved in the recording, and missed bits of a few other *Abbey Road* sessions, as he had been injured in a car crash in Scotland with

Yoko. The others just bashed on without him – something they would never have done seven years earlier. When John was eventually recovering, he and Yoko had a double bed from Harrods set up in the studio at Abbey Road. Yoko arranged for a microphone to be suspended over her head so she could offer her comments – which did not exactly thrill Paul.

In the manuscript, despite the limited number of words, George couldn't be bothered to write them all out so he used abbreviations like L.D. and H.C.T.S. He has written the words on what appears to be a sheet of headed paper with some sort of Eastern image and verses. (Could it be Sanskrit? Any suggestions?)

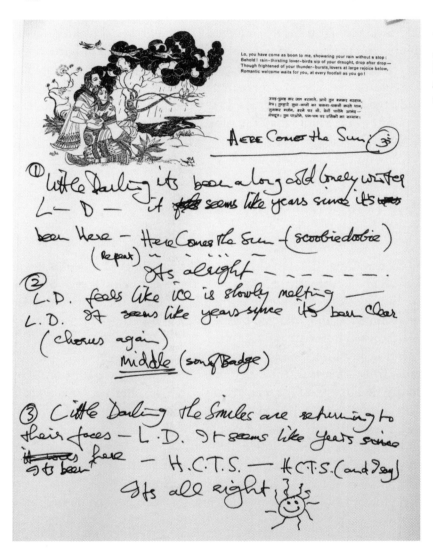

'Here Comes The Sun', from Abbey Road, *in George's hand, on mystical notepaper.*

Here comes the sun
Here comes the sun, and I say
It's all right

Little darling
It's been a long, cold lonely winter
Little darling
It feels like years since it's been here

Little darling I feel like ice is slowly
   melting

Little darling
The smiles returning to the faces
Little darling
It seems like years since it's been here

Sun, sun, sun, here it comes
Sun, sun, sun, here it comes

Little darling it feels like years since it's
   been clear

Because

Yoko was tinkling away on the piano, playing Beethoven's 'Moonlight Sonata' (she had studied piano as a gel, her father having hoped she would become a concert pianist). John was lolling, as ever, on the sofa, probably with a few relaxing medications to help him along. He asked if she could play some of the chords in the reverse order – and the resulting sounds inspired him to write 'Because'. The connection with Beethoven was well spotted by Wilfrid Mellers: 'The affinity between the enveloping, arpeggiated X sharp minor triads, with the sudden shift to the flat supertonic is, in the Lennon and Beethoven examples, unmistakable.'

In the early days, academic musicologists like Mellers tended to compare the Beatles' songwriting to Schubert's, so the Beethoven reference was interesting. One of their fave numbers in the Cavern days had been 'Roll Over Beethoven'. When asked what they thought about Beethoven, Ringo usually said he liked his work very much, 'especially his poems'.

The lyrics, once again, are sparse, just twelve lines, but they are quite poetic, combining Wordsworthian rhythms with modern usage: 'Because the world is round, it turns me on. Because the wind is high, it blows my mind. Because the sky is blue, it makes me cry.' It would have been easy to have mucked it up by having blue at the end, as they might have done back in 1962. Both Paul and George said it was their favourite song on *Abbey Road*. John was more matter-of-fact: 'The lyrics speak for themselves, they're clear, no bullshit, no imagery, no obscure references.'

Only five lines in John's hand have turned up, all a bit faded. They are written on the back of a business letter from John Eastman (representing Paul) to the other Beatles, during their interminable Apple rows. It gives us a date, 8 July 1969, and again reflects John's habit of writing lyrics on any old scrap lying around.

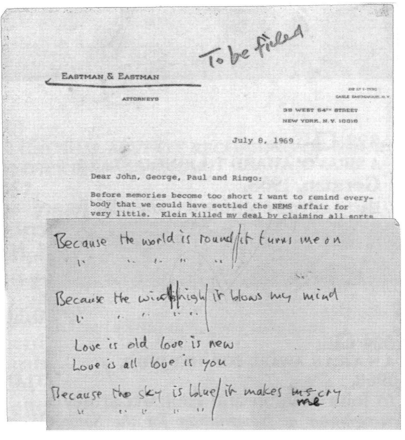

'Because', from Abbey Road, *five lines in John's hand, written on the back of a legal letter about yet another row concerning Apple, NEMS and Allen Klein, their one-time business manager.*

Because the world is round it turns me on
Because the world is round … aaaaaahhhhhh

Because the wind is high it blows my mind
Because the wind is high … aaaaaaaahhhh

Love is old, love is new
Love is all, love is you

Because the sky is blue, it makes me cry
Because the sky is blue … aaaaaaahhhh

You Never Give Me Your Money

This was one of those songs I could never get out of my head back when I first heard it. The opening four lines seemed to go round and round inside my brain. 'You never give me your money, you only give me your funny paper / and in the middle of negotiations / you break down.' Easy to sing, as it's almost all on the same note.

And then I could never remember how it went after that, the reason being that nothing really flowed on, nothing was connected. The song was made up of three if not four scraps of songs put together, using up leftovers.

The first part, about not being given the money, came out of the Apple squabbles. None of them ever seemed to have any real money, it was always bits of paper and forms purporting to show where it had all gone, where it was going. There might also have been a double meaning – Paul saying to John that you never give me yourself, now you are with Yoko. But that could be reading too much into it.

The next verse jumps rather awkwardly into the problems of a student, out of college, with no money. The last verse jumped again, to a sweet dream that had come true – meaning Linda, his loveheart, turning up to save him. So, quite a lot of scraps of lyrics, but not enough to make a whole song.

Sun King

We were now well into the second side of the album and from here to the end it is all short, unfinished pieces, filling up the side, unloading their minds, knowing it was going to be their last ever new album so better clear the decks in case we never come this way again. The songs run into each other, as a mad medley. In fact the working title was 'A Huge Medley'.

'Sun King' was a mere scrap, just seven lines – in fact three lines, with the other four made up of nonsense. The Sun King was Louis XIV of France. John, supposedly had been reading Nancy Mitford's biography of the Sun King, or at least a review of it.

For the final four lines, John reverted to singing gibberish, throwing in all the stupid foreign phrases he could think of: *mi amore, obrigado, quando, mundo* – in cod Italian/Portuguese/Spanish.

You could argue this was very avant-garde and revolutionary, like John Cage composing silent music, making a philosophical statement about the nature of art. Was John suggesting that words themselves were a nonsense? Who needs them, why do we tie ourselves to them, surely any words can be treated as lyrics, so come on, let's see if we can do it. Or was he just being bloody lazy? Or having a joke? Whatever the answer, it amused him at the time and filled two and a half minutes on the album.

Mean Mr Mustard

'Sun King' segues straight into 'Mean Mr Mustard' which then blends into 'Polythene Pam', and so on. They are connected in this way because they are all scraps, part songs, unfinished, embryos, not apparently good enough, or with no one willing enough to build them up and launch them as fully fledged, grown-up songs.

'Mr Mustard' was by John – 'a bit of crap I wrote in India' – based on a newspaper story about a miser who hid cash in his rectum, some sort of tramp, a dosser, a down and out. When John saw a homeless person sleeping in a park, or a dirty old man begging in the street, he used to say that he would probably have ended up that way himself, had the Beatles not come along. Perhaps he was thinking of his dad, Alfred, who wandered off to sea and survived doing odd jobs like washing up in hotel kitchens.

'Keeps a ten bob note up his nose' was not, John maintained, a drug reference, but the sort of thing he imagined Mr Mustard doing, to hide whatever money he had. Ah, ten bob notes, I remember them well. A real note, not a coin, which was worth half an old pound note, both of them long gone. In the song, mean Mr Mustard has a sister, originally named Shirley, but changed to Pam in order to lead us into the next song …

Polythene Pam

Also written in India by John. This one goes back to their dodgy, dingy Cavern days, telling of some insalubrious female fan who dressed up in polythene – a synthetic plastic material that had just become popular in the 1950s. Two different girls have come forward and said they were the original – one who ate polythene and the other who enjoyed three-in-a-bed sessions with John wearing nothing but polythene bags. The song finished with a 'yeah yeah', in a heavy Scouse accent – another period touch. Before merging straight on into the next song.

There is a manuscript for 'Polythene Pam' – not many from the Medley have survived or emerged – which has nine lines in John's best hand, but now a bit faint. In the final line there is a correction, but I can't read it. The rhymes are rather forced and the reference to the *News of the World* is now archaic (the paper closed in 2012).

Until I properly studied the finished lyrics – as they were not enclosed with the album – I had missed 'killer-diller', or at least failed to understand what he was trying to say, never having heard the expression. Now I see it written down, and have looked it up, I learn that it is American usage, coined just before the war, and refers to someone or something that is excellent, not to say fab. I wonder how John knew it? We never used it in Carlisle, and we were awfully cosmopolitan.

'Polythene Pam', from Abbey Road, *in John's hand but rather faint and some words hard to read.*

Well you should see Polythene Pam
She's so good-looking but she looks
    like a man
Well you should see her in drag
Dressed in her polythene bag
Yes you should see Polythene Pam
Yeah yeah yeah

Get a dose of her in jackboots and kilt
She's killer-diller when she's dressed to
    the hilt
She's the kind of a girl that makes the
    News of the World
Yes you could say she was attractively
    built
Yeah yeah yeah

She Came In Through The Bathroom Window

This is probably the best of the medley of short songs – written by Paul and based on a girl who actually did come through his bathroom window. She was one of the so-called Apple Scruffs who hung around Paul's house and the Abbey Road Studios, day and night, hoping for a glimpse. John, Ringo and George were usually spared this attention at their homes, living out in the suburbs in gated communities, but Paul was in the heart of London, and very handy for the studios. He also tended to indulge them, going out to say hello, pose for photographs, even asking the more sensible-looking ones to take Martha for a walk or do little jobs for him.

On this occasion, while Paul was away, some of them managed to find a ladder and climbed in through a bathroom window. Others poured in and went through Paul's clothes and belongings, one of which was a photograph of his father he particularly treasured. The neighbours spotted the girls, rang the police and each other – hence 'Sunday's on the phone to Monday'. The photograph was eventually returned.

After the first couple of lines, setting the narrative, the lyrics are a bit of a hotchpotch, not apparently connected, not meaning much, more like a John song, throwing in half-remembered phrases: 'And so I quit the police department' is said to have been inspired by a Los Angeles traffic cop named Eugene Quits. Or it could have referred to Pete Shotton, his boyhood friend, who did for a time become a policeman. But the tune is good.

The manuscript, in Paul's hand, on Apple Corps headed notepaper, looks like a version written out for somebody in the studio, perhaps George. At the end has been added: 'Another Lennon and McCartney original'.

She came in through the bathroom window
Protected by a silver spoon
But now she sucks her thumb and wonders
By the banks of her own lagoon

Didn't anybody tell her?
Didn't anybody see?
Sunday's on the phone to Monday,
Tuesday's on the phone to me

She said she'd always been a dancer
She worked at 15 clubs a day

And though she thought I knew the answer
Well I knew but I could not say.

And so I quit the police department
And got myself a steady job
And though she tried her best to help me
She could steal but she could not rob.

Didn't anybody tell her?
Didn't anybody see?
Sunday's on the phone to Monday,
Tuesday's on the phone to me
Oh yeah.

'She Came In Through The Bathroom Window', from Abbey Road, *in Paul's hand, again on Apple notepaper. There must have been a lot of it lying around, handy for writing out lyrics.*

Golden Slumbers

Paul wrote this at his father's house, 'Rembrandt', a rather smart villa with a conservatory and vines growing. Jim had moved there, thanks to Paul's financial help, abandoning their old family council house in Forthlin Road. By this time Jim had married Angie, whose daughter Ruth was learning the piano. Propped up on the piano was the sheet music of the well-known lullaby, 'Golden Slumbers'. Paul took the title and wrote his own version.

There are few words, just eight lines. The first two lines are Paul's – 'Once there was a way to get back homewards' – but the next six are taken almost word for word from the old lullaby, originally a poem written by Thomas Dekker in 1603. No sign of any credit for the words on the *Abbey Road* sleeve, but I suppose you don't have to worry about being sued when the author has been dead almost four centuries.

It's a sweet lullaby, nice melodies, but I never cared for the bit when he suddenly breaks into loud rocker mode, shattering the mood, before he goes back again to the soft going-to-sleep music.

Again, we move straight on, into the next tune in the Medley. Back before the shift in the balance of power, the Beatles had wanted to do a whole album where there were no breaks, but EMI had vetoed the idea, preferring songs to be clearly separated. On this their last album, the Beatles achieved one minor ambition.

Carry That Weight

As with 'You Never Give Me Your Money', Paul is feeling the weight of all the Apple arguments and the court cases, and his rows with Klein.

The notion of a weight having to be carried might also have been in Paul's mind in another sense, thinking of them as ex-Beatles: how would they cope, making music or anything else by themselves, saddled with the burden of having been Beatles. But this is probably a bit fanciful on my part.

After the first two lines – and there are only five lines in total – Paul reverts to the earlier song, and the words, repeating 'You Never Give Me Your Money' melody, but with slightly different wording, 'I never give you my pillow'. So it becomes a parody of his own parody.

And then goes straight on into …

The End

Which was the end, of the medley, of the album, and of the Beatles. They did record one more song after Abbey Road was completed – George's 'I Me Mine', but after Abbey Road came out in September 1969, the Beatles had effectively died.

Despite the lack of lyrics – just three lines, two of which are pretty good – there is a musical finale with the three guitarists doing battle. They each have a little solo – and even Ringo is persuaded, for the first time ever on a Beatles record, to do a drum solo. Then it all rises to a farewell crescendo, before Paul sings that final couplet: 'And in the end the love you take / is equal to the love you make.'

It sounds vaguely familiar, almost Shakespearian, but perhaps that's because it has been quoted so often. Paul said he wanted to finish, like the Bard, with a couplet, then exit left. Interesting that he went out on words, with a final lyrical flourish. Words did matter to them.

John thought the couplet was good, even if in talking about it to *Playboy* he got the words wrong, quoting it as 'the love you get is equal to the love you give'. But he did call it cosmic, which was praise enough.

Her Majesty

But, hee hee, having indicated it was the end, and done their farewells, and guitar flourishes, there is then quite a long pause. On the album sleeve it clearly lists the last song as 'The End', so clearly, nothing can be left. After all, with such an extended sequence of songs all strung together, it must surely all be over now. Then you suddenly hear Paul strumming away. It was originally part of the medley, then edited out. It supposedly appeared at the end of the master tape by accident. It lasts just twenty-three seconds, the shortest ever Beatles number.

And he has a good joke. He tells us that Her Majesty is a pretty nice girl, though she doesn't have a lot to say, but some day he wants to make her his. More affectionate teasing. As a schoolboy of nearly eleven, in June 1953, Paul had won an essay competition for the Queen's Coronation, writing about our lovely young Queen.

The Queen was still with us in 2014, and so was Paul and also Ringo – unlike the ten-bob note. And Her Majesty did knight Paul. So I am sure he would agree she was a pretty nice girl …

The Beatles' last 'public' performance on the roof of Savile Row in London in January 1969.

DISCOGRAPHY

Single playing records, by the Beatles, issued by Parlophone Records in England. All songs composed by Lennon and McCartney unless otherwise stated.

1962

Oct – Love Me Do/PS I Love You

1963

Jan – Please Please Me/As Me Why
Apr – From Me To You/Thank You Girl
Aug – She Loves You/I'll Get You
Nov – I Want To Hold Your Hand/This Boy

1964

Mar – Can't Buy Me Love/You Can't Do That
Jul – A Hard Day's Night/Things We Said Today
Nov – I Feel Fine/She's A Woman

1965

Apr – Ticket To Ride/Yes It Is
Jul – Help!/I'm Down
Dec – Day Tripper/We Can Work It Out

1966

Jun – Paperback Writer/Rain
Aug – Yellow Submarine/Eleanor Rigby

1967

Jan – Penny Lane/Strawberry Fields Forever
Jul – All You Need Is Love/Baby You're A Rich Man
Nov – Hello, Goodbye/I Am The Walrus

1968

Mar – Lady Madonna/The Inner Light (Harrison)

Single playing records issued by Apple Records

1968

Aug – Hey Jude/Revolution

1969

Apr – Get Back/Don't Let Me Down
May – The Ballad of John and Yoko/Old Brown Shoe
(Harrison)
Oct – Something (Harrison)/Come Together

1970

Mar – Let It Be/You Know My Name

Long playing records issued by Parlophone, England

1963

May – *PLEASE PLEASE ME*
I Saw Her Standing There; Misery; Ask Me Why; Please Please Me; Love Me
Do; PS I Love You; Do You Want to Know A Secret; There's A Place
Songs not composed by the Beatles:
Anna; Chains; Boys; Baby It's You; A Taste Of Honey; Twist And Shout

Dec – *WITH THE BEATLES*
It Won't Be Long; All I've Got To Do; All My Loving; Don't Bother Me
(Harrison); Little Child; Hold Me Tight; I Wanna Be Your Man; Not A
Second Time
Songs not composed by the Beatles:
Till There Was You; Please Mister Postman; Roll Over Beethoven; You Really
Got A Hold On Me; Devil In Her Heart; Money

1964

Jul – *A HARD DAY'S NIGHT*
A Hard Day's Night; I Should Have Known Better; If I Fell; I'm Happy Just

To Dance With You; And I Love Her; Tell Me Why; Can't Buy Me Love; Any Time At All; I'll Cry Instead; Things We Said Today; When I Get Home; You Can't Do That; I'll Be Back

Dec – BEATLES FOR SALE

No Reply; I'm A Loser; Baby's In Black; I'll Follow The Sun; Eight Days A Week; Every Little Thing; I Don't Want To Spoil The Party; What You're Doing

Songs not composed by the Beatles:

Rock And Roll Music; Mr Moonlight; Kansas City; Words Of Love; Honey Don't; Everybody's Trying To Be My Baby

1965

Aug – HELP!

Help!; The Night Before; You've Got To Hide Your Love Away; I Need You (Harrison); Another Girl; You're Going To Lose That Girl; Ticket To Ride; It's Only Love; You Like Me Too Much (Harrison); Tell Me What You See; I've Just Seen A Face; Yesterday

Songs not composed by the Beatles:

Act Naturally; Dizzy Miss Lizzy

Dec – RUBBER SOUL

Drive My Car; Norwegian Wood; You Won't See Me; Nowhere Man; Think For Yourself (Harrison); The Word; Michelle; What Goes On (Lennon, McCartney and Starkey); Girl; I'm Looking Through You; In My Life; Wait; If I Needed Someone (Harrison); Run For Your Life

1966

Sep – REVOLVER

Taxman (Harrison); Eleanor Rigby; I'm Only Sleeping; Love You Too (Harrison); Here, There And Everywhere; Yellow Submarine; She Said She Said; Good Day Sunshine; And Your Bird Can Sing; For No One; Dr Robert; I Want To Tell You (Harrison); Got To Get You Into My Life; Tomorrow Never Knows

1967

Jun – SGT. PEPPER'S LONELY HEARTS CLUB

Sgt. Pepper's Lonely Hearts Club Band; With A Little Help From My Friends; Lucy In The Sky With Diamonds; Getting Better; Fixing A Hole; She's Leaving Home; Being For The Benefit Of Mr Kite; Within You, Without You (Harrison); When I'm Sixty-Four; Lovely Rita; Good Morning, Good Morning; A Day In The Life

Long playing records issued by Apple Records

1968

Nov – THE BEATLES (THE DOUBLE WHITE ALBUM)
Back In The USSR; Dear Prudence; Glass Onion; Ob La Di Ob La Da; Wild Honey Pie; The Continuing Story of Bungalow Bill; While My Guitar Gently Weeps (Harrison); Happiness Is A Warm Gun; Martha My Dear; I'm So Tired; Blackbird: Piggies; Rocky Raccoon; Don't Pass Me By; Why Don't We Do It In The Road?; I Will; Julia; Birthday; Yer Blues; Mother Nature's Son; Everybody's Got Something To Hide Except Me And My Monkey; Sexy Sadie; Helter Skelter; Long Long Long; Revolution 1; Honey Pie; Savoy Truffle; Cry Baby Cry; Revolution 9; Good Night

1969

Jan – YELLOW SUBMARINE
Yellow Submarine; Only A Northern Song; All Together Now; Hey Bulldog; It's All Too Much (Harrison); All You Need Is Love. Not composed by the Beatles: Pepperland; Sea Of Time; Sea Of Holes; Sea Of Monsters; March Of The Meanies; Pepperland Laid Waste; Yellow Submarine In Pepperland

Oct – ABBEY ROAD
Come Together; Something (Harrison); Maxwell's Silver Hammer; Oh! Darling; Octopus's Garden; I Want You (She's So Heavy); Here Comes The Sun (Harrison); Because; You Never Give Me Your Money; Sun King; Mean Mr Mustard; Polythene Pam; She Came In Through the Bathroom Window; Golden Slumbers; Carry That Weight; The End

1970

May – LET IT BE
Two of Us; Dig a Pony; Across the Universe; I Me Mine (Harrison); Dig It (Lennon, McCartney, Harrison, Starkey); Let It Be (version two); Maggie Mae (arr. Lennon, McCartney, Harrison, Starkey); I've Got A Feeling; One After 909; The Long And Winding Road; For You Blue (Harrison); Get Back (version two)

Extended Players

1967

Dec – MAGICAL MYSTERY TOUR (Two EPs)
Magical Mystery Tour; Your Mother Should Know; I Am The Walrus; The Fool On The Hill; Flying (Lennon, McCartney, Harrison, Starkey); Blue Jay Way (Harrison)

NOTE: There were twelve other extended plays, but only one contains a song ('I Call Your Name' on the EP *Long Tall Sally*), not already on an LP or single.

Other songs written by the Beatles,

But recorded by other artists, not by the Beatles

LENNON/McCARTNEY

'I'll Be On My Way' (Billy J. Kramer)
'I'll Keep You Satisfied' (Billy J. Kramer)
'Bad To Me' (Billy J. Kramer)
'From A Window' (Billy J. Kramer)
'Tip Of My Tongue' (Tommy Quickly)
'Hello Little Girl' (The Fourmost)
'I'm In Love' (The Fourmost)
'Love Of The Loved' (Cilla Black)
'It's For You' (Cilla Black)
'Step Inside Love' (Cilla Black)
'One And One Is Two' (The Strangers)
'A World Without Love' (Peter and Gordon)
'Nobody I Know' (Peter and Gordon)
'I Don't Want To See You Again' (Peter and Gordon)
'Woman' (Peter and Gordon)
'Like Dreamers Do' (The Applejacks)
'That Means A Lot' (P.J. Proby)
'Thingumybob' (Black Dyke Mills Band)
'Catcall' (The Chris Barber Band)
'Penina' (Carlos Mendes)
'Goodbye' (Mary Hopkin)
'Come And Get It' (Badfinger)

GEORGE HARRISON

'Sour Milk Sea' (Jackie Lomax)
'Badge' (Cream)

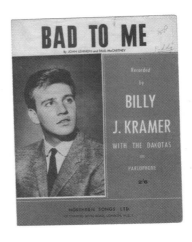

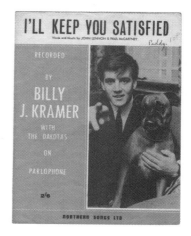

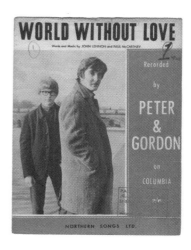

BIBLIOGRAPHY

Music Books

There must by now be well over 2,000 different books about the Beatles – by different I mean with their own ISBN numbers if nothing else. So many do repeat the same old stuff. On this project, it was the music that mattered to me, so I would like to recommend the following music books which I found most useful.

Steve Turner, *A Hard Day's Write*, Sevenoaks, 2012

Steve Turner, *The Gospel According to the Beatles*, Westminster John Knox Press, Louisville, 2006

Ian MacDonald, *Revolution in the Head*, Pimlico, 2005

Kevin Howlett, *The Beatles, The BBC Archives, 1962–70*, BBC Books, 2013

Wilfrid Mellers, *Twilight of the Gods*, Faber, 1973

Colin Campbell and Allan Murphy, *Things We Said Today: The Complete Lyrics and a Concordance to the Beatles' Songs 1962–1970*, Pierian Press, Ann Arbor, 1980

George Harrison, *I Me Mine: Genesis 1980* (limited edition), W.H. Allen, 1982

Stuart Madow and Jeff Sobul, *The Colour of Your Dreams*, Dorrance Publishing, Pittsburgh, 1992

William J. Dowlding, *Beatles Songs*, Fireside, NY, 1989

Stephen Spignesi and Michael Lewis, *100 Best Beatles Songs*, Tess Press, NY 2004

Jean-Michel Guesdeon and Philippe Margotin, *All the Songs*, Black Dog and Leventhal, NY, 2013

Biographies

Written by people who were there, or interviewed them:

Hunter Davies, *The Beatles* (1968); latest updated edition, Ebury, 2009, from which I have lifted quotes shamelessly.

Mark Lewisohn, *The Beatles: All These Years*, Vol. l, *Tune In*, Little, Brown, 2013

Barry Miles, *Paul McCartney – Many Years from Now*, Secker & Warburg, 1997

Olivia Harrison and Mark Holborn, eds, *George Harrison, Living in the Material World*, Abrams, 2011

George Martin and Jeremy Hornsby, *All You Need Is Ears*, Macmillan, 1979

Andy Peebles, *The Lennon Tapes*, BBC Books 1981

Jan Wenner, *Lennon Remembers*, Verso, 2002

David Sheff, *The Playboy Interviews with John Lennon and Yoko Ono*, Playboy Press, 1981

Jonathan Cott, *Days That I'll Remember*, Doubleday, 2013

Pete Shotton, *In My Life*, Coronet, 1984

Derek Taylor, *Fifty Years Adrift*, Genesis, 1984

Ray Coleman, *John Lennon*, two volumes, Futura, 1984

Reference

Mark Lewisohn, *The Complete Beatles Recording Sessions*, Hamlyn, 1988

Mark Lewisohn, *The Complete Beatles Chronicle*, Hamlyn, 1992

Julian Lennon and Brian Southall, *Beatles Memorabilia*, Carlton, 2010

Michael McCartney, *Remember, Recollections and Photographs*, Merehurst, 1992

Bill Harry, *The Ultimate Beatles Encyclopedia*, Virgin, 1992

Apple Corps, *The Beatles Anthology*, Cassell, 2000

Spencer Leigh, *Brother Can You Spare a Rhyme, 100 Years of Hit Song Writing*, Spencer Leigh Ltd, 2000

Keith Badman, *The Beatles Off the Record*, Omnibus, 2000

David Bedford, *Liddypool, Birthplace of the Beatles*, Dalton Watson, 2009

Stuart Maconie, *The People's Songs: The Story of Modern Britain in 50 Records*, Ebury, 2013

Help

If you know of any manuscript copies of Beatles lyrics (i.e. songs written and performed by them as Beatles) not included in this book, or if you think I have wrongly transcribed any of their handwriting, do please let me know: Johnlennonletters@hotmail.co.uk

ACKNOWLEDGEMENTS

Thanks

An unusual aspect of tracking down the originals of Beatles lyrics is that I came across several people who did *not* want to be thanked. Or at least their name revealed. Mostly they want a quiet life, with no one knowing that they have acquired something so valuable, which might get stolen or cause envy or total surprise amongst their family and neighbours, muttering well, I never, the sly old puss. The huge rise in the value of the best Beatles bits over the last thirty years has meant that relatively ordinary, not all that rich collectors and fans, if they have held on to their stuff, have often found they are sitting on small fortunes. Anyway, they all know who they are – so thanks a lot.

Apologies in advance to any owners surprised to see their treasures included here. I did try to contact every present-day owner where possible, but many of the items have passed through several hands over the years. Thanks to Sony, controllers of the copyright, for permission for publication, but I would also have liked out of courtesy to have been able to contact all the owners of the physical manuscripts. Sorry about that.

Those I would like to name and thank include the following:

Yoko Ono, who did like the idea when I first mentioned it, and Paul McCartney who has always wished the project luck. D.J. Hoek, Head of the Music Library at Northwestern University, Evanston, Illinois, USA, for his help, thoughts, suggestions. Northwestern have seven Beatles' lyrics, the most of any institution, apart from the British Library in London. And at the Brit Lib, a big thank you to Jamie Andrews, Head of English and Drama.

Colin Campbell, Emeritus Professor of Social Sociology at York University, England, was incredibly generous, letting me use material from his unpublished treatise on 'Eleanor Rigby', plus his thoughts on the Beatles lyrics. Thanks also to Professor Glenn Gass of the music school at the University of Indiana.

Amongst collectors and owners, family members and friends, plus expert fans who helped and to whom I am also grateful are: Maureen Cleave, Mike McCartney, David Birch, Marie Weston, Pete Shotton, Rod Davis, Jeff Leve, Philippe Leutert, Dave Ravenscroft, Howard Prosser, Dean Wilson, Peter Miniaci and Rick, Joachim Nosko, Thorsten Knublauch, Arno Guzek, Paul Drummond, James Breedon, Richard Hall.

Pete Nash, once again, for his research and saving me from some awful mistakes. Stephanie Connell and Stephen Maycock of Bonhams, Paul Wane and Jason Cornthwaite of Tracks, Spencer Leigh, Keith Badman, David Bedford, Steve Turner, Frank Caiazzo.

Alan Samson, Lucinda McNeile and Helen Ewing of Weidenfeld & Nicolson in London and John Parsley of Little Brown in New York – all a pleasure to do business with. Not forgetting Robert Kirkby of United Agents, for business and lunches.

The author and publisher are grateful to Sony, Harrisongs and MPL for permission to reproduce lyrics; to Charlotte Knee for photographing manuscripts; and to the following for their photographs or other images:

p.1, Photograph@Harry Benson; p.8, Sotheby's; p.9, Colin Hanton; p.11, Tracks; pp. 12, 150, 322, Hunter Davies collection; p. 18, Michael McCartney; p.23, Leslie Bryce; p.32, P. Drummond@Psy-Fi archive; pp. 15, 49, 356, Getty Images; p. 50, UPPA/Photoshot; p.57, Bill Harry; pp. 87, 328, Bad Handwroter/Arno Guzek; pp. 127, 131, 159, 160, 183, 242, British Library; p. 181, Ethan Russell; p.188, Jason Cornthwaite (Tracks); p.261, Mirrorpix; p.280, Ringo Starr; p.327, Caz Graham

INDEX